THE POPPY LADY

This book is dedicated to

... a husband

whose love and support have never wavered

... a Canadian

who asked, 'Who put the poppy on your lapel?'

... a go-between and a collaborator

... and many allies across the world

THE POPPY LADY

THE STORY OF MADAME ANNA GUÉRIN AND THE REMEMBRANCE POPPY

HEATHER ANNE JOHNSON

PEN & SWORD
HISTORY

AN IMPRINT OF PEN & SWORD BOOKS LTD.
YORKSHIRE - PHILADELPHIA

First published in Great Britain in 2022 by
PEN AND SWORD HISTORY
An imprint of
Pen & Sword Books Ltd
Yorkshire – Philadelphia

ISBN 978 1 39907 372 1

Typeset in Times New Roman 11/13.5 by
SJmagic DESIGN SERVICES, India.
Printed and bound in the UK by CPI Group (UK) Ltd.

Pen & Sword Books Limited incorporates the imprints of Atlas, Archaeology,
Aviation, Discovery, Family History, Fiction, History, Maritime, Military, Military
Classics, Politics, Select, Transport, True Crime, Air World, Frontline Publishing,
Leo Cooper, Remember When, Seaforth Publishing, The Praetorian Press,
Wharncliffe Local History, Wharncliffe Transport, Wharncliffe True Crime and
White Owl.

For a complete list of Pen & Sword titles please contact
PEN & SWORD BOOKS LIMITED
47 Church Street, Barnsley, South Yorkshire, S70 2AS, England
E-mail: enquiries@pen-and-sword.co.uk
Website: www.pen-and-sword.co.uk

Or

PEN AND SWORD BOOKS
1950 Lawrence Rd, Havertown, PA 19083, USA
E-mail: Uspen-and-sword@casematepublishers.com
Website: www.penandswordbooks.com

Contents

Introduction

Many people have published original, or duplicated, versions of the Remembrance Poppy history and, of course, Canadian John McCrae's 1915 poem 'In Flanders Fields' sits at the heart of these accounts. I agree it should hold an esteemed position, as many people empathised with it.

However, the continuing existence of Remembrance Poppy Days and poppies on lapels should be credited to one person alone, I feel. Madame Anna Guérin, 'The Poppy Lady of France', is the person I salute.

Soon after July 2015, I was asked, 'Who put the poppy on your lapel?' I knew that I had been brought up to respect the Remembrance Poppy; I knew why I wore a poppy; I knew why I placed poppy crosses in Belgium and France, for my three family members; I knew of the poem 'In Flanders Fields'; but I did not know the answer to that question.

A mature lady, Nancy McFarlane, asked that question of me. Fate decreed that I was introduced to her by a mutual acquaintance, Chris Stanfield. Nancy was seriously interested in local and national history; she was a proud Canadian; she was formidable; and, from her own limited research, she knew Anna Guérin had been forgotten.

Over the years, Nancy had come across Canadian archived newspaper articles about this French female enigma and gathered a couple of the jigsaw pieces, but she had not been able to identify this 'Poppy Lady', Madame Guérin. Nancy had reached a point in her life where she needed to hand over her quest to 'younger eyes', and they were mine.

I came to this research with no allegiances, but I soon discovered that contemporaries of this French woman had known the truth about her and her achievements: of her being a humanitarian for France and for the USA; and the only 'originator and propagator of Poppy Days'.

For me, this French woman, Anna Guérin, is the most significant personality. She saw the potential of a poppy emblem to help widows and orphans and those who survived the First World War, alongside the remembrance of those who had lost their lives in it. What singles her out from others is the fact that her dynamic personality drove her 'big idea' forward, to all Allied countries: where she led, so many others followed.

I became bewitched after reading article after article by others, who used descriptive words such as: audience moved to tears; vivid; dedication; sympathetic; vivacious; illuminating; intellectual; celebrated; expressive; graceful; tireless; illuminating; distinguished; eloquent; and 'The Spirit of France Incarnate'. How could anyone not be bewitched?

Anna was born in rural France. She married young, became a mother of two daughters, and ran a school in a French colony. She was determined that children, especially girls, should reach their full potential and was passionate about education, the French culture and language.

In 1911, Anna went to Great Britain, as an 'Alliance Française' lecturer. Not long before the First World War began, Anna committed to three years' lecturing in the USA and, not deterred by war, she arrived in New York in October 1914. Immediately but discreetly, because the USA had not yet entered the war, she began raising funds for France.

Once the USA entered the war, in April 1917, Anna could lecture openly for charities which provided relief in France. She campaigned on behalf of America's Red Cross and its War Bonds, for which she was dubbed 'the greatest of all the war speakers'. For her work in the USA and France, Anna was awarded several medals and wore them proudly.

Contemplating that First World War era, people saw the fragile scarlet poppies growing on battlefields, sent blooms home, or wrote about them. Contemporaneously with each other, many were emotionally moved.

An affinity with fragile red poppies quietly emerged. In England, in August 1915, a 'Poppy Day' was held at South Shields in aid of children and an Infirmary. In December, John McCrae's 'In Flanders Fields' poem was published. In 1916, artificial poppies were sold for more war effort causes; for instance, a 'Poppy Day' was held in Whitby, in aid of Sleights Red Cross Hospital and servicemen patients. Poppies became emblematic.

Was the first person to wear the bloom 'in remembrance' among them? Keeping silent, was a grieving mother in Whitby *remembering* her son, who had been killed in the early days of the war? Was she hoping her donation for a poppy would help care for another mother's son?

Anna Guérin was sailing back to France when the Armistice was signed. She thought her war work was over, but her reputation had gone before her, and she was called to Paris by the government. She returned to the United States and was given responsibility for organising an entire American branch of a new charity, which took the poppy as its emblem.

In 1919 and 1920, Poppy Days were held in each state that had been organised by Anna. In August 1920, she announced her 'big idea' – in effect, an 'Inter-Allied Poppy Day', which was taken to all Allied countries. American Legion veterans gave her the name of 'The Poppy Lady of France'.

This 'Madame Guérin' became an almost anonymous person within 'a fable agreed upon'. My quest is to enlighten anyone who may be interested in scrutinising the history of the Remembrance Poppy and the origin of the Poppy Day. My quest is to bring Anna Guérin out of the shadows.

I reveal an account that differs from that which has been circulating for too long, in the hope of dispelling some myths. I believe it was fate that Anna Guérin was there to work her magic with the symbolic scarlet bloom and take the sentiment of the 'In Flanders Fields' poem further, to another dimension.

My aim is to demonstrate that Anna Guérin was a leader, not a follower. As 'the Poppy Lady of France', full credit should be given to her; she should always be part of the history of the Remembrance Poppy, and her whole life needs to be known to appreciate her accomplishments.

Anna Guérin's legacy is the Remembrance Poppy we wear today, remembrance of all those who have lost their lives in conflict, and help for the families of the fallen and the survivors.

Honour the dead by helping the living.

Chapter 1

Childhood in France and Life in Madagascar

The woman who would become 'The Poppy Lady of France' was born on 3 February 1878, at Vallon, Ardèche, in south-eastern France. Her family name was Boulle and her first names were Anna Alix. Her parents were 'cultivateur' Auguste Boulle and his wife Anna, née Granier. Anna Alix was their second child and their first daughter.

Anna was born into a Protestant family rather than a traditional cultural Roman Catholic one. The Ardèche département is historically known for its Protestant connections. Going back to the sixteenth century, there were persecutions of Protestants in France and many of that faith emigrated because of harsh treatment. However, the Ardèche was peaceful and calm when Anna and her seven siblings were born into it. All five of the surviving children enjoyed a happy childhood and received a good education.

In 1881 and 1882, Minister of Public Education Jules Ferry made primary education free, secular, and compulsory. At the same time, high schools for young girls were created. Until then, education had to be paid for. Jules Ferry had several Protestant allies; the Protestant community welcomed secular schooling and the establishment of these schools was facilitated by Protestants. The first was in Sèvres and others followed.

The family home was a large and profitable farm on Rue du Mas des Aires, Vallon, now number 19. Auguste, with twenty-nine other people including nineteen Vallonnais, created a mutual fire insurance company in May 1895, called 'Mutuelle de Vallon'. As a respected member of the community, he was elected as a Vallon municipal councillor in 1904. Continually re-elected, he remained in this role until his death in 1913.

Auguste kept and raised pigs, poultry, and rabbits. To work the land, he must have owned either a horse or a mule. He may have also had goats, like many farmers in Vallon. The farm probably had olive trees, for the family's own consumption. The land also had mulberry trees for the breeding of silkworms.

1

On smaller farms, one upper floor or the attic of the farmhouse was the magnanerie, the silkworm nursery, for want of a better description. Nearly every house in Vallon had one.

A magnanerie was generally recognised by a small fireplace in each of the four corners of the room, where lit fires kept the silkworms at a temperature not lower than 18°C. The silkworms developed on mulberry leaves, atop wooden-framed racks with iron mesh grids. It was usual for women to be in charge of this silk production so, at the Boulle farm, it was probably Anna's mother who took on responsibility for this cottage industry.

At larger farms, like the Boulle farm, there was a separate building for this and magnaneries were on several floors. The cocoons were cleaned by the whole family and sold to spinning mills before the chrysalis came out.

Breeding silkworms was very important in the Ardèche. Olivier de Serres (1539–1619), known as the 'father of French agriculture', was born and lived in Ville-neuve-de-Berg, just 25 miles north of Vallon. He was very interested in silk farming (sericulture) and planted millions of mulberry trees in the Ardèche, in the Cévennes and the South of France, to use the leaves to feed silkworms. The Ardèche became a large producer of silk. In Vallon, there were important magnaneries until 1865, when a disease struck the silkworms. Many Vallonnais uprooted their trees, to plant vines. The invention of nylon in 1939 was the beginning of the end of silk production in the area. In Vallon, it lasted until the 1950s.

Today, the Ardèche is one of the most sparsely populated but most forested départements of France. Tourism plays a large part in the area's economy. Vallon became Vallon-Pont-d'Arc in 1948 – taking its new name from the natural arch bridge standing close to the town.

At the age of 14, in May 1892, Mlle Anna Alix Boulle undertook a school examination. She passed it and was awarded a scholarship at l'École Supérieure on l'Avenue des Marronniers, Largentière, Ardèche. The local Largentière Hôpital stands on the school's site now.

Anna is described as a petite, brown-eyed brunette, about 5½ feet tall. According to family lore, she was so dynamic and brave that she could dive from the Pont du Gard aqueduct (24m high, at the lower tier) into the River Gardon below. It is rumoured that, on one occasion, she dived for a film – understudying for a famous French actress.

On 13 July 1895, Anna graduated from l'École Supérieure, probably as a first level tutor, and this may have been her first employment. A photograph taken shortly after Anna's eighteenth birthday in 1896 places her in Ironbridge, Shropshire, England. Anna must have become a 'mademoiselle française'.

At the time, it was fashionable for a wealthy British family to have a foreign governess/mademoiselle and Anna, as a Protestant, would be ideal.

Twenty months later, on 6 November 1897, Anna married 26-year-old Cuban-born French national Paul Rabanit in Vallon – she was 19 years old. Paul was from nearby Les Vans and, it is suggested, privately funded by his wealthy father, who held a law degree and owned land.

Paul's father (Joseph Emile) Polydore Rabanit was known for being a 'globetrotter' because of his foreign travels. He had set up a home in Santiago de Cuba, Cuba. Paul's mother was Cuban-born Laurestine (née Savine). Paul was born on 23 September 1871, the first of eight children. All the children were French nationals by birth and, after mother Laurestine died on 16 June 1886, Polydore and his children had permanently made their home together in Les Vans, Ardèche.

It is deduced that, during the spring or summer of 1898, Anna travelled to the French-ruled Island of Madagascar, off Africa's east coast. Future North American newspapers would verify that the journey occurred when Anna 'was a bride', three months after Madagascar's conquest by the French. She may have travelled alone, as Paul's Army Reserve Record gives the date of 3 December 1898 for his change of address to Madagascar, but Anna was definitely there by September 1898.

Anna must have embarked at the Mediterranean port of Marseilles. The voyage to Madagascar (MG) was via the Suez Canal, on a Messageries Maritimes mail-boat usually. En route, ports of call were: Malta – Port Said (Egypt) – Suakin or Sawakin (Sudan) – Djibouti – Sansibar (now Zanzibar) – Diego Suarez (Antsiranana, MG) – Tamatave (now Toamasina, MG).

Anna and Paul settled in Tamatave, on the Island's east coast, which is now known as Toamasina. The French Général Joseph-Simon Gallieni, who would become known as the 'Saviour of Paris' in August 1914, had been made the Gouverneur of this new French colony.

Anna would spend nearly eleven years in Madagascar, which did not gain its independence from France until June 1960.

Anna Rabanit appears to have found her niche very quickly. She opened a private school, which received a Municipal Commission subsidy. This was the start of assisting Gouverneur Général Gallieni in his vision of bringing French civilisation and education to Madagascar.

Taking up his post, Général Gallieni had emphasised that all the indigenous Malagasy peoples should learn the French language with a view to becoming devoted associates of the French colonists – who had come to Madagascar to bring them civilisation and wealth. However, they were free to preserve their customs, religion, traditional dances, and so on. By the end of the century, Madagascar was at peace.

Evidence points to Anna's private school being open in 1898 because, in 1899, she was applying to the Municipal Commission for the continuation of a subsidy for the school she was already running. On 12 April 1899, it was announced that 100 Fr per month would be made available to her, to provide free education for ten needy students: 'ten children belonging to poor families in the city'.

In the future, an American newspaper would report: 'At the time Madame Guérin was in Madagascar General Gallieni, the "savior of Paris," was governor, and General Joseph Joffre was a member of his staff'; she 'became personally acquainted with these famous men'.

The Rabanit home, at 11 Rue Nationale, Tamatave, was called 'Vallon'. Family lore describes the property as having banana trees growing in the garden. 'Directrice' Anna had her private boarding school 'Pensionnat Rabanit' or 'École Rabanit' either at, or adjacent to, the Rabanit home. By June 1899, Anna's school was one of ten in Tamatave.

Gallieni considered education to be of the utmost importance, to establish French control, but he had inherited a problem. There was a continuing power struggle among religious groups in Madagascar.

The groups were English, American, French, and Norwegian Protestants, and French Catholics. Malagasy education was in these missionaries' hands, with more than two-thirds of schools run by foreign Protestants.

In order to achieve control of Madagascar, General Gallieni decreed that the French language was to be the basis of instruction and, if a Malagasy could not speak, read, and write French, they would not be employed by the French governing forces on the Island. As a means to that end, some of the mission schools and hospitals were taken over.

Initially, Gallieni's top priority was organising schools for Malagasy children. One school was in Antananarivo – the 'Myre de Vilers' school. The school was opened on 2 January 1897, 'to train interpreters, candidates for administrative functions and native teachers'.

However, numbers of European children were increasing and Général Gallieni had to turn his attention to structuring their education eventually too. He set about structuring the Island's education system at the start of 1904. There were already a small number of private schools following a fixed syllabus and Anna's school was amongst them. Gallieni wanted all schools to follow this method of teaching.

The schools had two levels: in the lower level, classes would correspond with French primary schools but a programme appropriate to Madagascar had to be included. Additionally, primary school classes had to include preparation for studies in French high schools and colleges.

The upper level was specialised, with four sections: General Education; Agricultural; Commercial; and Industrial. The pupils who followed the courses to that point were able to be admitted to the second cycle of France, because of this structure.

The earliest mention of Madame Rabanit, within the newspapers of Madagascar, was on 22 September 1898. Written in French, all mentions give an insight into the educational and social life Anna and other Europeans experienced on the Island of Madagascar. This aforementioned 1898 article reported that on Sunday, 11 September, Gouverneur Général Gallieni hosted some matinée entertainments, primarily for members of the municipal commission and the advisory chamber.

The event involved a dance, which continued into the night, and all the women wore charming and delicate dresses. Some specific society women of Tamatave were named, one of whom was Anna Rabanit, who wore a dress of black silk. This would be just one of the many marvellous balls that took place during Madagascar's annual social calendar. Thus, within months of Madame Anna Rabanit arriving in Madagascar, she was already part of the French social scene on the Island.

On 15 November 1899, Anna's first presentation of school prizes was reported on. The event was described as a lovely family fête in a very nicely decorated room, which was completely packed. In true school disciplinary fashion, it was reported that latecomers were forced to remain on the veranda. Anna's pupils presented the entertainment, which consisted of music, songs, choruses, and monologues.

Every year, Anna's prize-giving presentations were reviewed with descriptions such as: 'demonstrations of the excellence of teaching and education' at this school of 'special stature'; and 'appreciations of the excellent and happy results' of the Rabanit 'method of education'.

The school appears to have become very successful, very quickly. It was so successful, in fact, that Anna needed assistance: so she returned to the Ardèche, to Vallon, and collected her sister, Adeline Boulle.

Family lore offers an anecdote, recalled by Adeline in later life, about when the two sisters arrived in Marseille. Much-travelled Anna insisted Adeline go to the hairdresser before embarking for Madagascar. Reserved Adeline was shocked, because the village women of Vallon believed only women of little virtue went to the hairdresser!

However, the persuasive Anna succeeded in getting Adeline to agree to have her hair styled before the voyage. It was highly likely that Adeline had never ventured far from Vallon. What did she think, as her older, but enterprising and entrepreneurial sister whisked her off to the Island of Madagascar to assist in running the 'École Rabanit'?

Anna had two daughters with Paul Rabanit, during the early years of living in Madagascar. Raymonde Laurestine was born on 23 February 1900 and Renée Paule was born on 2 November 1901. The births of both girls were registered in the city of Tamatave.

On both girls' birth entries, Anna's profession was 'institutrice' (school mistress) and their father Paul's was 'commerçant' (trader). With a Cuban paternal grandmother, Raymonde and Renée were of mixed race. The family's pragmatic, non-prejudicial description of the two girls was quarteronne, an old-fashioned term for children of one white parent and one parent of mixed race, i.e. one-*quarter* mixed race.

In an article dated 20 September 1900, both Anna and Paul Rabanit appeared within a list of Alliance Française members in Madagascar. For Anna especially, given her obvious passion for the French language and culture, it is logical she would hold such a membership.

On 23 February 1901, the chief administrator of the Tamatave province reported on the situation in his constituency during December 1900: Tamatave was 'absolutely well equipped' with five schools. Schools were mentioned in order of importance: Anna Rabanit's school was third; with a Mme Panon's school fourth. Together, these two schools 'held 108 students, including 27 scholarship holders'.

Anna's school initially accepted 'young Creole or European children', but indigenous children eventually became scholarship pupils there.

Another article, relating to school pupils in the Tamatave province, appeared on 3 April 1901: 'schoolchildren, except in Tamatave, are not diligent. This neglect is most often attributed to parents who prefer to employ children in light cultivation work or the supervision of cattle.'

Also in 1901, during August, it was reported that, out of eleven candidates who passed the primary school examinations, seven were from Anna's 'Pensionnat Rabanit' school.

Anna Rabanit's school was gaining the reputation of being one of the best on the Island of Madagascar. The school was growing in status.

Anna's daughters were also growing. They attended fêtes and festivals too. At one fancy dress fête, in 1901, Gouverneur Général Gallieni laid on 'dances, puppet theatre, wonderful raffle of over two hundred toys, cakes and sweets' for the children. Raymonde was dressed as a butterfly, with four hand-painted gauze wings, which formed a 'beautiful illusion'. Her costume was described as 'very original and noticeable'.

When a fête was held the next year, Renée participated too. She was described as a baby, all in white; and wearing a large hat, called a 'capeline'. Raymonde was a ballet dancer, wearing: 'a very pretty pale pink silk muslin costume' with 'bodice trimmed with pearls', 'hair with fine pearls', and 'holding a pink fan and tambourine'.

Festivals for infants were often hosted by the Gouverneur Général. On another occasion, the 'most elegant' and 'most original' principal fancy dress costumes were reported upon. A list included a dragonfly, worn by Raymonde, and a multicoloured butterfly, worn by Renée.

After attending an 'Alliance Française' Grand Ball in October 1901, sister Adeline received attention also: 'Miss Boulle' impersonated a lady from Arles; she wore an 'Arlésienne black skirt and blouse, white muslin cloth headdress, flame colour neckerchief, black velvet in a regional hairstyle, a pearl necklace with several strands, rings and bracelets.'

On 17 July 1902, after taking leave in France, Gouverneur Gallieni arrived back into the port of Tamatave. Whilst attending to other business, he had been attempting to obtain more finance for his public works in Madagascar, including new roads and a railway line. Anna Rabanit's young girls and boys were part of his official welcoming party.

By the time 1902 ended, Anna's sister Adeline had been living on the Island of Madagascar long enough to have been courted, and proposed to, by Frenchman Jean Gerald Moreau. Jean was Madagascar's Principal Topographic Surveyor. Adeline Berthe Boulle and Jean Gerald Moreau married on 10 January 1903, in the city of Tamatave.

On 1 August 1903, it was announced a new judge had been appointed to the Court near the northern coastal port of Diego Suarez, 900 miles away overland from Tamatave. He was Constant Charles Eugène Guérin, who would become Anna's second husband seven years later. Always known as Eugène, he disembarked from the French mail-boat *Iraouaddy* at Diego Suarez, on 13 September. Today, the port is called Antsiranana.

During 1903, Anna Rabanit continued to be part of Tamatave's social scene. In September, she attended Général Gallieni's beautiful soirée at the Hôtel de France. It was a masked ball and a concert in the 'beautifully lit and decorated' great hall, with 'lovely ice sculptures'.

All individuals of 'the elegant society of Tamatave' were given an invitation. Anna Rabanit's attire was named among 'the costumes that achieved the greatest noted success'. She was impersonating Cléo de Mérode, the beautiful French 'Belle Époque' dancer.

By the end of 1903, Anna Rabanit's position in Madagascar's academic world was 'justly esteemed'. Her school was considered 'the premier one' of Tamatave; her efforts were acknowledged as being made 'in the interests of the city' and she deserved congratulations.

Going into 1904, the Rabanit boarding school's reputation and success confirmed 'the excellence of the methods employed'. Pupils' parents must have long known of Anna Rabanit's dedication to her work.

Anna's pupils continued to obtain Primary Education Certificates and the successes gave credence to the excellent reputation of her 'École Rabanit'. By May, the boarding school's pupils numbered thirty boys and forty girls. Fifteen of these children were in receipt of scholarships, which were funded from the municipal budget.

However, maintaining such high standards at Tamatave's 'most important' mixed boarding school must have been taking its toll and, on 3 July 1904, Tamatave's 'distinguished Director' took 'a well deserved leave of absence of six months in France'.

Being 'always devoted to her institution', Anna entrusted her school into the good hands of Mrs and Miss Courtois – the latter being a well-established teacher. Anna's school had been 'rapidly prospering' so she would want to retain the first place it was holding in Tamatave.

Anna reassured her families and hoped they would 'fully recognise her dedication, for seven consecutive years devoted to teaching ... by giving ... all their trust to Miss Courtois'. She planned to take a few months' rest in France and return at the beginning of 1905.

On the same day Anna began her temporary leave of absence, a most promising pupil of hers took an examination on the nearby island of La Réunion. This was the talented Eugène Bang, son of the Norwegian Consul to Madagascar. Being of 'first-rate intelligence', 13-year-old Eugène took an examination set for 16-year-olds. It was 'too rare and too unique' an occurrence in Madagascar not to be publicly announced.

It was reported that it was 'truly unfortunate that the departure to France of Madame Rabanit, necessary because of the state of her health' coincided with this 'brilliant and new success'. Anna was wished 'a full recovery of her health', along with 'a speedy return to her students'.

A cablegram from the island of La Réunion, during October 1904, delivered the good news that Eugène Bang had passed the examination. The magnificent result warranted congratulations being sent to Eugène, his parents and his 'distinguished teacher Mrs. Rabanit, whose enlightened care has shaped this young mind'.

During this leave of absence, whilst based in Vallon, Anna succeeded in acquiring a Certificat d'aptitude pédagogique (CAP). This award was announced in 'le Journal Républicain des Cévennes', on 11 March 1905. It qualified Anna to teach and test to a higher level.

Anna Rabanit arrived back at Tamatave on 6 April 1905 on the Messageries Maritimes mail-boat *Le Natal*. Institutrice Rabanit had returned to resume her teaching, after her leave in France.

It was announced on 25 June 1905 that Eugène Guérin was leaving Diego Suarez to be Deputy Judge at the Court of Tamatave. It is unlikely Eugène and Anna had met before he took up his post because even the shorter route via sea meant the two cities were 460 miles apart.

In the autumn of 1906, decisions were being announced relating to Anna Rabanit: by order of 7 October, she was appointed as a 5th classe teacher, with an annual salary of 3,500 francs; and, by order of 14 October, she was assigned as director of the girls' school in the Tamatave locality. It is interesting to note the pay in Europe was 1,750 francs, so it was financially rewarding to work in a French colony.

This appointment as 5th classe teacher was, in effect, a promotion. It would have been as a result of gaining her Certificat d'aptitude.

While Anna Rabanit's professional life continued to flourish and advance, her married life was not so successful. It can only be speculated upon but perhaps the latter was the result of the former.

Within the Vallon register, entries against the name of 'Anna Alix Boulle' not only document her birth and marriages, but also her divorce: 'Judgement of the first instance court of Tamatave April 15, 1907 following the judgement of 22 October 1906 granting the divorce.'

Anna's occupation was an 'institutrice', a schoolteacher, living in Tamatave. Paul was a 'prospecteur' living in Vatomandry, 115 miles north. Madagascar was rich in both gems and gold, but Paul was probably not physically prospecting himself. Given his wealth, he may have invested money in an expedition into the Island's unexplored interior.

The year 1907 must have been bittersweet for Anna because, for her dedication to France, she was awarded the French médaille of the 'Officier d'Académie' (Silver Palms) that year: 'By order of the Ministry of Education, Fine Arts and Religious Affairs, dated March 1, and on the proposal of the Minister of Colonies, are named: Officier d'academie Mme. Rabanit, Head Teacher of a private school.'

In later life, it would be recorded that this award was in recognition of her school work, writings, and organisational work, whilst living and working on the Island of Madagascar.

Reportedly, it was Général Gallieni who recommended Anna for the médaille and Général Gallieni who presented her with it. Apparently, it made her one of the youngest people to hold that particular award.

In August 1907, still being referred to as 'Madame Rabanit', it was declared that Anna was to take another period of convalescence in France: 'A three-month convalescence leave, full balance in Europe, was awarded to Mrs. Rabanit, teacher, to enjoy in France.'

In later life, Anna described her work with Malagasy 'slave' girls,

> reared there with no other aim than to be the mistress of some man. They were brought in from the provinces when they are thirteen or fourteen and sold like animals in the streets of Madagascar. I helped to establish schools where they were taught sewing and housework and various occupations that would enable them to earn a living.

Anna's name appeared in Malagasy articles on numerous occasions. They had told of her dedication; prize-giving events; quality of instruction; charmed audiences; pupils' displays of sewing and drawings; pupils' singing, acting, piano playing; visits to horse races; attendances at children's fêtes, with her daughters; attendances at soirees; and so on. Anna had become very well-known as a member of the 'société élégante'.

However, on 14 September 1909, Anna left her Tamatave teaching position. The consensus is that the announcement of her departure is translated as a dismissal from her 5th class teaching post.

Anna probably knew that day would come, sooner or later, once she became divorced. Her prestigious reputation within the Island's education system may have allowed her to survive longer than another person might have but, eventually, it had to happen.

French bourgeois society would have frowned upon Anna's new divorced status. Although a perfectly legal position, being divorced would have unjustly lost her the reputation she had worked so hard to attain.

Divorce in France was first legalised in 1792 but it was revoked in 1816, when Louis XVII declared the state religion would be Roman Catholic. After a handful of attempts beforehand, divorce became legal again in 1884. Regardless of whether one is an opponent or an advocate, legalising divorce is looked upon as a first step to the slow emancipation of French women.

When Anna divorced, the status was still frowned upon, and it is highly likely that it was felt inappropriate for a school principal to be a divorcée. She may have been ostracised by many who had once applauded her.

On 17 October 1910, Anna married Alsace-born French national Eugène Guérin in Vallon. Eugène was noted as a Judge/Justice of the Peace with extended jurisdiction. He was 'domicilié à' 8th arrondissement of Paris, France, meaning legally resident there, but 'demeurant à' Kayes, meaning temporarily staying at Kayes.

At the time, Kayes was capital of French Sudan, now Mali. After marrying, Eugène returned to the Sudan and resumed his duties at court. Eventually, he became Court President at Conakry, French Guinea.

It has been suggested this marriage might have been, in part, one of convenience. As a married woman, rather than as a divorcée with two children, Anna's social standing would be more respectable. Bearing in mind her future work, which would involve travelling alone most of the time, being a married woman was much more satisfactory.

As far as their relationship was concerned, Anna's and Eugène's lives would rarely converge, and they would separate in the late 1930s.

All references to Anna would now be as 'Madame E. Guérin'. This followed the era's cultural and formal etiquette, whereby a husband and wife were deemed to be one person – with a husband taking priority.

Chapter 2

Lecturing in Great Britain 1911–1914

Having left the teaching profession, the new 'Madame E. Guérin' embarked on another career along similar lines. Anna would not have expected Eugène to support her two daughters. That aside, research shows Anna was not a person to remain idle for long.

Anna Guérin was an independent, strong, resilient woman and not afraid of hard work. There is little doubt that impersonating at the odd soirée and producing performances at her school in Madagascar gave her the belief and confidence to use her talents and charm to embark upon a career as an illuminating, artistic lecturer for the Alliance Française organisation.

Lecturing in Great Britain would be Anna's next big adventure and during that period, apparently, she was awarded the French médaille of l'Officier de l'Instruction Publique by the then French Ambassador to London. This would have been (Pierre) Paul Cambon (1843–1924) who was the French Ambassador between the years 1898 and 1920.

In the absence of evidence to the contrary, it is reasoned that Anna Guérin arrived in England early in 1911, with her two daughters Raymonde and Renée Rabanit. To date, the earliest mention found of Anna is 9 March 1911. She gave a lecture on Madagascar, at the private Girton House girls' boarding school on the Mall, Ealing, London.

Two days later, the *Middlesex County Times* printed: 'There was so much of interest in the admirable lecture given by Madame Guérin in Girton Hall ... The address admirable in composition and diction...'

In the 1911 Census (2 April), the two Rabanit girls were 'Girton House' school boarders. Eight miles away, one 'Anna Guérin' was a visitor to French couple Maurice and Yvonne Roux, at Gt. College Street, London NW. Yvonne's birthplace was Reims and therein lies a question mark, because this Anna's birthplace was also entered as Reims.

However, incorrect information was often entered in Census returns and this Anna's signature compares favourably with that of our would-be Poppy Lady, so I have a sneaking hunch that this was probably Anna.

On 19 May 1911, Madame E. Guérin gave another lecture on the subject of 'Madagascar' at the Ealing Grammar School for Boys.

Also in May, Anna gave the first of four Napoleonic-era matinée littéraire lectures at l'Université des lettres française, Marble Arch House, London. For those lectures, Anna performed under the pseudonym of 'Madame Sarah Granier'. Her first subject was: 'The Two Empresses, Joséphine de Beauharnais and Marie Louise'.

The *London Times* reviewed it: 'Certainly, few things could be more charming or more sympathetic, or more delicately pictorial'; 'a speaker of beautiful prose'; 'interesting and vivid'; 'most charming and refined'; and 'little stories told with a charming demure humour.'

L'Université opened in 1910. It was the initiative of Marie d'Orliac, a young French woman. She introduced French artists, writers, etc. to London society. It is now known as l'Institut français du Royaume-Uni.

Anna's second Université lecture, on 2 June, dealt with the 'celebrated women of the Empire, the Sisters of Napoleon – the lectrices, and the actresses'. The weather was bad but it was well attended. The *Times* reviewed: 'Mme. Granier is a speaker of beautiful prose, and speaks it with fine art. Her matter is always interesting and vivid, and she enlivens it with little stories told with a charming demure humour.'

Mme Granier's fourth Université lecture was in December. It dealt with 'The Times of Napoleon Bonaparte'. Joséphine de Beauharnais, his Empress, featured. Anna wore a high-waisted gown of pearl-white silk girdled with gold, which was a copy of one made by Joséphine for herself. She took Napoleon from babyhood to his desolate life on St Helena.

Anna used the artistic stage name of 'Sarah Granier' for only a short time in Great Britain. She may have deliberately combined names of two famous French actresses – Sarah Bernhardt and Jeanne Granier.

That said, with 'Granier' being Anna's mother's maiden name, there could have been a more personal reason for taking that last name. Interestingly, throughout her professional life, Anna was often found described as 'the Sarah Bernhardt of the lecture platform'.

In the November and December of 1911, 'Madame Guérin' gave at least two lectures – one at the Bedford Grammar School, the other at Hastings and St Leonards Ladies' College. Both the lectures were about Madagascar – the three-week voyage and the places 'touched at en route' were described. Anna always used limelight/magic lantern slide views to illustrate her performances, which were all given in French and in costume.

A newspaper review noted that the Bedford lecture 'concluded with an eloquent peroration about the flowers and the fruit and the beauty of the land, and Madame Guérin was warmly applauded'.

After 1911, Anna Guérin seems to have abandoned 'Madagascar' as a subject for her lectures and concentrated on significant women in French history – namely, subjects such as the 'Heroines of the French Revolution' (Marie Antoinette, Charlotte Corday, and Madame Roland of Bordeaux); 'Jeanne d'Arc'; 'Joséphine Bonaparte'; and so on. Slowly but surely, Anna increased her popularity and became more well-known.

Wherever Anna lectured in Great Britain, performances received glowing reviews. Observations made were a feast for the imagination, for example, 'eloquent'; 'intellectual treat'; 'audience moved to tears'; 'declamatory force'; 'vivacious'; 'sympathetic'; 'graceful'; 'dramatic'; 'intellectual treat'; 'celebrated'; 'expressive'; 'attractive'; and so on.

Anna Guérin's first UK tour probably finished in spring 1912. Anna was not found again in British newspapers until November of that year. The content of future articles appearing in US newspapers indicates she may have been spending time with her husband in Africa whilst away, 'to develop the educational facilities of the territory'.

On 9 November 1912, 'Madame Guérin' was in Scotland. She gave a lecture to the French society 'Les Amis des Annales' at Gartshore Hall in Edinburgh. Anna's subject was Marie Antoinette. The *Scotsman* described Anna and the lecture with phrases such as 'an interesting and dramatic recital'; 'it was enlivened'; and 'an admirable elocutionist'.

By the end of the month, Anna Guérin was back south of the border again, in England, giving the first of three French Artistic Lectures in Bath. Somerset. Ahead of the series, the *Bath Chronicle & Weekly Gazette* newspaper was informing its readers that Madame E. Guérin had 'already given 400 French Artistic Lectures all over England'.

At a guess, Anna Guérin probably stayed at the Milsom Hotel when she was in Bath, because it was at this hotel that particulars about the lectures could be obtained. As time went on, it became the usual practice for Anna to use hotels for such a purpose: sometimes giving lectures, interviews, and basing her 'Poppy Day' headquarters in them.

However, in this particular instance, Anna's first Bath lecture was delivered in the city's Assembly Rooms, with the second and third lectures delivered at Bathwick Ladies School, Pulteney Street in Bath.

The first lecture's subject was 'Jeanne d'Arc, Heroine and Martyr'; the second lecture (18 December) was about 'Heroines of the French Revolution – Madame Roland, of Bordeaux, and Charlotte Corday'; and the third lecture (22 January 1913) concentrated on 'Les Impértrices de France; les femmes de Napoleon I – Joséphine and Marie Louise'.

Anna Guérin's lectures were reviewed afterwards in Bath's local newspapers. The first lecture's review reported on her impersonation of the shepherd's daughter Jeanne d'Arc. She 'was attired in a costume of a style that prevailed in France 500 years ago … When she reached the final scene of martyrdom … many in the audience were moved to tears…'

In all, Anna had four changes of costume when she portrayed Jeanne d'Arc: (1) as Jeanne, the shepherdess; (2) as Jeanne, listening to the voices; (3) as Jeanne, the girl-warrior; and (4) as Jeanne, the Maid of Orleans, wearing a sackcloth gown as she was led to the stake.

Anna researched her subjects in depth, studying old engravings and searching through hundreds of books in her quest for authentic costumes. In a 1914 interview, she told how the suit of armour she wore, as Jeanne d'Arc, 'was made in France 500 years ago'.

In Bath, it was noted that Anna 'displayed considerable charm of manner, and a decided sense of humour'; 'recited … with excellent feeling and declamatory force'; and 'it was noticed that many in the audience were moved to tears by the touching recital'.

To quote from the review of Anna's third lecture, 'Madame Guérin thanked her audience, and asked them to accept souvenir postcards.' Some of these cards survive and some of their images are featured in this book.

Throughout the professional life of 'Madame E. Guérin', these souvenir postcards served as promotional keepsakes but, today, they serve to document that part of Anna's life.

These souvenir cards illustrate exactly how she portrayed her subjects and how her audience saw her, in the flesh – with authentic costumes, accompanying her historical storylines.

Back in Edinburgh, Anna had a second lecture engagement (3 December) entitled 'The Empresses of France' ('Les Impértrices de France'). This included a sketch on Napoleon's wives Joséphine and Marie Louise.

A third Edinburgh lecture, on 15 February 1913, was called 'The Princesse de Lamballe and Mme. Vigée-Lebrun, two friends of Marie Antoinette'. The *Scotsman* newspaper printed this advertisement, in French, ahead of that lecture: 'LES AMIS DES ANNALES. – CONFERENCE par Madame GUÉRIN le Samedi, 15 février à 8 heures, GARTSHORE HALL. "Mme. Vigée-Lebrun et La Princesse de Lamballe—deux amies de Marie Antoinette." Non-members, 1/6.'

Only one voice of dissent has been discovered in Great Britain, during research. In June 1913, two East Riding of Yorkshire newspapers informed their readers that Hull Education Committee had been asked to permit

Miss Rowland, of the Secondary Girls' School, to pay a fee of three guineas for a French lecture to be given by Madame Guérin.

The fee in question, which was the equivalent to £350 in 2019, was called 'a waste of money' by one Mr Coult, but he received no support for his opinion. Several committee members spoke 'of the excellence of Madame Guérin's credentials' and Canon Lambert 'thought such a lecture would be of great educational value'.

Anna continued to lecture and travel around Britain during 1913, lecturing again in Edinburgh and in places such as Derby and Stevenage.

Lectures in 1914 began in Northern Ireland, in January, and Anna's 'high reputation' had preceded her. Her lectures were in Belfast: the first in Victoria College's Common Hall; the second in the Lodge, Fortwilliam Park; and the third at the Municipal Technical Institute. The first two lectures were about Marie Antoinette and the third was about Napoleon.

It is within reviews of that second Belfast lecture that we learn about Anna Guérin's plan to go to the USA. The *Belfast News Letter* and the *Northern Whig* newspapers both enlightened:

> Madame Guérin's lecture was warmly applauded, and thanks were conveyed to her through the pupils; whilst Miss Rentoul expressed her regret that a three years' lecturing engagement in America would preclude the audience from soon again hearing another of those addresses which had won for Madame Guérin a high distinction from the French Government.

For the next four months, Anna Guérin travelled up and down England, from Northumberland down to Devon, and so on. If she lectured in Wales, no proof has ever been discovered within newspaper reviews.

Chapter 3

Lecturing and Fundraising in the USA

Anna Guérin's last known lecture in Great Britain was in May 1914. As was usual, she returned to France for the summer. In Paris, it is presumed Anna purchased costumes from the Paquin fashion house and finalised arrangements for her forthcoming 'Alliance Française' American tour. Afterwards, she would have taken her daughters back to Vallon, to be under 'the supervision of her aged mother' for the foreseeable future.

Eventually, Anna travelled to see her husband Eugène in Lyon, where he was acting as a French attaché at the World's Fair, manning 'Le Pavillon Des Colonies'. It had opened on 1 May 1914, and should have run until 1 November, but the outbreak of the First World War forced many countries to abandon their pavilions a while before that.

In Lyon, she purchased some more authentic-looking costumes from the Kayser fashion house and had photographs taken, attired in some of them. On 4 August 1914, Great Britain declared war on Germany and, by default, British Empire dominions followed. However, despite that, Anna would honour her commitment to the US tour.

Anna returned to Great Britain to cross the Atlantic on 3 October 1914, embarking from Liverpool. She sailed on the *Lusitania*, arriving in New York six days later. The ship's manifest recorded: 'Mme. E. Guérin Lecturer'; last residence 'Lyon'; nearest relative 'E. Guérin, 33 rue Franklin, Lyon, France'; with a destination of 'St. Regis Hotel NYC'.

Eugène was 44 years old when the First World War began but, at his request, he was mobilised on 5 July 1915. Presumed an Alsatian-German dialect speaker, being born in Guebwiller, Alsace-Lorraine, Eugène began his war service as a translator at 'Camp des Prisonniers Alsacien-Lorraine', Saint-Rambert-sur-Loire. He served there until 6 December 1916.

Consequently, Anna and Eugène's lives continued to be continents apart but that was always going to be the case and it would continue long after the war ended. Eugène would carry on his judicial duties in French-governed African countries and Anna would divide her time between the United States of America and France.

In her hastily written 1941 *Synopsis*, Anna described her position when she arrived in the USA:

> As the U. S. were neutral I could not call myself a WAR LECTURER and could not speak about the War in public places, but I lectured in Universities ... etc in many Colleges ... etc and many private schools and Seminaries and Convents. After the French lecture I was making an appeal for the French and Belgium refugees and the money collected for them was sent directly to THE SECOURS DE FANCE in Paris. But when the U. S. entered the War, I became a War lecturer, and lectured for the Red Cross throughout the Country.

This would become Anna Guérin's next big adventure.

In the first days of research, I thought I had found the correct woman and, after finding living relatives of Anna, that was substantiated. By the time I came to read Anna's *Synopsis*, I had already created a fact-based timeline for her, of considerable length. Her *Synopsis* confirmed it all. My research proved Anna's own words to be a truthful and factual account and, in return, she gave my research authenticity.

In essence, all content within the *Synopsis* and American newspapers offers an accurate method of documenting Anna's work in the United States of America and beyond. It would be naïve to think that every single thing will be discovered about Anna because new facts come forward regularly. However, enough essential elements of Anna's life are known, proving her to be an exceptional humanitarian.

It can honestly be said that 'Madame E. Guérin' wasted no time, after disembarking in New York. At the time of writing, the earliest date discovered for a lecture given by her in the USA was 23 November 1914. She was attending the Misses Hebbs' Girls' School in Wilmington, Delaware, for an Alliance Française lecture. Her female subjects were Marie Antoinette, Charlotte Corday, and Marie-Jeanne Roland.

We learn a little about Anna Guérin's underlying intent from the next day's review. Anna

> spoke concerning the fishermen and their families of Brittany, for whom she devotes half the proceeds of her lecture receipts. ... Mme. Guérin comes from a little village in the Cévennes ... In order to send some Christmas cheer to the poor children in the village Mme. Guérin asked for any old toys or

children's clothes that those in the audience could spare, adding
that she would be very glad to use them for that purpose. Mrs.
William C. Speakman of No. 1201 Delaware avenue, will
gladly forward anything that is donated to this cause.

The last paragraph gives us an insight into the future, in relation to Anna's
lectures and proceeds collected from appeals. Not only did Anna raise
funds for official charities, but also for other causes known to her. She
never handled any donation because she gave that responsibility to a locally
respected, honest individual and/or a local bank official.

It was the head of Wilmington's branch of the 'Alliance Française',
Swiss-born Marie Speakman née Vuillenmier, who took responsibility for
the donations at that lecture. Marie was the wife of respected dental surgeon
William Cyrus Speakman. They would both go out to serve in France in
1916, before the USA entered the war.

This prestigious school's pupils, Mrs Speakman, and Wilmington as a
whole were already raising funds for the Red Cross War Relief Committee
but they were generous again, for Anna.

Even at this early stage, Anna was making good allies and, although she
did not know it at the time, distinguished people like the Speakmans would
help her with her future children's charity and her future Poppy Drives.

In 1919, William Speakman would return from war a highly decorated
veteran and become American Legion State Commander for Delaware.
Both William and Marie would become important to Anna.

Delaware would be the first state Anna Guérin organised for her
Children's League, in 1919. The 'indefatigable' Marie Speakman became
Delaware State Committee Chairman and, as the State's American Legion
Commander, William Speakman became a committee member.

Anna Guérin's next lecture was at Rumford Hall, 50 East 41st St., New
York City, at 8.15 pm, on 1 December. This was probably a private lecture,
not an 'Alliance Française' one. It was jointly organised by New York's
Museum of French Art and 'Joan of Arc Statue Committee'.

Just before the First World War had begun, a committee was formed
to honour the 'Franco-American Alliance'. As a result, a statue of Joan of
Arc was commissioned, and the committee set about fundraising. Anna's
lecture, about Joan of Arc, formed one small part in that campaign.

The statue was dedicated on 6 December 1915. The stones which formed
the statue's base, it is documented, were brought from France: from the
Rouen prison, where Anna's heroine Jeanne d'Arc had spent her last days,
before being burned at the stake.

A week later, Anna appeared at the Waldorf Hotel. A week after that, the *New York Tribune* printed a large feature article about her. It was accompanied by photographs of Anna, one in which she was dressed as Jeanne d'Arc the shepherdess, and one as the warrior she eventually became.

It was an article entitled 'The Women of France Have Always Been Feminists', written by a critic attending one of Anna's 'Jeanne d'Arc' lectures. Perhaps it was the Waldorf lecture. It was the first American article I discovered, and it was a revelation.

Such was the riveting description of the performance, and the sympathetic interview afterwards, that it suggested a total captivation of the critic and much is learnt about Anna the woman and Anna the lecturer. For me, it was an enlightening and momentous article to read.

Anna made many bold statements in the interview: 'The women of France have always been feminists'; 'As wives and mistresses of Kings, they ruled France'; 'Today the real officers of the French Republic are the wives of the ministers'. Anna hailed the French heroine Jeanne d'Arc as 'the greatest feminist of France', 'the greatest in the world'.

Anna had portrayed Jeanne in her usual way, through all stages of her life. The genuine authentic costumes Anna wore were described. Her five-century-old armour was mentioned, as possibly worn in the Hundred Years' War between France and England.

'French women have always been the equals of their husbands,' Anna Guérin said. 'It is because men and women have worked together that there is no really distinct "feminist" movement in France, as there is in England,' she added.

Anna stated how glad she was that New York was to have a statue of Jeanne d'Arc. She was quoted as saying: 'Women now are beginning to have her courage in obeying the voices that come to them, the voices that are unseen and unheard by others.' By example, she was one of them.

Anna was asked if she believed Jeanne d'Arc had heard voices. In her answer, Anna confessed: 'Indeed, I do. There are always voices hovering about us trying to be heard, trying to advise us and direct us. But few of us lead such pure, simple lives as did Jeanne d'Arc, and that is why we do not hear them. Then there are some who do, and who are afraid of ridicule and dare not let the world know they have heard.'

This is the article aforementioned, which reported on how Anna helped the plight of slave girls within the culture of Madagascar: 'I won my appointment to the Academy through work on behalf of the slave girls of Madagascar,' she further explained in the interview.

She also spoke of her French countrywomen taking the places of their husbands at home, who had gone off to fight in the war. Of course, the same situation faced many women in each of the Allied countries, but Anna was only appealing on behalf of France, and no other.

Did Anna Guérin consider herself to be a feminist? If she believed her statement 'the women of France have always been feminists', then she must have believed she was! Certainly, I do feel evidence suggests that Anna heeded *her* own voices and persevered with each commitment she made, dedicating herself to *her* cause – just as Jeanne d'Arc had.

Anna's first tour of the United States of America appears to have been confined to the states of Connecticut, Delaware, Massachusetts, New Jersey, New York, and Pennsylvania. She is known to have lectured in colleges, schools, and universities, at least. Apart from the Joan of Arc Statue Committee lecture, the 'Alliance Française' was involved and some collections were 'given for the benefit of the Red Cross society'.

Lecture subjects included 'Jeanne d'Arc', naturally, but 'Marie Antoinette' and 'Les Trois Heroines – Victims de la Revolution' (Marie Antoinette, Charlotte Corday, and Jeanne-Marie Roland) were also reviewed. Lectures were packed full of spectators and content – to give examples, Anna had five costume change intervals during her Marie Antoinette lectures and during those, or during intervals, magic lantern slides of the relevant historical subject matter were shown.

Anna would have travelled everywhere by train and, perhaps, someone connected to her forthcoming lecture/s might have met her at the railway station of every destination. Along with her costumes, magic lantern equipment, and sometimes an overnight bag, Anna must have been accompanied by quite a lot of luggage on all her journeys.

Anna's first US lecture tour probably ended in May 1915. She travelled at least 1,600 miles. The exact date on which she left New York is not known. However, it is reported, Anna usually spent 'from May to October helping the people of her district. Week after week she lived near the trenches, in order, she says, to renew her courage at the real source – by the unquenchable courage of the poilus', when back in France.

Anna Guérin returned to the USA in early to mid-September 1915, with her eldest daughter Raymonde. This is evident because, on the 30th of that month, Anna's youngest daughter Renée arrived in New York.

Renée set sail from Bordeaux, France, on the 19th. Renée was to join her mother and sister at the Waldorf Astoria Hotel, in New York City.

Thus, Anna's second tour began and, as discreetly as before, Anna continued to raise funds to send to France. Her daughter Raymonde was often to be found assisting her. Anna gave her illustrated historical lectures in more states. She is known to have toured Illinois, Connecticut, Delaware,

Kansas, Massachusetts, Missouri, New Jersey, New York, Pennsylvania, Wisconsin, and Washington DC, giving Alliance Française lectures at colleges, universities, academies, schools, and so on.

Many lectures were repeat bookings. Institutions, 'having so much enjoyed' her 'exquisite Impersonations' during that previous first tour, had 'eagerly' looked forward 'to her rendering of a character which offers even wider scope for her genius' and they had booked her again. Anna's lecture subjects included 'Conference, Artistique'; 'Jeanne d'Arc'; 'Les Trois Heroines – Victims de la Revolution'; 'Le Salon de Mme. de Rambouillet la cour de Louis XIV'; 'Marie Antoinette'; and so on.

In November, Anna gave another lecture for Wilmington Alliance Française. Mrs Marie Speakman was supportive once again and at the end of the lecture, after Anna had spoken, Marie announced that her Alliance Française branch would send a Christmas box to French soldiers at the Front, including articles of clothing, caps, knitted goods, chocolate, and so on.

Invariably, an Alliance Française branch would make a newspaper announcement to invite members, and anyone interested in all things French, to attend. Reviews, after Anna's impersonations, would illustrate her gift of engaging advanced students with the language but also enabling those with no or limited knowledge to understand the subject matter.

One review, from Andover, Massachusetts, stated: 'Throughout her lecture, Madame Guérin was so dramatic, her gestures so expressive, that she was easily understood and the interest of her audience was kept to the end. Indeed, a Phillips [Academy] youth was heard to say that she spoke so entertainingly that he hardly glanced to the fair Abbot [Academy] girls, whom he at first intended to watch.' Praise indeed, from a young lad.

On 8 December 1915, Canadian Lieut. Col. John McCrae's poem 'In Flanders Fields' was first published in *Punch*. He was compelled to write it after his friend Alexis Helmer was killed. After the war, a comrade in arms, Cyril 'Cy' L. C. Allinson, regularly sat at the Canadian Legion 'Bullshit Table' in Uxbridge, Ontario, telling his story about the poem. When John McCrae threw the poem away, not valuing its worth, it was Cy who retrieved it and gave it to his commanding officer. It was that poem that Anna and her representatives would come to recite so often.

John McCrae's first line read 'In Flanders fields the poppies grow' initially, but Punch acquired permission to change the last word to 'blow'. But it was that original first line which became an integral part of Anna Guérin's Poppy Drives, after she began organising them in 1919. Anna's League's poppy sellers' badges and white sashes carried the words in red: 'In Flanders Fields the Poppies Grow'.

The word 'grow' was used as often as 'blow' within US newspaper articles mentioning Madame Guérin.

After the 1915 Christmas festivities, a new year dawned and Anna Guérin continued with her US lecturing tour, accompanied by her daughters Raymonde and Renée. Famous French women from history remained the subjects for her lectures. Initially, Raymonde assisted with the lectures, but Renée soon appeared on the lecturing platform scene.

During this tour, most of Anna Guérin's engagements probably continued to be arranged through the Alliance Française. Interestingly, the Alliance has been described as 'most vital and active' during the war years. Perhaps it approved of Anna's collections, even encouraged them.

Occasionally, organising bodies sent a review to a newspaper in French rather than English, for the benefit of members or students. One such review appeared after Anna lectured to the language department of the University of Missouri on 11 February 1916, on three heroines of the French Revolution. 'Ce n'est pas une etude d'histoire que je vous apporte ce soir, mais je veux simplement evoquer pour vous les trios heroines de cette époque lugubre, dit Madame Guérin...'

'This is not a historical study that I bring you tonight, but I just want you to evoke the dismal period of these three heroines,' she began by saying. Anna described how 14-year-old Marie Antoinette arrived in Paris to be crowned the dauphine of France. The people cried 'Vive Marie Antoinette, vive la reine' but she threw herself into pleasure, while her people starved and 'The words liberty, equality and fraternity were heard from all sides.' The ten-paragraph review was long and emotive.

Anna's next lecture was at Fraser Hall Chapel, University of Kansas in Lawrence, and the anticipation was high: 'There is another language besides that which employs the lips and the tongue, or writing and the printed page. It is the language of acting, through which Madame E. Guérin, a noted French speaker, expects to make herself understood.'

Analysing newspapers up until then, articles reported that Anna had given 1,200–1,400 lectures to 500–650 establishments within England, Scotland, Northern Ireland, and the United States of America. However, it will never be known how many lectures and fundraising events Anna Guérin carried out in any given year, in any given country.

The following establishments give an idea of those included in Anna's 1915/1916 'Tour of Duty': Mount Saint Mary's College, Bridgewater, NJ; Assembly Hall and Boys' High School, Hartford, CT; Bryn Mawr College, Bryn Mawr, PA; Washington DC; Stratfield Hotel, Bridgeport, CT; Rogers Hall School, Lowell, MA; Abbot Academy, Andover, MA; Normal School auditorium, Oshkosh, WI; Fraser Hall Chapel, University of Kansas, Lawrence, KA; University of Illinois, Chicago, IL; Morrow Hall, Urbana, IL; University of Missouri, Columbia, MO; the Winchester School and Pennsylvania College for Women, Pittsburgh, PA; Miss Cowles' School, Highland Hall, Hollidaysburg, PA; Greensboro College for Women, Greensboro, NC; and High School, Montclair, NJ.

The last known 1915/16 tour engagement was on 15 April 1916, in New Jersey. It is estimated that Anna Guérin travelled at least 5,000 miles during that tour. The date when Anna and her daughters left the USA is not known but leave they did, probably in late April.

If Anna Guérin looked back on any accumulated newspaper cuttings, she must have been proud of the comments she read. Here is just a selection of them: 'celebrated'; 'inimitable'; 'so dramatic'; 'well known speaker'; 'easily understood'; 'audience was kept to the end'; 'clear enunciation'; 'careful articulation'; 'There is another language besides that which employs the lips and the tongue, or writing and the printed page. It is the language of acting, through which Madame E. Guérin, a noted French speaker, expects to make herself understood'; 'the sincerity and refinement of a cultivated woman'; 'a historical and literary student of known attainments'; 'so expressive'.

After the summer in France, Anna arrived back in New York on 26 September 1916. She had embarked at Bordeaux, south-west France, on the *Rochambeau*. The regular route of the *Rochambeau* had been in and out of Le Havre but, between 1915 and 1918, its route became Bordeaux–New York–Bordeaux. Because of the war raging in the north of France, Bordeaux was the safest shipping route between France and North America. However, that route was not without risk either.

Anna was back for her third lecture tour of the US. She arrived with her 16-year-old daughter Raymonde. The Manifest gave Anna's 'Last Permanent Residence' as 'Vallon'. The nearest relative was her husband, who was still an interpreter. Two months later, Eugène was moved to Africa, to settle German business for the French government.

Anna and her daughter Raymonde's destination was the Waldorf Astoria Hotel in New York, where they would get ready for another tour. The first known engagement for Anna was on 27 October 1916. With Raymonde assisting her, Anna gave a lecture at the St Mary's Academy, a boarding/day convent school, in Windsor, Ontario, for the Alma Mater society. As was usual, she lectured in French and gave selected 'episodes in the lives of illustrious French men and women'.

There were new venues, such as the private Presbyterian Wilson College, Chambersburg, Pennsylvania; Nashville's St Cecilia Academy, a private

Roman Catholic girls' school; and the Columbia Female Institute, both in Tennessee. The *Columbia Herald* stated: 'Madame Guérin will make a special appeal, because she comes in the spirit of a patriot, and while no allusion will be made to the crisis through which her country is passing, it is a labor of love for France victorious.'

Anna had repeat bookings, such as in Hollidaysburg at the Miss Cowle's school. It was Marie Antoinette last time but, on 8 December, students were treated to Jeanne d'Arc. Fifty magic lantern slides were mentioned, with explanations in the English language. 'The speaker's impersonation in costume ... gave the spectators a vivid idea both of French peasant dress and of French armor of the fifteenth century.'

In February 1917, lectures were on Marie Antoinette at both the Sophie Newcomb College in New Orleans, Louisiana and the St Agnes Scott College in Atlanta, Georgia. Ahead of Atlanta, the Atlanta Constitution newspaper wrote: 'The costumes worn are from the shops of Paquin, Paris, and Kayser, Lyon, and are not only beautiful but historically correct. Between acts the vividness of the setting is enhanced by stereopticon views.'

I often describe Anna Guérin as 'forgotten' and, it seems, Jeanne Paquin is labelled the same. Paquin has been described as the 'forgotten dressmaker'. During this same era, she was at the height of her success, reportedly employing 2,000 workers, and internationally known for her eighteenth century-inspired dresses/costumes. Even less is known about couturière F. Kayser of Lyon, today. However, both fashion houses must have held a similarly high status in their respective cities, given the quality and beauty of the costumes Anna Guérin wore for lectures.

Engagements in North Carolina happened next. Anna Guérin was giving two performances a day sometimes, and the 'St Genevieve of the Pines College', in Asheville, NC is an example: Jeanne d'Arc was portrayed in the afternoon and Marie Antoinette was portrayed in the evening.

> It is difficult to give any adequate idea of Madame Guérin's perfect impersonation ... extraordinary delicacy and accuracy of her interpretation was heightened by the wonderful charm of delivery and by her quick transition from one phase to another ... She is marked off from lecturers and readers by the originality of her technique.

The State of Massachusetts was next, where a 'third and final' lecture at Boston's High School was given on 23 March 1917. The States of New York, Iowa, Tennessee, and Ohio followed: Elmira College chapel, NY; St Cecilia auditorium at the Immaculate Conception Academy of Davenport in Iowa; St Cecilia Academy in Nashville, TN; and the Academy of Notre Dame in Dayton, OH, respectively.

Anna continued lecturing in French, but stereopticon slides were introduced in English. Occasionally, her pseudonym 'Sarah Granier' appeared alongside 'Madame E. Guérin' within the same newspaper article. Daughter Raymonde continued to assist and impersonate such characters as Princess de Lamballe, a confidante of Marie Antoinette.

The 1916/1917 tour venues included: St Mary's Academy, Windsor, Ontario, Canada; Pennsylvania College for Women, Pittsburg, PA; Miss Cowles' School, Highland Hall, Hollidaysburg, PA; Wilson College's Thomson Hall, Chambersburg, PA; St Cecilia Academy Concert Hall, Nashville, TN; The Institute, Columbia, TN; Sophie Newcomb College, New Orleans, LA; Decatur, Atlanta, GA; Saint Genevieve's College, Asheville, NC; High School, Boston, MA; The Elmira College Chapel, New York; Immaculate Conception Academy, Davenport, IA; St Cecilia Academy, Nashville, TN; St Cecilia Academy, Dayton, OH.

On 6 April 1917, the USA formally declared war on Germany and began mobilising its troops, ready to join the existing Allies. Anna Guérin would now be able to go public with her war effort fundraising.

Looking back on any collected newspaper cuttings, Anna Guérin must have been proud of the comments she would see. Here is just a selection of them: 'most fascinating impersonations'; 'was a pleasure to all who listened'; 'so deliberate, so nice in her enunciation'; 'her lectures have met with great success'; 'a rare treat'; 'in the spirit of a patriot'; 'educational in its inception'; 'vividness'; 'remarkable French artiste'; 'extraordinary delicacy and accuracy'; 'originality of her technique'; 'eloquent speaker and a talented dramatist'.

It is estimated that, by the time their tour came to an end, Anna Guérin and her daughter Raymonde had travelled at least 7,600 miles. They sailed from New York around late April 1917, on the ship *Rochambeau*.

During her next 1917–1918 tour, Anna talked about returning to France on the *Rochambeau* at the end of her previous tour. She spoke of the ship narrowly escaping being hit by a torpedo in submarine-infested waters.

It is assumed this torpedo encounter was the one that is documented as occurring at 3.00 pm on 30 April 1917. According to an eyewitness account, which was cabled to the *Philadelphia Inquirer*, it was the ship's first encounter of the First World War. When the torpedo was seen, Captain Juhaum ordered a fast change of course and it was said that the torpedo missed the stern by only ten yards. With sun in the gunners' eyes, they opened fire and $340 was collected afterwards for them. Apparently, 90 per cent of the passengers were on the deck watching and 'The calmness of the men, women and children was marvellous.'

Did Anna Guérin get relief from lecturing, back in France? Future articles reported that, during that summer, Anna gave 'many talks before the French, in response to a request of the French government, telling them of the kind of people in America upon whom they were to pin their faith.' '"Some of them thought still that you were Indians," said she laughingly.' Humour is often associated with Anna: 'Delightfully humorous touches lighten the gloom of what she has to say…'

As is recorded, whenever home, Anna always updated herself on the dreadful situation France found itself in. She needed to return to the USA, knowing the dire circumstances of devastated France.

On 25 October 1917, Anna arrived back in New York, on the ship *La Touraine* with her sister Juliette Virginie Boulle. Anna was to 'lecture in U.S.', as a 'Teacher'. They had each travelled from Vallon and were heading to the Washington Hotel in New York City.

Frenchman François Robert le Breton Oliveau was also on the ship *La Touraine*. Interesting, his brother François Jean le Breton Oliveau had arrived in August, on a 'foreign mission'. Anna, and one of these brothers, had been officially appointed by the French authorities, to appeal on behalf of 300,000–400,000 invalided soldiers of France, who were unfit for military duty, disabled in service, and who had been discharged without a pension. These were soldiers categorised as French Invalids Class No. 2. For the purpose of the lecturing circuit, the Frenchman took Robert Oliveau and Robert Arbour as his pseudonyms. So was Anna's companion Robert or Jean?

The Oliveau boys were born in Bordeaux, France: Robert in 1890 and Jean in 1895. Together, they entered the USA in 1912, heading for Canada. Jean married and, in 1914, his son Roy Henry was born in New York.

Both served France during the First World War. Articles noted 'Oliveau' served with the 9th Regiment of Algerian Tirailleurs; he fought in the Marne, Aisne, Ypres, and Somme battles, and was cited for bravery. This was Jean and, on returning to America in 1917, he was recovering from wounds. After being in the USA, Jean returned to France, returned to the 9th Tirailleurs, became intoxicated by gas on 17 July 1918, and was wounded again on 13 October 1918.

Robert served in the 3rd Tirailleurs. He was not wounded or cited for bravery. When he arrived on Anna's ship, he was a medically discharged veteran. Thus, the conundrum is: did Jean lecture, using Robert's name, or did Robert lecture, describing Jean's service?

Both brothers would serve in the Second World War. Robert became a member of the French Resistance, directing escape routes through Spain. Jean was in the 65th Infantry Regiment. He was recorded as captured on 23 October 1940 and interned in the Frontstalag 194 camp, in Châlons sur Marne.

It is deduced that Anna Guérin and le Breton Oliveau spent November preparing for their lecture tour and meeting with their agent, or 'advance representative', as Joseph Theodore Buddecke was often described. This pairing demonstrates why it was good for Anna to be a married woman, rather than a single woman, travelling with Oliveau.

Joseph was a well-known New Orleans-born gent. Primarily, his career was in journalism, having progressed from reporter to editor to prominent publisher. However, in 1917, Joseph had temporarily based himself in New York and donated his services to the two French lecturers, having 'put aside his business to devote all his time to this work'.

The first engagement for the two French lecturers appears to be 11 December 1917. They were in Montclair, New Jersey, at a monthly Alliance Française soirée. Anna was already known; she had lectured there before and she was 'chief speaker'. However, this time, her lecture was very different: she spoke in English and the subject was 'La France Immortille' (Immortal France): 'Mme Guérin is familiar with the war conditions and has new and interesting things to tell about the thrilling realities that dwell behind the phrase "somewhere in France".'

Anna's practice of showing magic lantern slides continued to play a part in this Guérin-Oliveau lecture tour but, for this fundraising, scenes were very graphic. They were actual photographs taken at the Front, pertinent to appealing to the hearts and pockets of an audience.

The Grunewald Hotel Convention Hall in New Orleans, on 21 January 1918, was another engagement. Anna was described as 'a lecturer of international reputation' and she told of the war conditions, as she knew them. Oliveau gave a 'stirring talk' about the French invalids and he personally passed the collection plate around. This collection resulted in a 'substantial contribution' to the soldiers' fund.

Natchez, in Mississippi, was next. Lectures were given at the Red Cross headquarters, Baker Grand Theatre, and Cathedral Hall. Venues were typical of those organised by Joseph Buddecke. Oliveau told of 'thrilling experiences at the battles of La Marne, Aisne and Ypres'.

Anna was described thus: 'a woman of charming personality'; 'wife of a judge of the French court'; 'famed speaker'; 'a typical distinguished French lady'; 'her personality is striking'; 'her emotional talent is great'; 'holds her audience spell-bound'; 'has secured her the greatest success on the platform'; 'she quickens the morale if her auditors'; 'she illumines and strengthens the ties between France and America'.

By February 1918, it was reported that Anna had spoken in twenty-two states east of the Mississippi, since her arrival in October 1914.

Still in Mississippi, Vicksburg followed for a couple of days. On 8 February, Anna and Oliveau lectured at the Bijou Dream Theatre. On the 9th, Anna addressed school children at the Carnegie Library at 11.00 am and, at 8.00 pm, both spoke at the Library. Judge Harris Dickson introduced Anna as 'an intensely interesting speaker' and 'paid a high tribute to services which she is rendering to her people'.

Anna explained: 'I have just returned from a long journey through our war stricken country. The scenes which confronted me inspire me more than ever to urge everyone to their full share towards bringing this terrible war which is for humanity, liberty and civilization to a successful end.'

Emotive quotes and descriptions were so numerous and so frequent, wherever Anna visited, it is very difficult not to try to use them all, but that is just not possible. As the tour continued during February, compliments flowed in for Anna, as she and Oliveau arrived in Shreveport, Louisiana: 'she retains her youth, her beauty and vitality'; 'to hear her is an instruction, to meet her is a high privilege'; 'Although she spoke in broken English, her address was forceful and at times the audience was moved to tears, when she would speak of her "beloved France," of heroic Belgium or of the atrocities of Germany. When her address was finished the cheering lasted for several minutes.'

Anna and Oliveau lectured in Shreveport for three days. Anna visited the local schools, St Mary's Convent, St Vincent's Academy, and the Shreveport Chapter of the Red Cross, offering invitations to the joint talks. At the latter, Anna was described as looking 'disarmingly handsome'.

At the City Hall Auditorium, Anna also gave a special matinée to school children and their mothers. Lectures were sometimes free but, on this occasion, admission was 10 cents for a child and 25 cents for an adult. She gave a solo evening lecture in French, under the auspices of the French Mutual Aid and Benevolent Society of Shreveport.

On 14 February, St Valentine's Day, Anna and Oliveau arrived in Alexandria, Louisiana. Immediately, on that day, Anna set to work and spoke to ladies of the Rapides Chapter American Red Cross headquarters 'in the interests of the wounded and helpless soldiers of France'. It was the next day that a joint lecture took place at City Hall.

The next day, at 4.30 pm, Anna gave a solo lecture at the Fraser Hall Chapel, Kansas State University in Lawrence. No mention was made of raising funds for the French soldiers. Her lecture was on Jeanne d'Arc and was given in French, to the French students. It is logical to assume it was either an engagement for the Alliance Française or a private one.

Apart from one day in Natchitoches, Louisiana, the pair's campaign moved to Texas for three weeks. The touring duo visited Dallas, San Antonio, Houston, Austin, Marshall, Texarkana, and Marshall, in that order. In San Antonio, they gave separate lectures: Oliveau's subject was 'Warfare in the Trenches'. He described the French soldier's life, with the aid of stereopticon slides. He told stories of bravery.

Anna's lecture was 'Present Conditions in France'. She told of the condition of the civilian population and how French people were 'bearing up under the war and showing the truest type of patriotism'. It may have been a Patriotic Speakers' Bureau lecture. On an unknown date, perhaps during this tour, Anna had become a Patriotic Principal Speaker.

Anna and Oliveau spent five days in Houston, 20–24 February inclusive. There was a series of five lectures benefiting soldiers and tubercular patients. Most took place at the Rice Hotel. Anna's sister Juliette and Joseph Buddecke joined and assisted them.

In Houston, Anna was described as: 'a woman of rare charm'; 'Sarah Bernhardt the second'; 'a most interesting speaker'; and 'her subject certainly cannot fail to stir the sympathies of her audience'. Under the auspices of the city administration, Anna gave a solo lecture at the city auditorium. This was probably a Patriotic Speaker lecture for her.

In Austin, descriptions of Anna included: 'a high type of French woman, serious, yet with the graceful, attractive social manner that is one of the French woman's chief charms'; 'speaks in English with an adorable accent'; 'can be understood perfectly'.

On 10 March, Oliveau went to Hot Springs, Arkansas, to lecture to 2,000 people, while Anna remained in Marshall, Texas, where she was given an informal reception in the afternoon, by Club women. In the evening, she gave a lecture on behalf of wounded soldiers at City Hall.

The pair rendezvoused in Little Rock on 12 March. Over three days, comments about Anna included: 'an orator of unusual capacities'; 'well-known French patriotic speaker'; 'a brilliant conversationalist'; 'very charming and gracious manner'; and 'The Great French Patriot'.

Pine Bluff, in Arkansas, was the next engagement for Anna and Oliveau. Sister Juliette and Joseph Buddecke had gone ahead of them to make arrangements for the lectures the pair would make there.

Afterwards, Anna and Oliveau parted company for a few days again. Anna went to lecture in Muskogee, Oklahoma, and Oliveau went to Kosciusko,

Mississippi. They came together again in Tulsa, Oklahoma, on 2 April. It was here that a group of oil millionaires got together and subscribed to an expenses fund for Anna. In the future, she spoke of raising a lot of money in Tulsa and of the millionaires willing to help finance her.

Two days later, Anna and Oliveau were both in Bartlesville, Oklahoma. They gave lectures at the High School. Anna gave a 'pathetic description of the wasted condition of the French land'.

On 8 April, Oliveau gave a lecture at Central High School auditorium in Tulsa. It was probably his last lecture of the joint tour. Anna headed to Kansas and Missouri.

Anna spent the next two months speaking in these two states. It is presumed she began by canvassing for the Third US Liberty Loan Drive, before campaigning for French widows and orphans under the auspices of the American Red Cross. Anna may have begun wearing her signature blue-grey uniform already, beside uniform-wearing Oliveau, but she was definitely wearing it immediately afterwards, with her French medals.

Anna's costume mimicked the blue uniform of the French soldiers. It was a tailor-made suit, with a hat of the same fabric: styled on the uniform of the Chasseurs Alpins, nicknamed the 'French Blue Devils'/'les Diables Bleus'. Anna stated she did not consider it a uniform but wore it for convenience. Apparently, the suit was designed for Anna, as near to what the French soldiers wore as she could get it.

Anna wore the suit with the French government's consent. Usually, the outfit was completed with a leather army belt and cross-shoulder strap. On one occasion, it was reported, she entered a hotel restaurant wearing 'an evil-looking gun strapped to her uniform'. It was written: 'the waiters dropped their dishes in fright and hid behind the restaurant pilasters'. Guns had to be checked-in at the door, but it was Anna's travelling gloves hanging from her belt that were mistaken for a gun.

The American Red Cross held War Fund Drives during May 1918. The second Kansas Red Cross Drive was officially held between 20 and 27 May, although it included a few days either side of that week. The nationwide drive's goal was reported at $100,000,000, with it being exceeded by 70 per cent. Anna contributed to that, speaking so many times during those days.

Anna emerged as an even greater tour de force during this period. On one particular day, it is reported she 'made nineteen speeches' and 'raised $32,000 in a territory which already had been canvassed'.

Anna spoke every day and every evening. The Campaign Director for Kansas State, Mr James C. Nichols, wrote a letter to thank her for all her great work. Anna was made the guest of honour at a special reception at one of the country clubs.

Kansas State's Lieutenant Governor, William Yoast Morgan, heard Anna speak in Kansas City. The American newspaperman and politician told his friends, 'she is the greatest of all the war speakers'. He found it was possible to book her for a patriotic meeting in Hutchinson, his hometown, and immediately wired to make the arrangements.

After the Kansas Red Cross Drive finished, Anna began a tour on behalf of French widows and orphans. She began travelling deeper into these two states. Still continuing as Anna's 'advance representative', Joseph Buddecke arranged just as many engagements for her.

All the fundraising donations and subscriptions were sent to France to relieve widows and orphans via the American Red Cross. Appearing around now, though, is a 'Madame Guérin's Appeal' fund, although its funds still went via the Red Cross.

We barely know about the fund because it is rarely mentioned. The *Neosho Daily News* asked: 'Will those, whose pledges to Madame Guérin's fund have not paid, please call at Bank of Neosho and redeem same.' Additionally, the *New York Times* included it within a list of the American Red Cross donations in 1918: only four individuals gave a higher donation than Anna.

On 6 June, while Anna was working in Kansas and Missouri, an Associated Press article was circulated. The *New York Tribune* and Kansas's *Hutchinson News* were amongst the newspapers that printed it. It described American soldiers decorating steel helmets 'with poppies from the fields' before going into battle at Veuilly-La-Poterie, Aisne, France. Poppies were continuing to become emblematic with Americans.

For the rest of June, Anna lectured at: Grand Avenue Church, Great Bend, Kansas; Tabernacle, W. Eleventh St, Baxter Strings, KS; High School, Neosho, Missouri; First Presbyterian Church, Emporia, KS; Congregational Church, Aurora, MO; High School Auditorium, Kansas City, KS; Auditorium, Topeka, KS; Commercial Club, Leavenworth, KS; St Joseph, MO; Methodist Church and Claflin Hall, Salina, KS; Albert Raylor Hall, Emporia, KS; Wichita Library, KS Wichita, KS; and Convention Hall plus stores and theatres in Hutchinson, KS, at least.

In Hutchinson, funding was further explained. Yes, some expenses came from the French government; she also used her own money; but, if necessary, financing was taken over by a group of philanthropic men. These were her thirty-five Tulsa millionaires, of course.

Words used to describe Anna and her lectures were many: 'most winning smile'; 'great speaker'; 'delicious foreign accent'; 'her lectures are said to quicken the patriotism of her hearers'; 'wonderful little woman'; 'distinguished'; 'enraptured audience'; 'vivacious, magnetic; attractive face and figure'; 'In voice deep toned as a bell, eyes flashing, now softened, gracefully gesturing'; 'she paints word pictures and sways her audience at will'; 'Speaking in her own inimitable way'; 'has all the natural charm and animated play of feature'; 'Her magic is tragic, full of hope and courage'; 'the Sarah Bernhardt of the lecture platform'; 'gives vivid word portrayals'; 'a decidedly interesting speaker'; 'one of the best known French-women of today'; 'most directly appealing manner'; 'although of a slight build her voice carried well'; 'a patriot'.

Such phrases entice a person to imagine what it must have been like to hear Anna's powerful speeches. Propaganda played a part, of course, but I feel her raison d'être went deeper than that. She genuinely knew her kinsfolk's plight. She told of working in a hospital but knew she would not make a good nurse. But she was serving her country by doing what she was good at: lecturing and raising funds.

Speakers, including Anna, built their patriotic speeches around the tough reasoning that France had helped America when it was fighting for its independence in 1776, and it was time for America to repay the debt by helping France in *her* hour of need. There is no doubt that Anna's speeches complimented her American audiences. Undoubtedly, she would flatter any country she visited, if it meant helping France.

To use Anna's Baxter Springs Tabernacle speech as another example of her prowess, the seating capacity (of 1,500) was full and many had to stand. In her 'vivacious, emotional, dramatic' manner, Anna stated 'I have come across the seas to thank America.'

Sometimes, I regret that I will never know how Anna might have praised *my* country of birth, my British kinsfolk, had there been the need to make her appeals for help in Britain during the Great War.

Anna told of

> the coming of the Sammies. France bleeding, stumbling about, almost crushed in body – mourning in every home, weary, but struggling on in the unquenchable, unconquerable spirit of France – welcomed the coming of the Americans as the saviors of the cause and spread the path of the marching Sammies with flowers. We love those brave boys of America and we give them the best ...
>
> I can see thousands of wounded soldiers, towns burning, and women and children fleeing from the Germans ... But we

shall hold them. The Germans shall never pass. The sons of
France are dying and the women and children are suffering
and sacrificing. But they are glad to do it – for France. They
know what defeat means.

She spoke of

atrocities perpetrated upon the French, their finest boys taken
prisoners and innoculated with the bacilli of tuberculosis sent
home to die and spread the horror among their families. The
daughters of France thrown back across the borders, outraged
and broken ...

But Anna also told listeners of things she knew personally. She told of 'the
sad story of the neighbor man gassed by the fiends of Prussia, who toiled
in the fields to support his three little children and died in sorrow with the
hungry and unprotected faces of his little ones about him.' Other stories
were told by Anna which 'brought moistness to the eyes of the audience'.

Anna brought 'the horrors a little closer home', by producing 'a letter
from the Governor of Missouri verifying her statement of the little American
nurse who was captured by the Germans and sent back into France maimed
for life ... to be the mother of a child by a German officer'.

She stated: 'there is 200,000 people in France who are destitute and
starving at this time'. 'In fiery manner and voice', Anna repeated the watch
word of France: 'They Shall Not Pass!' – 'Ils ne passeront pas'.

'At the close of the meeting a liberal collection was taken up for the French
helpless and the destitute...' The review for the speech was practically the
whole length of one column of that Kansas State broadsheet newspaper. It
feels totally unfair to Anna to only quote what is cited above from it.

Some atrocity stories used as First World War propaganda would be
discredited, but at least Anna could relay stories personally told to her. After
the war ended, French communes officially recorded locally witnessed
atrocities to prove they had happened.

Anna's passion, at this point, was promoting the plight of the *fatherless
children of France*, but this turn of phrase resulted in, at least, a couple
of misunderstandings during her US tours. The first problem occurred
simultaneously: in Topeka and Wichita, in Kansas.

Anna was due in Topeka, Kansas, on 24 June. She was to speak there
and receive 'an elaborate reception' at State Governor Capper's home. Also,
she was due in Wichita on 26 and 27 June, but during his 'advance' visits,

Joseph Buddecke stated that Anna was working on behalf of the 'fatherless children of France'. People misunderstood and thought she officially represented the Fatherless Children of France organisation. To confuse matters further, the Wichita lectures had been arranged by the local FCF committee chairman, Mrs Thor Jager.

With official status disputed, Topeka and Wichita regarded Anna Guérin with suspicion and cancelled her engagements. Immediately, Anna visited Governor Capper. She explained the facts of her tour to the satisfaction of everyone; she was

> working for the widows and orphans of France. Her expenses
> are paid from a special fund, and do not come out of the proceeds
> of her lectures. All the money collected from her lectures is
> sent directly to the American Red Cross, Washington, D.C.,
> which forwards it immediately to France …

Anna's status was further verified because she was authorised by the Speaker's Bureau of the Red Cross. After the upset, one Wichita date was able to be reinstated and Anna was given a special luncheon when she visited. The Topeka engagement was rearranged for 31 June.

The Fatherless Children of France organisation was, in essence, a sponsorship scheme for French war orphans. It is quoted as becoming operational in the spring of 1916, but the concept was being promoted in the USA in 1915. It held, at its heart, the welfare of children of French soldiers. In 1917, keeping its name, it was reorganised and became part of the Fraternal League for the Children of France, affiliated to the American Society for the Relief of French War Orphans.

France needed this young generation to thrive because its future depended upon it. It was imperative that the French language and culture survived beyond the war, with that generation. Americans were asked to 'adopt' a French child for at least 10 cents a day. Basically, those who adopted were committing to sponsor a child or children.

The principles were that French orphans should be brought up in their French homes, their father's religion, and with mothers and siblings, if possible. In the absence of family members, responsible guardians were appointed. Fatherless Children of France committees in villages, towns, and cities were formed to administer funds, in order that these orphaned children's lives were sustained for as long as need be.

Regardless of deliberate intent, news articles must have pricked consciences. Lists gave the names of local adopters; the number of children adopted by each (it could be two, three, or four, but the norm was one); and donation amounts. In 1917, in Marin County, California, the question was asked: 'Is your name amongst those on the following list?'

Normally, at this time of year, Anna would not have been in the USA but, because the war was still raging, Anna felt she needed to remain and carry on raising more funds for France. She announced she would 'take no rest'. As a result, her schedule increased by at least another 100 lectures throughout the summer of 1918:

> After having given more than sixty speeches or lectures in Kansas City for the benefit of the American Red Cross drive, Madame Guérin gave some special lectures in order to send some money to the mayor of a village in the center of France. This money will allow him to hire horses or machinery to help the poor women and children to gather their crops.

The men were away and, apparently, the Germans were ready to 'rush to Paris'. Anna's heart was 'bleeding for all the women of France, but especially for the women of this village, every one of whom she knows personally'. Surely, this must have been Anna's Vallon.

Trustworthy Scottish-born Andrew Young handled the donations from Anna's personal lectures. He was the Manager at Kansas City's Montgomery, Ward & Company, a wholesale catalogue store.

Another Kansas speech, in Emporia, alludes to the magnetism felt on hearing Anna:

> Vividly and with an earnestness which evinced a determination to achieve victory at any cost, Madame Guérin gave a true and characteristic manifestation of the spirit of France ...
>
> Without a desire to incite to hatred, yet with a belief that Americans ought to know what war with Germany means, she told of the horrors Germany had committed upon the civil populations of France and Belgium.

Another long review of the Topeka speech wrote of Anna having a 'long trail of friends' in the twenty-eight states she had already visited. Again, as on other occasions, Anna spoke in English, even though she had 'only recently learned to speak the English language'. But she 'held the attention of her audience from the moment she raised her voice in grateful appreciation of America's aid, to the close of her talk'.

Some of Anna's phrases appear sharp when seen written down in black and white:

> Do not think this is charity. The French people do not want charity. Don't say that you have given many times before, but you will make another sacrifice. Don't dare to use the word sacrifice here. Don't dare to think of the giving of money as sacrifice. Only those boys who are offering their lives for their country and humanity, only their mothers and wives, are making any effort worthy to be called sacrifice.

But whichever words she used, wherever they were spoken, and in whatever charitable causes, Anna was always successful in bringing out the best of her audiences. They always found themselves digging deep into their hearts and deep into their pockets.

Occasionally, reviews mentioned Anna's accent and recorded that her English was not easily understood, but it appears that it mattered not.

In June, at the end of one of her patriotic Kansas speeches in Baxter Springs, Anna appealed to the audience for good-quality clothing and shoes for men, women, and children in war-stricken France. As a result, the response from Baxter people was generous and 350 items of clothing were sent to the French Relief Society HQ in New York.

On 2 July, Anna headed for Nebraska. It was the next state that Joseph Buddecke had arranged for her and she made Lincoln her headquarters. Anna had given one isolated lecture there before, on 26 June, when she had a free day because Wichita was cancelled.

It was, perhaps, during that first week of July that Anna met one Anne Parker Miner, who was staying with her sister Mrs W. G. L. Taylor in Lincoln. Anne, who lived in Chicago, was the Western Division and Illinois Deputy for the Food for France Fund (FFFF). The Fund was the next charity that would benefit from vivacious Anna's energy. She would continue to uphold the 'greatest of all the war speakers' title.

The Food for France Fund had been started in New York, on 14 July 1917, by Miss Carita Spencer. She had personally visited many of the military hospitals in France and noticed there was a lack of proper nourishment. Before setting up the Fund, Carita received $10,000 from an American donor and this demonstrated to her that she might succeed in offering aid. She was commissioned to raise funds in the USA by Justin Godart, the French Under-Secretary of State and head of Service de Santé.

The Service de Santé was, and still is, responsible for French armed forces' health needs. In the First World War, it offered relief to sick soldiers in French military hospitals but funds for these were not large enough to meet the demands on it. Apart from soldiers, the Service also assisted civilians and refugees – three groups dear to Anna.

Apparently, the equivalent of only 25 cents was allocated, per day, for each French soldier. That had to cover care, medical treatment, and food. The Fund also provided some support for medically discharged soldiers, who Anna and Oliveau had been raising funds for.

It was reported the Fund did not conflict with, or duplicate, the work of the American Red Cross, nor any other American War Relief Committee sending food, because its goods were sent directly to the French government for distribution to military hospitals.

Apart from money to buy goods, canning and preserving products were requested. Members of the National League for Women's Service, also known as 'The Housewives' Army', were asked to donate some of their preserved food. Other articles requested included animal fats; beans; butter (tinned); chicory (dried); chocolate; cocoa; coffee (green); fruits (dried); flours; honey; lard; meat juice; macaroni; milk (condensed); peas; prunes; rice; sugar; tapioca; and vegetables (dried).

France badly needed more food: bakers' shops had closed because of lack of flour; fruit trees and crops had been destroyed by the war.

Many boxes of goods were sent to a Paris warehouse, for distribution to sick and wounded soldiers in hospitals, civilian adults, and children in the devastated areas, who were all underfed and hungry. Thus, the Food for France Fund was an ideal charity for Anna to work with, alongside her lecturing for her Red Cross French orphans' fund.

No doubt keeping to Buddecke's schedule, on 3 July, Anna gave a stirring appeal at Lincoln's Commercial Club 'for close co-operation and warm friendship between the United States and France'. She said the four years of war had left France exhausted, with thousands of men and boys dead in the trenches, one million wounded, crippled soldiers, plus one million widows, and more than two million orphans.

Articles in Nebraskan newspapers, for instance the *Lincoln Star* on 7 July, gave Anna headlines such as: 'Our Boys in France and the French. Free Lecture with Lantern Slides. MADAME E. GUÉRIN. "The Spirit of France Incarnate."' This wording was typical of what editors used, to promote or review Anna's lectures at this time. Clad in her formal blue-grey uniform, as usual, she spoke with passion and brutal honesty:

I am just back from a long journey through my war-stricken, bleeding France. I am here to thank you and to tell you that in spite of all that France has endured, never has her courage been greater than at this moment ...

I am here to thank you and to tell you that you must not forget now that American boys and French soldiers are fighting in the same trenches, for the same aims, shoulder to shoulder, heart to heart. Do not forget that the French soldiers are dying for the Stars and Stripes of your flag as the American boys for the Tri-colors of France ...

I am here to ask help as I should do to a brother, to a sister, for people who have every right to ask it, because they have given everything they have for this great cause by in giving their lives, their husbands, their fathers. Don't call it charity but duty. Bless the privilege that God gives you in a blest country. Be a soldier here at your place as your boy is over there. Be ready to give until it hurts you as it hurts the boy to be wounded or killed. ... Give your money as you do not give your life. Do not be a slacker.

However, it was often reported that Anna's 'delightfully humorous touches' lightened the gloom.

Anna was described as being rather small of stature, but she made a striking appearance, nevertheless. Her large eyes had been 'saddened by the pictures of suffering they had witnessed'. It was noted that both of her daughters were safe in Switzerland, her husband was in Africa, and there she was 'on her errand of mercy in America'. She was 'giving the people a real conception of what the war is, by telling of the conditions, not only in the French army, but of the American'.

The same day, the *Nebraska State Journal* printed a similarly long article about Anna. It mentioned her sister, Mlle Juliette Virginie Boulle. Juliette, or 'Yette' as she was known in the family, was in Kansas City giving lectures. She was following on from Anna's great work during the Red Cross Drive there.

The Journal's article informed readers that Juliette was giving audiences 'a new comprehension of France', having carried out Red Cross work in France, and England, before arriving in the USA. It is interesting to note, at this point, that Juliette was lame in one leg.

Again and again, it was made known that Anna was presenting the terrible plight of her people under the auspices of the American Red Cross and the money raised was handled entirely through it. The local Red Cross chapters sent it directly to Washington DC HQ, solely for work to be carried out in the devastated regions of France.

The Sedgwick County chapter of the Red Cross, in Kansas, is a good example to quote because, after a plea from Anna, those facts were printed along with an announcement that a cheque for $304.61 had been forwarded to those headquarters. Throughout her lecturing, Anna appears to have been scrupulously honest. She did not, and would not, handle donations, in order to be beyond reproach, to be above suspicion.

By this point, it was noted that Anna had travelled to, and lectured in, twenty-eight states. It was reiterated that she travelled on a special expenses fund, provided by the French government.

Anna described incidents which made her audience realise that not even children are exempt from the ravages of war. She told of a five-year-old girl, who had her hands cut off above the wrists and, it was said, as each person passed her hospital bed, she would ask, 'If I will be very, very good, do you think that my hands will grow out again and get well?' Anna would say 90 per cent of atrocities were not known. Such propaganda was convincing and compelling but not always verified.

For the next few weeks, Anna would be lecturing all over Nebraska. She visited and gave speeches at places such as Omaha, Fremont, Cedar Bluffs, Alma, Grand Island, Aurora, Raymond, Panama, Roca, Prairie Home, Denton, Emerald, Hickman, Firth, Plymouth, and Havelock, and these were all regularly interspersed with lectures in Lincoln, where she was making many new friends.

Anna stayed at the Lincoln home of renowned American General John Joseph Pershing's sisters, May (Anna Mae) and Mary (widowed Mrs Daniel Mercer Butler). They were raising their brother's son. The General's wife and three daughters had suffocated in a fire at their home at the Presidio Military Post, in San Francisco, in 1915. His son had been rescued alive. An investigation into the fire concluded that hot coals, from an open grate, had fallen and set the home alight. There were long-held concerns that the Post's old wooden buildings could be fire-traps.

Such was Anna's reputation that, when she spoke at Lincoln's City Auditorium on behalf of fatherless children in France, the building was arranged to accommodate an audience of over 100, but chairs were taken long before she was due to speak, extra chairs had to be placed on the actual stage, people had to stand in aisles, and many had to be turned away, disappointed. She spoke for two hours, almost overcome with emotion at times. Pledges and collections amounted to $1,153.

During her lectures, Anna spoke of all French men, aged between 17 and 45, having to fight. Those not fit to fight had to carry out work behind the lines. She spoke of the 'valor and courage' of the 'Sammies', and said that they were fighting like lions beside the French.

On at least one occasion, she read part of a letter sent from Albert, her 43-year-old brother:

> I take back everything I said to you about your American friends last summer. When I saw them in Bordeaux so well equipped – always laughing, joking, always so generous with their dollars – when I said to you I wished to see how they would act under fire, those Yankees. I have seen them and they are wonderful, wonderful in their power of resistance, in their obstinacy, in their seriousness ...

On 12 July 1918, Anna arrived in Omaha, Nebraska, to hold a fundraising drive, including speaking at a mass meeting on 14 July, France's Bastille Day. However, another misunderstanding faced Anna over her credentials. It was described as a 'tangle' but it was soon unravelled. At the time, she was working on her own account and her advance letter had stated, correctly, that funds would be sent to the Red Cross. It was wrongly assumed she was officially representing the American Red Cross, but Omaha Red Cross leaders knew nothing about her. Luckily, Lincoln's Commercial Club Secretary, Walter S. Whitten, was in Omaha at the time and he vouched for Anna. All ended well.

Anna made Omaha her temporary home for a while, giving speeches eight days running. Sometimes, it was several speeches a day, for instance: on 13 July, she spoke on the Omaha streets during the day and spoke at six city theatres during the evening; on 14 July, she was the principal speaker at Red Cross mass meetings that were held at the Elmwood, Manawa, and Miller Parks. Omaha's Bastille celebrations continued beyond this, though. Anna spoke also at Hanscom Park, Gifford Park, the Chamber of Commerce, and the Brandeis theatre.

Even though they were far from their native land, Bastille Day continued to be celebrated by French immigrants to the USA. In 1918, Omaha celebrations included a picnic; concert, jazz, and orchestra music; patriotic readings; folk singing; a merry-go-round, with organ playing French airs; and 'La Marseillaise' was sung. The French 'Tricolore' was prominently displayed all over the city.

Another Omaha speech was held at the Stock Exchange, on 19 July. An article, partly headed 'MADAME GUÉRIN STIRS SYMPATHY', began: 'It is not often that business men, accustomed to dealing with the practical side of life, are giving to weeping, but tears stood in the eyes of many a veteran of the Stock exchange … Madame Guérin stirred the hearts of the stockmen as no other speaker had done.'

At this Stock Exchange event, donations received from businessmen came partly from the selling of small buttons. These are also known as pin/button-badges. Apart from reviewing the speech, the article also described how the badges bore the American and French flags and the inscription 'United in Liberty's Cause'.

This description was important, as it enabled me to identify the badge when I came across one. The words 'I helped the French orphans' also appeared on the buttons or badges.

Perhaps after a recommendation, the buttons were ordered from M. F. Shafer & Co., of Omaha. It was only three months earlier that the company had moved into a new modern factory. Buttons/badges were amongst the assorted 'Advertising Specialities' that the company produced, along with utility specialties, leather goods, business calendars, signs, etc. The buttons were sold at all the Omaha events Anna spoke at, for any amount a person so desired to donate.

Before returning to Lincoln, Anna carried out a couple more engagements at locations close to Omaha. One was in Fremont and the other was in Council Bluffs, which is 4.5 miles east of Omaha, just over the Missouri River border into Iowa. In her lecture at Fremont, Anna Guérin 'painted a graphic word picture' of the suffering that her people had 'been forced to endure' during the war. She appealed for money for French orphans, saying, 'A child can be fed for 10 cents a day in France. A mother and two children can be fed for a week for $1.'

At the lecture's end, a collection raised $152 and anyone wishing to further donate was asked to do so at three trusted locations: the First National Bank, the office of lawyer Seymor S. Sidner, or Fremont Red Cross Chairman of Relief Work, Mrs Rose S. McGiverin.

On 24 July, it was announced in papers that Anna had been taken ill in Omaha, perhaps with exhaustion. Anna went quiet for a month, re-emerging on 22 August, when she gave a lecture at the Cedar Bluffs Opera House, 240 miles west of Lincoln. Her next attendance was at Grand Island.

Reportedly, arrangements had been made with the National Committee of the Food for France Fund for Anna to speak throughout Nebraska. She continued that commitment at the Nebraska State Fair ground at Grand Island, 'enlisting interest in the enterprise'.

The State Fair was held on 4, 5, and 6 September and Anna definitely attended on the first two of those days, if not all three. She was accompanied by sister Juliette and local ladies.

It appears Anna and Juliette spent some time at the FFFF booth and some time walking the fairground, selling the buttons/pin-badges. Whilst doing the latter, Juliette had to frequently return to the booth with her 'tray heaped with coins' and take out more supplies of the badges, because they sold so quickly. Cigar boxes were also used as a means of collecting money and this practice would feature in the future.

On 5 September, the fair's second day dawned. It began cloudy and chilly but became increasingly warm as the day went on. In the morning, there was a circus parade which was described as a 'judiciously generous exhibit of wild animals', with camels, elephants, and so on.

Anna spoke at Lincoln's Commercial Club luncheon and attended the fair on the afternoon of the 5th. She joined Juliette and other ladies at the FFFF tent and, at the fair's auditorium, Anna gave another speech under the auspices of the Food for France Fund organisation. It was stated the money came in freely when Anna brought her speech to a close.

More badges were sold on the last day, Friday the 6th, but the supply soon became exhausted and, on two occasions, more supplies had to be ordered from Omaha. It is logical to deduce that these fair badges were identical to the Shafer ones sold in Omaha.

At the fair, badges were being sold for the fixed price of 10 cents. It was a clever ploy to equate the 10 cents price for a badge, to the same amount which would provide 'a French child's food for one more day' and that was the cry that had gone out at the fair.

The Food for France Fund organisation, the National League for Service, the Red Cross, and the Young Men's and Young Women's Christian Aid war fund were reported as having been 'gathered together fraternally' at this Nebraska State Fair.

Interestingly, in some accounts, Anna is described as a secretary or representative of the French YMCA or YWCA. Certainly, within its Archives at the University of Minnesota Libraries, there is no card for her. The archives also hold newspapers detailing its war work, and she is not found there either. Additionally, neither YMCA France nor World YMCA, in Geneva, have any document filed for her.

The organisation and Madame Guérin are only linked with other parties, for example, on 27 February 1918 (*Austin American*), Anna paid 'tribute to the American Red Cross, the Y.M.C.A., the canteens and other

American organisations working' in France. On 7 July 1918 (*Lincoln Star*), it was noted that Anna visited French and American armies and YMCA HQ in Paris, to determine the conditions of the war. As above, at the Nebraska State Fair, on 15 June 1919 (*Beatrice Daily*), Anna's agent arranged a lecture for her, 'under the auspices of the Y.W.C.A. and a committee of the ministerial association'. YWCA members helped on some Poppy Days with other organisations. I have only found proof she was hired by the French government.

On the evening of 6 September, Lincoln honoured the French General Lafayette, who had played a part in the American Revolution. At the city's auditorium, this big public patriotic meeting celebrated 'Lafayette Day' and 'Battle of the Marne Day'. The first part of the programme was a community singing festival, which culminated in singing of 'La Marseillaise'. Then Anna was introduced.

Just like the Omaha badge, the *Nebraska State Journal* headed a lengthy review the next day with 'UNITED IN LIBERTY'S CAUSE' plus 'Mme. Guérin Stirs Large Audience at the Lafayette-Marne Anniversary Program'. Anna was greeted with a packed house ready to hear her again. She began by acknowledging that they were all there to honour the 161st anniversary of the birth of Lafayette, as he was known in the USA, and the Great War's First Battle of the Marne.

The date of 6 September commemorated both, the former in the year 1757 and the latter in 1914.

Lafayette was the Marquis de LaFayette, Marie-Joseph Paul Yves Roch Gilbert du Motier. He was a wealthy Frenchman and, when he inherited his grandfather's estate, he became even wealthier. To cut a long story short: he became a King's Musketeer at age 13; by marriage, aged 16, he became part of one of the most politically powerful families in France; and, aged 19, he took his wealth to help support the USA in its struggle for independence from Great Britain.

In that fight, France supported the USA 'in liberty's cause'. Anna spoke of Lafayette arriving with one million dollars, with his entire fortune, and with thirty young officers. The Americans fighting alongside the French in the First World War were helping France in her liberty's cause. The USA was paying its debt.

Anna described how her people had been driven from their homes and seen them destroyed. They had endured unspeakable atrocities. At the end of her speech, Anna was met by the Havelock Home Guards as she left. She stopped and 'gave them a little talk on "Keeping the Home Fires Burning," setting forth their opportunities and duties as a home guard.'

Only men aged 35 or over, and men who had been rejected for enlistment, could apply to be in the Home Guard. Home Guard units were, as the name implies, home defence bodies similar to those in the UK.

Anna loved Lincoln and Nebraska and the feeling was mutual. To quote her: 'I am so grateful for the generosity of Lincoln that I am a great admirer of this city, the head and heart of Nebraska.' It was reported that she was trying to encourage Juliette to stay in Lincoln, to organise classes to teach the French language to anyone entering war service in France. It seems that Anna was successful because, within days, Juliette was offering French classes to the local Student Army Training Corps.

Juliette placed advertisements in the papers too: 'French Private Lessons given by Mademoiselle Y. Boulle Studio: 311 Neb^r State Bank Bldg. Phone B-4979.' It was reported that she wanted to permanently locate to Lincoln because of the educational atmosphere in the city. (Y was Yette.)

Apart from Anna speaking on behalf of the French orphans and the Food for France Fund, she had made a commitment to raise funds for the US Fourth Liberty Loan. As a Principal Speaker, her next obligation was to tour Nebraska's Lancaster County, which had Lincoln at its centre. She began on the evening of 28 September, by speaking at Raymond.

Until 12 October, Anna's Liberty Loan itinerary took her to many places, including: Lincoln (Methodist Episcopal Church); Panama; Roca; Prairie Home; Denton; Emerald; Lincoln (Cotner University and First Methodist Church); Hickman; Firth; Lincoln (Auditorium); Plymouth (Congregational Church); Havelock (shops and railroads); and Beatrice (Opera House).

She had the odd day off but, to compensate for that, she spoke more than once on other days. The cry went out: 'Do not fail to hear the noted Frenchwoman.' On three occasions, Anna was joined by one John T. Prince. John was the Lancaster County Chairman of Publicity. In his pre-war professional life, John was an actor, a theatrical manager, and a theatre 'play writer', and was ideally suited to a stage environment.

At two lectures, Chicago veteran Harry Douglas accompanied Anna. When the First World War broke out, Harry had enlisted in the Canadian army, as many Americans did. During his seventeen-month service, Harry was wounded three times: in the right arm; the left shoulder; and the right leg, where shrapnel still remained. After being medically discharged, he returned to the USA. Like Frenchman Oliveau, lecturing with Anna allowed Harry to continue serving his country.

Lancaster County's Liberty Loan quota was $2,700,000 and, by 16 October, that amount had been exceeded by $500,000. Independently,

Lincoln had a quota of $1,934,250 and had raised a total of $2,375,830. The campaign closed on the evening of 19 October.

After participating in this Loan campaign, Anna expected to continue her lecture tour under the auspices of the Food for France Fund, but the tour had to be cut short because of the 1918 influenza pandemic.

This Spanish Flu pandemic was worldwide but had been moving across the USA after some of the first cases appeared in the Kansas military Camp Funston, during March 1918.

In the States, by October, public gatherings were either being restricted or banned completely and public places closed. According to Walter S. Whitten, secretary of the western division of the FFFF, these closures interfered with Anna's future speaking dates.

In Nebraska, for instance, many schools were closing, and a strict quarantine was established wherever the influenza was diagnosed. It is said that more people died from this influenza than died as a result of the First World War. In her 1941 *Synopsis*, Anna wrote: 'the epidemic of Influenza [stopped] all gatherings, so I decided to return to France, in order to gather new material for other lectures.'

On 20 October 1918, the *New York Times* documented the activities of the American Red Cross during the influenza pandemic. The article also listed 240 donations of $100 and over, acknowledged the week before. Anna's donation amount was $1,326, under the Food for France Fund heading, one of twenty-three charities noted. Listed as 'Mme Guérin's appeal', only four individuals donated a higher amount. In 2021, Anna Guérin's $1,326 donation would have a value of more than $25,200.

A week later, the *Lincoln Star* brought its readers up to date with Anna's future plans. After living in Lincoln for several months, she had left but had every intention of returning to Nebraska around Christmas or in the 1919 New Year, 'with new facts and new inspiration'. At some point, whilst Anna had been lecturing in Nebraska, a local Baptist pastor, the Rev. G. F. Fink, became her advance agent. It was he who would arrange a speaking itinerary for her, before her arrival back in the USA.

The article wrote about an offer that Anna was making to the people of Nebraska. She would not sail from New York before 2 November and, if messages or parcels were sent to her at the Waldorf Astoria Hotel, she would personally post them in France – at the nearest station to where the American boys would be.

In Lincoln and other Nebraskan towns, so many people sent items through to Anna that it proved impossible for her to confirm receipt of all of them. Before returning to the USA, she planned to place a notice in the official American Expeditionary Force newspaper, *The Stars and Stripes*, stating that she would bring 'trinkets and keepsakes gathered by the boys back to their home folks' in Nebraska.

On 7 November 1918, Anna left New York for Bordeaux. She took with her two large trunks full of letters and 290 packages from people in Nebraska, for passing on to their American soldier relatives serving in France. She left the USA with the war still raging but, when she was halfway across the Atlantic, the Armistice was signed.

Anna arrived in Bordeaux around 16 November. On the 17th, she wrote to Nebraskan Myrtle Cull. In her letter, Anna wrote she was back in France, and the hundreds of packages she had taken back to France with her had been sent off to the American soldiers.

Anna thought her work was over, but she was wrong.

During that last tour of duty, it is estimated that Anna travelled at least 8,800 miles. She had spent twelve months travelling and campaigning within the United States of America.

However, Anna would find herself returning to the USA and working tirelessly again for the benefit of the widows and orphans in the devastated regions of France. In the future, it would be reported that 'she had been with her family just five days, when she was called back to Paris and told she was to have entire supervision of the work in America.'

Chapter 4

The After-War Work

Foundations for the 'After-War Work' must have been laid down in Paris, as soon as the Armistice was signed on 11 November 1918. With Anna Guérin being called to Paris so soon after returning home, she was considered important enough to consult. She was needed to cross the Atlantic again to do what she did best: lecture and raise money.

Eventually, however, she would be organising a new children's relief charity in America. She had never done such work before, and it would be a great challenge. Throughout the First World War years, Anna would have certainly discovered how American society worked. She would have had the knowledge to pinpoint the important people she needed to help her succeed in her quest, to help her pave the way.

In the future, Anna would be reported as saying that France

> felt the need of organizing an After-War-Work which would continue the splendid relief given by all these great war societies who, alas, found it necessary to close its books. Something big, worthy of France and of America, should be built: then was conceived the idea of the American Star, the American and French Children's League.

Before Anna left France in March 1919, she visited the Meuse and Aisne départements in Northern France to discover the conditions as they were then. In a Wisconsin interview, in June, Anna described what she saw there as an 'awful nightmare'. She told of interviewing General J. J. Pershing and, after gaining his permission, she visited the battlefields of Chateau Thierry, Saint-Mihiel, and Belleau Wood, speaking to American soldiers who had fought there before the Armistice.

On 31 March 1919, Anna arrived back in New York City. She had sailed from Le Havre, on the *La Lorraine*. She had stayed 50 miles away, at Vendeuvre, prior to embarkation. On the ship's manifest, she was a 'professor' travelling to sister Juliette 'care of' the Lincoln Commercial

Club, Nebraska. While her husband Eugène continued with his judicial duties in French Sudan and her daughters were in Vallon, in the care of her mother, Anna began her next big adventure.

On this quest, Anna would not return to France for another twenty months. It is estimated she travelled in excess of 24,000 miles. Her work ethic, documented in so many local newspapers along the way, proves how committed to this French cause she was.

If Anna did go direct to Juliette, she was not with her for very long before she went off to Chicago. She was there to lecture as a Council of Defense Speaker, for the fifth Liberty Loan campaign and for the Fraternal League of the Children of France. Anne Miner Parker was US National Chairman for this Fraternal League.

After this work, Anna would start to establish her League.

The 'Final Report of the Missouri Council of Defense 1919' shows Anna was one of the Principal Speakers. The accompanying text reveals how important these speakers were: 'No activity of the Missouri Council of Defense yielded more tangible results than the sustained campaign to carry the message of the Government and State by the spoken word' and 'the various County Speakers' Bureaus, performed an indispensable task in conducting our people through the successive stages of education as to why we were at war and how and why the individual could best serve and contribute to the winning of the final victory.'

A selected Committee on Public Information list provided most of the speakers, many possessing 'unusual advantages for the observation of war conditions in Europe'. The speakers' purpose was to stimulate patriotic service and mobilise public opinion. Vivacious Anna Guérin, with her first-hand knowledge, was an ideal person for this work.

Anna's first known public appearances in 1919 were on 12 April, on behalf of the Fraternal League of the Children of France: she gave a free lecture at Chicago's Fullerton Hall Art Institute, called 'A Pilgrimage in Northern France'; the Alliance Française gave a luncheon for her; and, at an afternoon reception, in the Fine Arts building, Anna spoke on 'The Fraternity of Children of Different Nations'.

On the same day as those lectures, a press release came out of Washington DC. Not for the first time, Americans would read about the poignant symbolism of the 'Allied flower' – the red Flanders poppy.

The article began: 'In Flanders fields the poppies blow, Between the crosses, row on row, That mark our places,' and continued: 'Immortalized by a soldier-poet, himself buried in France, Flanders poppies already are symbols of the nation's hero dead of the world war, says a bulletin from the National Geographic Society.' It explained the poppy was to receive semi-official recognition because it was being planted in government parks in Washington DC, as 'memorials to men who sleep under the crosses and poppies of Flanders'.

Anna next visited Shelbyville, Illinois. As the Principal Speaker, she gave an 'intensely interesting' address at a Victory Loan mass meeting at the Court House, on 16 April. She was introduced as 'an eloquent French woman fresh from the battle-ravaged France'.

At this meeting was another speaker, Lieutenant Frank McGlinn, who was one of the local 'Reilly's Bucks'. McGlinn had served in Chicago's 149th Field Artillery Regiment, under Colonel Henry J. Reilly (war correspondent/soldier). Frank spoke about his sixteen months' service.

Some of Reilly's men had returned from the war in January. Reilly was a well-known Chicagoan journalist. He had left for France in 1914, where he initially drove an ambulance with British and French forces before the USA entered the war. Even Henry J. Reilly was on this speaking circuit.

An automobile parade was often a feature of soldiers' homecoming celebrations and, sometimes, a lecture from Anna followed.

When Anna stayed in Chicago, during this or past and future visits, she may have booked into the Blackstone Hotel, on South Michigan Avenue and E. Balbo Drive. On one visit, Anna had a professional photograph taken at the Lewis-Smith Studio, which was based in that hotel. This was one of many photographs Anna used to promote her work.

Based in Chicago, and introduced as official representative of the Fraternal League of the Children of France, Anna Guérin spent most of April and May lecturing for the Loan. Some lectures were entitled 'My Visit to the American Battle Front', still illustrated with lantern slides, perhaps those shown on the Guérin–Oliveau tour.

In a review of one of her Chicago speeches, Anna was described as 'vivacious and eloquent, with flashing eyes, and when she talks of what the French people have suffered and still keep up their courage, she seems typical of the spirit of that country.'

In April, Anna's Loan lectures were largely in and around Chicago but there were odd visits further afield, which were received as if a great honour had been bestowed upon those who issued the invitation. For instance, the chair of the woman's division of the Victory Liberty Loan committee in Muncie, Indiana, stated: 'We had not hoped to be able to give the people of Delaware county a treat like this when we started out to find a speaker of national importance for our big meeting.'

Anna was said to be 'the best woman speaker on the war that has ever come to this country and the local committee feels itself most fortunate in obtaining her for an engagement here as it is one of the few places she will appear outside of Chicago.' She spoke at the High School auditorium at 8.00 pm and, previous to that, she spoke at a dinner given for women of Muncie at the Delaware Hotel, where she had been the guest of honour. After her dinner speech, newspapers announced subscription pledges of $87,400 had been made to the Loan.

Ahead of a large mass meeting for the Loan in Iowa, Anna was introduced as the 'French Woman Said to Be Greatest of All War Aid Orators'. Those present heard her tell 'of horror created by the Hun, of the children crazed, the mothers murdered, homes wantonly destroyed'. She returned to Muncie in December, to create a State Committee.

Anna's last known Loan lecture was on 1 May. From then on, she concentrated on her new League's orphans. On 6 May, she spoke at a meeting of Le Cercle Français at 3.00 pm in the Fortnightly Rooms of Chicago's Fine Arts building. On 13 May 1919, the Chicago Daily Tribune notified its readers: 'Mme. Eugene Guérin, official lecturer of the Fraternal League of the Children of France, will speak this evening at the Oak Park club. It will be guest night, and there will be a program of French and American music.' For the rest of May, she lectured in Chicago.

On 30 May 1919, US Memorial Day, some First World War Allied nations showed solidarity with the United States. France and Great Britain commemorated it alongside the USA. For instance, Lord Derby, Great Britain's Ambassador to France, attended the Memorial Day ceremony at the American cemetery in the Paris suburb of Suresnes.

The British Embassy's Assistant Military Secretary, Capt. Malcolm Bullock, who would become Lord Derby's son-in-law a few weeks later, also attended. Their two paper boutonnières survive from that time: they each hold a Marguerite de Paris daisy, cornflower, and poppy. These are symbolic of the flowers of First World War battlefields. They are archived in Lord Derby's Collection at Knowsley Hall, Merseyside.

Special memorial services were held in many parts of Great Britain on that Memorial Day, to remember all the American sailors, soldiers, and nurses buried in British cemeteries. American Red Cross nurses placed wreaths and flowers on the grave of Florence Nightingale.

In June, Anna found herself in Wisconsin, Michigan, and Nebraska. In Wisconsin, one of the places she visited was Madison. She was the guest at 'La Maison Française' ('The French House').

An interview with Anna began:

> 'I don't like to be interviewed and explain about myself and
> my work,' declared Madame E. Guérin, the charming little
> French woman now in Madison in the interests of the Fraternal
> League of the Children of France, 'but just after the signing of
> the armistice, I went into the northern part of France and saw
> the awful nightmare. Then I could no longer keep silent. No
> one could.'

It continued:

> 'The purpose of my coming to America in the interests of
> the league,' said Mme. Guérin, 'is to create a link of durable
> affection between the American people and the hundreds of
> thousands of French children, who being under the yoke of
> the Germans, have never received any help, and have been
> underfed and miserably clothes for the past four years. This
> organization must not be thought of as interfering in any way
> with the Fatherless Children of France,' she continued. 'Its
> purpose is to help those children who have not been reached.
> This is a last appeal to America to help build up what she
> has already saved, to save in its final sense, the children of
> France.'

It concluded:

> 'I am not used to going out and organizing societies. I am only
> a lecturer,' she confided, 'and I was not at all looking forward
> to coming to Madison for that purpose, but I have met with
> such kindness and real sympathy here, and I expect to return
> soon to give lectures.'

This was a significant interview to discover, early in Anna's quest. It
demonstrates how she was feeling: motivated but wary; continuing to
distance her particular charity from the Fatherless Children of France, so as
not to cause more confusion; and personally doing the groundwork for her
League, slowly but surely, everywhere she went.

You get the sense that visiting 'La Maison Française' in Madison,
Wisconsin, helped to strengthen Anna's resolve when she was so warmly

welcomed at a luncheon, on Frances Street. If her expressed worries were real, she must have felt more confident afterwards.

The University of Wisconsin's 'La Maison Française' was founded in September 1918. Anna visited the original Delta Upsilon house. In 1922, it moved to 1105 University Ave. Today, 'La Maison Française' still exists, in a modern building on the shore of Lake Mendota. It remains a francophone cultural centre, where students sign an all-French rule and enjoy living 'en français'.

On Saturday, 21 June, a Tag Day was held in Belding, Michigan. Anna, described as 'a French lady of some importance', had been in the city five days beforehand, to organise it. 'The Campfire Girls' ran it. The Campfire Girls was the female equivalent of Boy Scouts. Both groups of youngsters would help Anna in the future.

On 22 June, Anna was in Beatrice, Nebraska, at the Christian church. It was third time lucky, as a lecture had been cancelled twice in 1918, because of her illness and the pandemic. Anna's agent Rev. G. F. Fink arranged it with the backing of the YWCA and a committee of the ministerial association. Rev. Fink stated: 'the story she tells in her lecture is a very vivid one and takes a strong hold on her hearers.'

A momentous event occurred on 28 June 1919, when the First World War officially ended with the signing of the Treaty of Versailles. However, it did not result in an end to people's suffering in the war-torn countries that had been occupied, nor did it make fundraising superfluous. Thus, Anna (and others, of course) could not sit back and relax. She continued her quest to raise money for devastated regions of France.

By mid-July, Anna was in Michigan, telling people in Detroit about thousands of starving, destitute, tubercular children in northern France. A reporter wrote that she was 'Extremely picturesque in her leather-belted suit of horizon blue, the breast pocket of which is decorated with three medals awarded by the French government.' With pride, Anna pointed to the medal beside her French ones. It was her US Victory Liberty Loan Medal, one of many made from a German cannon awarded for patriotic service by the US Treasury Department.

'You see,' Anna said,

> I have served your country as well as my own. I have worked for every Liberty loan drive, and for all the national drives and war relief fund [of] the war. … I have delivered more than 500 lectures, in 30 states. And now I shall have a chance to tell of the greatest tragedy of my own country, the tragedy of its children and to ask your help for them.

She told of crossing the Atlantic Ocean nine times during the war years and of returning to France each summer, to visit the men at the Front 'to obtain inspiration for her American lectures'. Ships' manifests, for one crossing or the other, survive to prove that.

Anna spoke of being engaged in 'the greatest work that lies before France'. It was her duty and she was dedicating her life to it. After the Armistice, she said, the veil over northern France had been lifted but thousands of children still lived in cellars, holes, ruins, shacks, and tents. Children were a 'mere mockery of childhood', pitifully undersized.

By late July, Anna was in Duluth, Minnesota. She gave lectures, arranged a Tag Day, to be held on 2 August, spoke to Rotary Club men, and made an 'eloquent plea for assistance in safeguarding the mental and physical health of children in the war-stricken areas.' She stayed at the Spalding Hotel, whilst she was in and near Duluth.

In the Spalding Hotel's parlour, at 10.00 am on the morning before Duluth's Tag Day, Anna addressed her Tag Day 'captains' and workers. They were given their instructions, their seller badges, and supplies. Every eventuality was covered: if a girl could not attend at 10.00 am, she could come at 12.30 pm, 5.00 pm or 6.30 pm. Any other girls who wished to help were invited to the hotel on the morning of the Tag Day, where they would be 'most cordially welcomed'.

This practice became part of Anna's Tag Day or Poppy Day routine. Her Poppy Day headquarters was often the hotel she was staying in locally, or another suitable nearby site. It is not known what either the sellers' badges or the tags actually looked like because neither has been found described. Nor is it known how much that Tag Day raised.

In a speech she gave in France, in 1920, Anna would speak highly of Minnesota and of the time she spent lecturing there. Certainly, in the months of August and September, I did not find her lecturing in any other state. In the same speech, she exclaimed with affection: 'I wish I had time to tell you some of thing done for us by the schools of Dubuque and Burlington (Iowa) – the response from the schools of the Iron Range in Minnesota. I would like to name every one of them: Tower, Aurora, Biwabick, Gilbert, Eveleth, Virginia, Mt. Iron, Buhl, Chisholm, Hibbing, Keewatin, Nashwark, Marble, Coleraine, Grand Rapids…'

That one circular Iron Range lecture tour, out of Duluth, would have been about 345 miles. Anna told the French, in 1920: 'These names are nothing to you: to me they are as sweet as the people were kind.'

On 26 September 1919, when Anna Guérin was again in Duluth, she spoke at the Central High School. She had returned, as promised, to establish her Children's League committee there.

After a few lectures in Bemidji, Minnesota, during a short visit at the end of September, Anna was 'called back' to Chicago. It can only be speculated as to why that happened. Perhaps she had been notified that her Paris Committee was fully functional and ready to accept funds, as and when each American State Committee was formed. Who knows?

Anna Guérin was about to begin another big adventure.

Chapter 5

American and French Children's League

Perhaps it is good to backtrack here to late November and December 1918, when the foundations must have been laid down for 'La Ligue des Enfants de France et d'Amérique' in Paris, affiliated to the French government. Anna Guérin's reputation had gone before her and she was summoned to Paris, soon after she had returned from New York. Her country may have been at peace now, but it still needed her.

Although Anna's quest was to create a totally new American branch of a children's charity, on returning to the USA in March 1919, she arrived as the 'Official Lecturer' for La Ligue Fraternelle des Enfants de France (Fraternal League of the Children of France or FLCF).

Early in 1919, Anna lectured for both the Fifth Loan, via the Woman's Victory Loan Committee, and La Ligue Fraternelle des Enfants de France. Of the latter, Anna recounted how Madame Poincaré was then 'head' of La Ligue Fraternelle des Enfants de France.

La Ligue Fraternelle des Enfants de France charity was founded by one Lucie Rose Séraphine Èlise Faure, around 1896. It attempted to halt depopulation, by providing assistance for poor disadvantaged children. In July 1919, it was described as an organisation '23 years old'.

Lucie was born at Amboise, on 3 May 1866. Her father, Félix Faure, was President of France from 15 January 1895 until his death on 16 February 1899. Not inconsequential, her mother was Marie-Mathilde Berthe (née Belluot). On 10 November 1903, Lucie married Georges Goyau at Saint-Honoré-d'Eylau Parish Church, Paris.

Madame Lucie Goyau died on 22 June 1913 in Paris, aged 47. Coincidentally, Raymond Poincaré became President of France that same year. It was then that his wife, First Lady Henriette Adeline Poincaré (née Benucci), took over the role of Honorary President for La Ligue Fraternelle des Enfants de France, along with other causes.

On 21 September 1919, the Fraternal League ('La Ligue Fraternelle') was being written about in the *Chicago Tribune*. Miss Anne Miner Parker of Chicago was the United States Committee's National Chairman. Subsequently, its US headquarters was 434 First National Bank building, 38 South Dearborn Street, Chicago. As already mentioned, Miss Parker had been Illinois and Western Division deputy for the Food for France Fund, with links to Nebraska and Anna.

Others on the American FLCF committee were: George A. Kelly, general secretary; Mrs Jessie Ozias Donahue, executive secretary; George Acheson of New York, national treasurer; and Mrs Frederick W. Masters, mid-west executive treasurer. Margaret Masters, as she was, had Irish and French-Canadian roots and was known to love all things French. Margaret would become Anna's League Business Manager.

In the US, the Fraternal League of the Children of France had been endorsed by the National Investigation Bureau of New York and Incorporated under the laws of Illinois, with its headquarters in Chicago. Facts and clues suggest the US branch of the FLCF metamorphosed into Anna's American-Franco Children's League within a month.

'La Ligue des Enfants de France et d'Amérique', as the American-Franco Children's League, was incorporated in Maryland. 'Mrs George Corbin Perine' of Baltimore became State Chairman. In her own right, this was Mrs Tyler Ione Perine and she would become Anna's National Chairman.

Anna's League was associated with 'La Protection des Enfants des Régions dévastées' ('Protection for Children of the Devastated Regions of France'), which had been created to reach the vulnerable children that existing war charities in France were failing to protect; so many were being overlooked. It was attached to the Ministry of the Interior and was the main 'Beneficiary Organisation' of Anna's League.

French politician Alexandre Millerand, who would become President of France on 23 September 1920, was the 'Active President' of 'La Protection des Enfants des Régions dévastées'. Aforementioned Madame Henriette Poincaré was Honorary President.

We know there was no affiliation to the Fatherless Children of France charity, where Americans sponsored French orphans. That had been founded by American philanthropist Edward Shearson. Its French Committee was associated with 'La fraternité Franco-Américaine'.

During the First World War years, numerous similarly named societies were founded, operating between North America and France. Any one individual charity could be referred to by any combination of names, often lost in translation between French and English. It must have caused as much confusion at the time as it has in research.

Anna would state her League became official in October 1919, with her Committee in France not becoming active until November or December. That said, Anna's groundwork had begun earlier, without her realising. Through Mrs Speakman, Delaware was the first state to send money to Paris in December. Its dollars converted to 9,600 Frs.

I wondered in the very early stages of research if Anna Guérin had controlled La Ligue des Enfants de France et d'Amérique in its entirety, i.e. in France as well as the USA. But, as more information was discovered, I realised that it was more than enough work for her to just create a branch in the USA, with all that entailed. It was for others, in Paris, to be responsible for distributing of her hard-earned funds.

The archives of Nebraskan professor Hartley Burr Alexander have proved crucial. The Nebraska State Historical Society (RG4028) holds some of these. They give a valuable insight into Anna, as a personal friend of Alexander, and into the operational business of the League.

One Alexander document is a 1920 Nebraska Committee leaflet for 'The American and French Children's League'. Each Committee must have printed a comparable leaflet, specific to its own state.

The State of Nebraska is a very good example of the prominent and respected people that Anna would conscript onto League committees. Most names will mean nothing to the reader but it is worth recording them here, to have them represent all the Committee members Anna had: Miss Mae Pershing (sister of US General J. J. Pershing) was President; Mrs John Slaker (Woman's Club President – née Awana H. K. Painter) was Vice-President; Mrs George H. Holden (Chairman, Abolish Capital Punishment in Nebraska organisation – née Lulu Ida Kennard) was State Chairman; Mrs T. J. Doyle (1918 Woman's Club President and President, Women's Democratic League – née Eliza A. Remine) was Vice-Chairman; Mrs Paul Bartlett (Chairman, Girls' Canteen Service – née Rose A. Murray) was Secretary; and Professor H. B. Alexander was Treasurer (later President).

Lincoln's Executive Committee: Donald Miller (Veteran, ex-US Ambulance Service, WWI); Mrs J. E. Miller (Nebraska Legislative Ladies' League, wife of the mayor); Mrs D. M. Pershing-Butler (sister of US General J. J. Pershing); Mrs Charlie Klose (ex-Patriotic War Worker – née Nellie Mahler, Swiss-born); Professor Fred Morrow Fling (European History, University of Nebraska); Professor Louise Pound (Linguistics, University of Nebraska); W. T. Irons (ex-Chairman, United War Work Campaign, Lincoln and President, Lincoln Commercial Club); Ernest B. Chappell (Commander, Lincoln Post American Legion); Alfred F. Larrivee (Chairman, Entertainment Committee, American Legion).

The Committee of Honor consisted of: Samuel McKevie (Nebraska State Governor); J. E. Miller (Mayor of Lincoln); W. E. Hardy (Lincoln Chairman of the Red Cross); E. C. Hardy (President, Lincoln Commercial Club); R. V. Pepperberg (President, Lincoln Rotary Club); W. L. Anderson (President of Lincoln Kiwanis Club); Dr Harry Everett (Lincoln Physician); and John M. Matzen (State Superintendent of Public Instruction/Schools).

The leaflet documents the League's original structure and ethos. 'Present help' was children of the devastated regions of France; it was for the 'future friendship' of the United States and France; the 'plan and the work' was supervised by the French government; and 'after war' came reconstruction of homes, justice, and friendship.

It stated the United States of America owed three duties to France:

Homes – aid was needed for the children still living in ruins.

Justice – the American government promised this.

Friendship between the two nations – from 1776 and 1917 – which should never end.

The plan was: to form a League Committee in each US state; for each of the states, to raise at least $10,000; for the French government to receive these monies and distribute every single dollar, via recognised French organisations, for urgent relief of children; and, finally, to nurture the American-Franco relationship.

France would play its part too: where a state's quota was raised, each assisting school and club received a certificate, which entitled its community to free annual lectures by French lecturers; and, when the immediate crisis was over, a permanent endowment would be committed to – offering the lectureships to the whole of the USA. In helping the League now, America was paying for lectures in advance.

The Nebraskan Committee leaflet stated America had helped free France from the 'Iron Fist' and it must help to free the country from 'Disease and Death, Desert and Devastation. The German is gone, the veil is lifted, and what is left of four million enslaved French haunt the ghosts of their plundered and broken homes.'

The leaflet told of the horrible plight of children. They had lived in cellars and holes for four and a half years, and were still doing so. Thousands were suffering from wounds and the effects of poisonous gas, rheumatism, and tuberculosis. Only precious care could save them.

There were 'multitudes with tense, unsmiling faces that have broken the hearts of so many observers. There are children under the 'teens who have lost their minds, children a little older who have forgotten how to read and write, how to speak, how to smile – and these are "the Hope of France!"'

France was doing all it could, but it carried a heavy burden and the United States of America had to help by giving nursing and schooling, because each week saw many a child die: 'many a child laid under the poppies who might have been saved to France.'

The children were 'the martyrs of the war' and, in that description, you can hear Anna Guérin. The leaflet concluded with the words: 'We can never forget! Our DEAD ARE OUR MEMORIALS.'

On 23 September 1920, the Prime Minster of France, Alexandre Millerand, became President of the French Republic. His wife Jeanne, the First Lady of France, was already being publicly named as Active President of Anna's French Committee.

Another document in Hartley Burr Alexander's papers is a headed sheet of paper, confirming Anna's position as far as the USA is concerned: under 'National Officers in the US', she is 'Director'; she is prominently listed as 'Founder of the League in the United States'; and, significantly, the link between her League and the government of the French Republic is proved.

Perhaps it is best to look further ahead into the future now, in this chapter, and explain how Anna Guérin's 'American and French Children's League' benefited many needy causes. The money raised in the USA was directed to three Beneficiary Organisations in France:

1. Protection of the Children of the Devastated Regions (attached to the Ministry of the Interior);
2. Committee of Assistance for Alsace-Lorraine; and
3. Bidart House, a sanatorium for children, near Biarritz, left to the care of the Children's League by Mrs Dorothy Canfield Fisher.

The following is a translation of Ligue Americaine Française des Enfants' Reglement, or Regulation. It is a document dated December 1919, and it was reproduced on the back cover of the February 1921 edition of *Le Semeur*, of 650 Downing Street, Denver, Colorado, which was the Literary Review published under the patronage of the French Ministry of Foreign Affairs and the Alliance Française organisation.

The edition also reproduces, on pages 11–16 inclusive, facts from La Ligue's first annual report (October 1919–October 1920). They describe the proceedings at the Committee meeting held at the Élysée Palace in

Paris, on 9 December 1920. Madame E. Guérin, Anna, gave her report in the presence of La Ligue's President, Madame Millerand, the Committee members, and guests. Jeanne Millerand's husband, Alexandre, had become President of France only eleven weeks earlier.

Various pieces from *Le Semeur* appear later in this book.

French American League of Children: Regulation

ART. 1 – An Association was formed in the United States under the title 'The American and French Children's League' with the aim of: the maintenance and development of the bonds of affection between the two nations. Help for French organisations, approved by the Government, which offer to help and protect children from devastated regions.

ART. 2 – This Association, constituted in accordance with the laws of the United States, is represented in France by a Committee, the members of which are also part of the general office of the Association.

ART. 3 – The Association's Headquarters is in the United States. The Headquarters of the Committee are in Paris, at the place fixed by it, and transferable at will.

ART. 4 – In addition to its titular members appointed in accordance with US law, the Association may include a Franco-American Honorary Committee.

ART. 5 – The French Committee is made up of at least 5 members and at most 10. The members of the office are:

President—MADAME MILLERAND
Vice-President—ANDRÉ LEBON
          —DU VIVIER DE STREEL
Secretary General—ROGER SCIAMA
Treasurer—GÉNÉRAL LEGRAND GIRARDE

ART. 6 – This Committee's mission is to receive donations and receipts of any kind, to ensure their distribution among the various organisations to control their use, to provide the

League as well as to the donors all justifications making it possible to verify that the donations have received a destination in accordance with the goals that the League has proposed.

ART. 7 – The committee pays administrative expenses and all commitments made on its behalf out of revenue, in accordance with Article 12 below.

ART. 8 – The Committee decides on the admission of organisations to the benefit of its allocations; it fixes the share of the revenue to be allocated to each of them.

In principle, no subsidy is granted without the benefiting work having previously informed the Committee of its use.

The Committee determines the nature of the justifications for requests from beneficiary organisations and the use of funds or objects allocated to them.

ART. 9 – The accounts of the allocation and use of funds received by the Committee are drawn up, sent periodically by it to the League Headquarters, and possibly to the donors for the part that interests them.

ART. 10 – The functions of the members of the Committee are free.

ART. 11 – This Committee meets when convened by its President whenever the needs of the work so require and at least once a month. Minutes of its meetings are kept.

ART. 12 – The Committee may delegate to its President or to one of the members specially designated for this purpose the authorisation to exercise one or more of the functions which have devolved upon it.

The President signs the correspondence, represents the work in court and vis-à-vis third parties, appoints or dismisses employees, settles current expenses. It can delegate all or part of its functions to one of its members.

ART. 13 – The decisions of the Committee are taken by majority vote, that of the President was decisive in the event of a tie.

ART. 14 – The Treasurer periodically presents to the Committee, and at least once per quarter, a statement of the receipts and expenses carried out by him: he submits for its approval and receives discharge of its operations. The funds received by the Committee are deposited in a bank designated by it. December 1919.

Not all the needful causes that were given aid by Anna's American and French/American-Franco Children's League will ever be known. However, an archived list in Hartley Burr Alexander's papers does identify some of the work carried out from 1919, into 1920, as a result of Anna's fundraising. The following is the transcription of that list:

WHAT THE 'AMERICAN STAR' (American-French League of children) has done for the children of the Devastated Regions of France 1919–1920:

1. Excess nourishment, Montescourt (Aisne).
2. Purchase of cows at Verdun.
3. Founding of an organisation for the distribution of milk. Senones.
4. Establishment of a lying in hospital at Roye (Somme).
5. Aid for tuberculous children (Aisne).
6. Treatment of children at the Sea-Side (Merville-Nord).
7. Purchase of cradles and baby carriages Saint-Laurent-Blangy) [Pas-de-Calais].
8. Purchase of baby outfits at Saint-Quentin (Aisne).
9. Financial Assistance to Boys-Scouts.
10. Treatment of children at Sanatorium (Arras).
11. Purchase of medicines and medical Supplies (Ternier-Nancy).
12. Purchase of clothing and boots (Fourmies) [Nord].
13. For the home at Bidart (Lille) [Nord].
14. For the home at Sainte-Pierre-d'Albigny (Lille-Verdun).
15. Purchase of clothing (Varennes-Meuse) [Argonne].
16. Purchase of cows at Senones (Vosges).
17. Founding of preventorium at Sissonne (Aisne).
18. Treatment of children in the country.
19. And at the Sea-Side (La Capelle-Pas-de-Calais).
20. Widows and orphans under medical care (Lille-Moyenmoutier) [Nord-Vosges].

Hartley Burr Alexander was Professor of Philosophy at Nebraska University in Lincoln. He and his wife Nelly became very good friends with Anna Guérin. People like the Alexanders embraced Anna and she them. Hartley began as Nebraska State's Children's League Committee Treasurer but he became Anna's National President in the end.

Lincoln was Hartley Burr Alexander's birthplace, on 9 April 1873. He was a son of Methodist preacher George Sherman Alexander from Rhode Island, who had initially been a Quaker. His mother Abigail had died when he was three years old and, apparently, this set in motion a sense of abandonment, which he felt all his life.

Father George remarried and bought a newspaper, but continued to preach. Hartley's stepmother was musical, artistic, and spoke French. Perhaps Hartley could speak French; he had lectured in Paris, after all. In his first year at university, 1893, Hartley's stepmother died. A year later, after suffering long and painfully, he lost his father to facial cancer.

It is documented that Hartley gradually turned away from the religious environment he had been brought up in. While still in high school, the Wounded Knee massacre of Sioux Indians by US military troops, in December 1890, affected him very deeply.

As a protest against that atrocity, he wrote the poems 'To a Child's Moccasin'; 'The Only Good Indian is a Dead Indian'; and 'Her Robe is Broidered'. This led to a lifetime of empathy for America's indigenous native people and a passion for everything connected to their culture.

Hartley had been Professor and Dean of Philosophy at Nebraska University, in Lincoln, since 1908, when Anna met him. For his work for French orphans during (and perhaps after) the war, Hartley was awarded the Chevalier de la Légion d'Honneur in 1936. He went on to help establish California's Scripps College for women. Hartley's accomplishments are too numerous to document here but he is internationally recognised as an author of books, papers, poems, and so on, and a noted educator.

When Hartley died in 1939, newspapers stated his death 'brought widespread mourning'. Before his funeral service, he lay in state at Scripps College in Claremont, California.

As mentioned, the main Beneficiary Organisation (1) of Anna's Children's League in the USA was 'Protection des Enfants des Régions dévastées', with its first President being Alexandre Millerand. He was a lawyer by profession, before entering politics. He was Minister of War for France twice, during the Great War. He was Commissioner General de la République (March 1919–January 1920), with the responsibility of reorganising the three former departments of Alsace-Lorraine.

The second Beneficiary Organisation (2) was the 'Committee of Assistance for Alsace-Lorraine' and Madame Poincaré was one of the Honorary Presidents of it. Of course, Millerand had held responsibility for Alsace-Lorraine and his wife had joined La Ligue des Enfants de France et d'Amérique Paris Committee which directed aid to it. Charities were interconnected by personalities, like a spider's web.

Millerand's professional link to the law, the war, and Alsace-Lorraine might indicate that he had a longstanding acquaintance with Eugène and Anna Guérin, before La Ligue was created. Eugène was a judge, with a personal interest in Alsace-Lorraine, and Anna had worked as a war lecturer for the French government for years.

The third Beneficiary Organisation was 'Bidart House' (3), on the south-western French coast, at Bidart, near Biarritz. In reality, 'Bidart House' was 'Maison Maurice-Pierre'. 'Bidart House' was a sanatorium for children from the war-torn regions of France. It was founded by the American Mrs Dorothy Canfield Fisher and run by UFF (Union des Femmes de France), which would become part of the French Red Cross.

Dorothy was born Dorothea Frances Canfield, in Lawrence, Kansas. Dorothy's father became Chancellor of a small college in Lincoln and, under his stewardship, it excelled. It secured the grand status of the University of Nebraska. Nebraska knew the Canfields well.

Dorothy was educated in France and the USA, gaining a PhD in modern languages. She became well-known as a reformer of education, adapting the Italian Maria Montessori's innovative teaching methods to suit the needs of Americans. In 1915, her husband John joined the American Volunteer Ambulance Corps, going overseas.

In September 1916, Dorothy took her two children and followed him to France. She rented a house near Paris and, for two years, she and John carried out their respective war relief work.

Amongst all the Nebraskan letters and packages Anna carried with her on her voyage back to France in November 1918 were letters to Dorothy Fisher. When Anna became acquainted with Dorothy's work at Bidart, she conferred with the League's committee members in Paris and it was decided 'Bidart House' must be one of the institutions that benefited from the American funds. Dorothy was another of the many confident and esteemed women Anna became associated with, during her humanitarian work.

Dorothy's accomplishments, and other causes she championed, are too many to document here. The relief work of the Great War, together with Nebraska, linked the two women together.

Through this relationship, Dorothy transferred 'Bidart House' over to Anna's League. The Nebraska Committee requested that funds raised in the state, or 'such part of them as should be necessary', should be given to 'Bidart House' and, by October 1920, that totalled 90,000 francs.

The Bidart Home had taken children from Paris initially but, when Anna's League took it over, it was greatly improved and was devoted to thirty-five weak children from the devastated regions, including Lille. Two inscriptions, 'Nebraska' and 'Pueblo' (Colorado), on the Home's porch pillars reminded the children that the majority of funds were donated by these two places, which gave 'precious help to the Institution'.

The children's stays varied from four months to sometimes more than a year. They received a good education from a qualified primary teacher; learnt 'good habits of voluntary discipline'; and had, if at all possible, their shattered health restored by devoted nurses.

A homely atmosphere and education was provided for girls aged from 6 to 14, and boys from 6 to 10. The climate enabled children to live an almost exclusively outdoor life. There were rhythmic breathing exercises on the beach. From 5 June 1919 to 1 November 1922, the Home put a roof over the heads of 255 vulnerable children.

Another cause was the Fatherless Children of France organisation. Towards the end of October 1920, it was preparing to close its books. According to Hartley B. Alexander, Anna's Children's League would carry on the work when the Fatherless Children of France ceased to exist, which it did in the December of that same year.

It is quite ironic that Anna's Children's League would carry on the important work of caring for the orphans left vulnerable by the charity that Anna had, so often, deliberately distanced herself from.

Reportedly, in total, the Fatherless Children of France provided 60,000 French orphans with sponsorship from American godparents. Also within Hartley Burr Alexander's archive, Anna's own hand confirms the 'American and French Children's League' state structuring:

In each state organized we have at the Head of our Committee:

The Governor of the State

The State Superintendent of the School

The Commander of the American Legion

The President of the Federation of Women's Club

And in each town we have as Chairman the Mothers or a relative of an ex-soldier. And with their help we have for the benefit of these children of devastated France what we call 'Poppy Days.' camouflage for tag days – the tags being a Red Poppy of Flanders – the badges of the girls inscribed:

'In flanders fields the poppies grow.'

As each state was organised, its Committee began raising funds, recruiting members, and having Poppy Days. Anna, or a representative, would visit the Governor, to request his endorsement to hold Poppy Days in his state. Within each state, mayors had to be approached for their permission too and these were publicly proclaimed in newspapers too. All these authorisations enabled cities and towns to be canvassed.

Each place was asked to raise a percentage of the state's $10,000 quota. For example, in the state of Utah, Salt Lake City aimed to raise $3,000 and Ogden aimed to raise $500 from their individual Poppy Days.

On 2 December 1919, Anna's Children's League fees were printed in the *Des Moines Register*: Associated Membership $1; Sustaining Membership $5; Foundation Membership $10; and Life Membership $100.

At least 85 per cent of all donations were cabled, as soon as possible, to the Bank Credit Foncier d'Algerie et de Tunisie, 43 rue Cambar, Paris. Fifteen (some sources say five) per cent was held in the USA as an expenses fund. Expenses incurred in France came from the bank deposit interest.

Between October 1919 and October 1920, Anna's organised states had raised the following amounts, with outstanding sums carried over: Delaware 47,390 Fr; Maryland 4,720 Fr; South Dakota 77,078 Fr 50; Nebraska 96,835 Fr; Wyoming 31,835 Fr; Colorado 91,867 Fr 90; Utah 90,388 Fr 40; Idaho 43,988 Fr 75; Washington 119,142 Fr 40; Montana 30,203 Fr; California 247,100 Fr; Arizona 36,305 Fr; Missouri 1,755 Fr.

Anna Guérin's strategy would be successful from the offset. Those first Poppy Tag Days would evolve into Anna's 'big idea'.

Chapter 6

The USA Children's League and the Poppy

Chapter 4 finished in September 1919, in Chicago, and this chapter resumes at that point. Anna's Loan lectures were over, and the Chicago Loan Headquarters wrote to her, stating her work had 'stood out as among the very best done' during Liberty Loan campaigns.

But now the war was over, Anna believed that it would be much harder to raise money for the orphans. Yes, she thought, Americans still admired and loved France, but so many of them wanted to forget the war now. However, she did not blame them for feeling so.

Chicago remained Anna's base. Whilst speaking to Evansville's War Mothers, 290 miles south, she was asked to go to the second convention of the War Mothers (also known as Gold Star Mothers), in Baltimore.

It is a good idea to write a little about the Gold Star Mothers at this point. It was not a government or official name, but the general public's term of endearment. It originated from the family tradition of hanging a US service flag (also known as the 'Blue Star Flag') in the front windows of homes where a family member was serving in the military.

In an era of home sewing, flags were usually homemade and had any number of blue stars sewn upon them, relevant to the number of family members who were serving in the armed forces.

If ever a family member was killed serving, one blue star was covered up by a gold star, thus begetting the name. After the war, families could choose to have their loved ones repatriated to the USA or buried 'over there', the government paying for either option.

Around two-thirds of Gold Star Mothers' loved ones were repatriated to the USA. Alternatively, some mothers and widows were able to cross the Atlantic and make pilgrimages to the graves, under a government scheme which paid travelling expenses.

The War Mothers' Baltimore convention began on 6 October at the city's Emerson Hotel. On the 8th, the Mothers marched through Baltimore. At Druid Hill Park, the march stopped and each state's members dedicated a tree within a 'Grove of Remembrance' to their fallen heroes. It was reported that the silence was broken only by the sobs of the Gold Star Mothers. The Ambassador and Mrs Jusserand, of France, were also present at this commemoration. There is a plaque standing at the Grove, commemorating the event.

Additionally, on this day, these War Mothers voted to change the organisation's name to the 'Service Star Legion'. The change, however, was not welcomed by every member. It was noted that the Pennsylvania delegation, of 100 members, wanted to keep the original name and abstained from voting. Regardless of its new official name, members continued to be affectionately known as War Mothers.

Another point of business was choosing a 'Symbol in Memoriam'. Many speakers suggested an idea: one Mother suggested a small flag; one suggested a daisy, which grows naturally in the USA.

When Anna addressed the Mothers, probably on 8 October 1919, she told of the plight of French orphans and she also read John McCrae's poem 'In Flanders Fields'. She suggested the poppy as the emblem for the Mothers. Anna's idea was accepted 'with great emotion'. This was heartwarming, given that Flanders poppies (papaver rhoeas) are not native to the USA.

Anna felt the War Mothers would 'keep alive the Memories of the Heroes of the War' and the Mother who invited her told her: 'We shall help you all over the country after [the convention], as the War Mothers are coming from every state.'

The 1919 poppy success was shortlived. At the Service Star Legion's 1920 convention, in Des Moines, Iowa, the carnation (for mother love) and the red rose (for blood and sacrifice) were adopted instead. However, that decision would not prevent the War Mothers from supporting Anna.

On 19 October, the *Baltimore Sun* published a full page spread of photographs depicting many of the important women who attended the War Mothers (Service Star Legion) Convention in Baltimore. The outgoing President, Mrs A. W. Roach, and 'distinguished French visitor' Anna Guérin held the prominent central position.

Anna resolved that on each State Committee organised, a Gold Star Mother, in other words a War Mother, could be Committee President of her Poppy Days, if possible; and, with the aid of Poppy Days, she would raise 1,000,000 francs, for children in devastated France.

Anna proceeded to make a replica poppy of silk and took it to a local manufacturer of artificial flowers. This may have been the company of L. Snellenberg & Son (on the south-east corner of Aisquith and Oliver Streets). Certainly, in 1919, this was the only one advertising in the

Baltimore Sun: it promoted 'neat light work for neat bright girls'. With her own money, Anna placed an order for 10,000 poppies.

While waiting for the poppies, Anna spoke at a luncheon held on the roof of the Emerson Hotel, given by the Advertising Club. Anna probably stayed at the Emerson, as it became her Poppy HQ. The *Baltimore Sun*, on 23 October, reported she was in the city to create a Franco-American Children's League.

On 25 October, Anna's first Poppy Day occurred in Baltimore. More poppies were ordered for a poppy tag day in Rockville, 38 miles from Baltimore. The two days raised $5,000 for French children. War Mothers and other patriotic organisations assisted.

By the beginning of November, Maryland became the League's second State Committee to be organised. Mrs Tyler Perine became its Chairman; would later become League National Vice-Chairman and, eventually, National Chairman. Tyler's husband, George Corbin Perine, was a descendant of President George Washington's family.

On 5 November, Anna addressed her new Maryland Committee at the Emerson Hotel. The two Maryland Poppy Days were such a great success that another was planned for the first anniversary of Armistice Day that year. Anna went back to Chicago, to form a committee to organise stocks of poppies for future Poppy Days.

In her 1941 *Synopsis*, Anna wrote that Albert Loeb, millionaire vice-president of Sears-Roebuck & Co., gave a donation towards the expenses of that Poppy Committee. Albert may be the 'Mr L' who gave Anna a postcard in 1919. He knew she would like the Flanders Poppy printed on it. The card also held an 'Answer' poem to John McCrae's 'In Flanders Fields'.

This poem was written by Miss Moïna Michael of Athens, Georgia, in November 1918. There were many such poems written in 'Reply' to 'In Flanders Fields' but this was called 'The Victory Emblem' (later named 'We Shall Keep the Faith'). Anna was given Moïna's address and she wrote, complimenting her.

Another poem, published earlier (May 1918 onwards), was popular at the time. It was 'America's Answer' by Robert W. Lillard. It concluded: 'Fear not that ye have died for naught; / The torch ye threw to us we caught: / Ten million hands will hold it high, / And Freedom's light shall never die! / We've learned the lesson that ye taught / In Flanders fields.'

Another poem was 'An Answer', written by one C. B. Galbreath. The *New York Times Book Review*, in November 1918, considered it the best known. The poem began 'In Flanders Field the cannon boom, / And fitful flashes light the gloom, / While up above, like eagles, fly / The fierce destroyers in the sky; / With stains, the earth wherein you lie, / Is redder than the poppy bloom, / In Flanders Fields.'

Anna's 1941 *Synopsis* would be written to Miss Moïna Michael, ahead of the publication of Miss Michael's autobiography, about which more is written in Chapter 12. It was sent by Anna, to validate her claim that there was only one 'Originator of the Poppy Day', and Anna believed that was her: Madame E. Guérin. The seven typed pages gave a detailed timeline account of her campaigns in the USA, from the day she landed in New York, on 9 October 1914, until 1923/24.

Returning to 1919, Armistice Day arrived but, in Baltimore, so did the rain. Poppies were red, white, and blue but they, and hundreds of Campfire Girls, were not out on the streets because Poppy Day was postponed until Saturday, 15 November. A number of prominent society girls had been asked to distribute souvenir pamphlets and these pamphlets described the work of the Children's League but all the preparations had to wait until the next tag day. In Bemidji, Minnesota, 1,300 miles away, a Poppy Day did go ahead that day, however.

Delaware, Anna's first organised state, always referred to her League as the 'American Star'. Delaware's committee was also blessed with an aristocratic member, Mrs Irene Sophie DuPont.

Irene DuPont's husband, Irénée du Pont, was President of the DuPont company. DuPont had been the country's largest producer of munitions during the war. Of Irene, Anna wrote she 'did a lot to help us in every way' in the League campaign. Wilmington's 'indefatigable' Mrs Marie Speakman became Delaware's Secretary and Treasurer.

Anna's next lecture was in Wilmington. 'Her Visit Through Liberated France' was held at the Washington Heights New Century Club there. She told of 1,000,000 fatherless 'Tiny Tots' and made an impassioned plea for French children in liberated France.

Anna spoke of German propaganda suggesting France had negative attitudes towards the USA but, she said, that was false. She gave examples of the goodwill that existed between the two nations, telling of how the French Government had set up a Bureau to help American women find their loved ones' graves in France.

Whereas, during the war, Anna praised the splendid American soldiers' supreme sacrifice, now she began to compare it with French losses. America's wounds were 'too few or too light', which was obviously good for the USA but, for the country, 'the trial had been too short', she said. Their short time in Flanders' fields had not allowed Americans to understand the suffering of the French.

Anna wasn't criticising American soldiers per se. She called them 'splendid men'; 'formidable with energy, man power and money'; and 'they finished the war six months at least before any one could expect', but she needed to impress upon her audience just how much the French soldiers and people had suffered under German occupation.

From then on, Marie Speakman, as any League Chairman did, went out promoting the Children's League, recruiting members, and raising funds. She would campaign on the basis she was justly qualified to help the French with her appeals to Americans: she was born in the French-speaking part of Switzerland, educated in Paris, and, with 'heart and soul', she had adopted America as her own.

Marie followed Anna's lead, passionately describing children who were emaciated, that 20,000 orphans did not know their names, and that they had no prospect of any Christmas. Along with her husband, she had seen this personally and knew it to be true.

At the beginning of December, Anna was still announcing that Madame Raymond Poincaré was the League's Hon. President. In the USA, Mrs T. Parkin Scott was now National President. She was also Maryland's Service Star Legion President. The League was now listed as 'American and French Children's League'.

Iowa was the next state on the list and, at this point, Anna spent a week in the state capital, Des Moines. An interview with Anna, in the *Des Moines Register*, described her as pretty, eloquent, and a maker of epigrams. To quote: 'Through the medium of epigrams she evokes interest, sympathy or smiles.' The interview touched on the usual reasons for Anna visiting, but politics was mentioned too.

Anna spoke of French government ministers' wives being thrifty, wearing cotton skirts, rather than silk, and wearing cheap shoes. She thought that, if Georges Clemenceau were not the next French President, it would be someone he named. That statement proved accurate because Alexandre Millerand received Clemenceau's patronage.

Anna was asked if France wanted the USA to join the League of Nations. She replied, 'Ah, oui. The feeble, are they not always ready to accept aid from the strong?' Anna added by quoting Clemenceau: 'Fear not if America should not sign. With or without a signature or treaty, America will never stand aside when justice calls.'

People from all walks of life were debating whether it was right to join the League, or not. Although the League of Nations was the idea of US President, Woodrow Wilson, America was declining to sign up.

It is presumed Anna spent Christmas back in Chicago. Directly after the festivities, Anna went off to Sioux Falls, South Dakota, to set up another State Committee for her 'American Star', her 'American and French Children's League'. She stated in an interview that she planned to hold Poppy Tag Days everywhere next April.

Anna was in Sioux Falls between 27 and 30 December. Speaking to men and women at the Commercial club rooms, in the National Bank building, tears streamed down her face as she addressed her audience.

As with each state, South Dakota was asked to raise $10,000 in total and Sioux Falls' quota was approximately $3,000. All the state's women's clubs took part and raised funds.

After just a week, on 17 December, Sioux Falls was announcing that approximately two-thirds of its $3,000 quota had already been achieved and the remainder was expected through within the following few days.

South Dakota's State Drive began on 9 January 1920, after Sioux Falls' campaign finished, in an attempt to start raising the requested $10,000. In the newspaper, all those who pledged money were urged to send in their cheques so that money could be sent to France. Most of the Drive's Poppy Days in South Dakota occurred during August.

It is not known where Anna spent New Year. I have always thought she might be travelling on a train, thereabouts, because she has not been found in the US Census, which began being taken from 1 January 1920. Anna may have been either in Lincoln or en route to it, because she was back in the city's news on 5 January.

In Nebraska, the enumerators began their work on 2 January but, given that they took nearly the whole month to complete their work, it seems Anna successfully dodged being captured.

On 5 January, at Lincoln's Temple Theatre, Anna spoke to a special meeting of the Woman's Club about forming a State Committee for her League. Another year had dawned, with more new challenges. In four weeks, Anna would be 42 years old.

It made the newspapers that Anna had met with a Mrs Bessie Dredla, in Lincoln. Bessie was from nearby Crete and a prominent local woman. She had led the area's women in their war work.

Bessie Dredla was a member of the Masonic Order of the Eastern Star, Crete's Woman's Club, and the First Christian Church. Bessie would become one of Anna's founding committee members in Nebraska.

Bessie's husband, Anton, was as community spirited as his wife. Anton was mayor of Crete a total of seven times. Both Bessie and Anton were born in Bohemia (now the Czech Republic) and had each arrived in the USA in the late 1890s. Both sets of parents were seeking freedom of opportunity, through homesteading.

Nebraska had strong Czech enclaves at the time. In fact, part of nearby Omaha was known as 'Little Bohemia'. Today, the state of Nebraska continues to celebrate its strong Czech heritage with many annual festivals, museum exhibitions, and so on. The culture of the Czech heritage is actively encouraged and promoted.

On 19 January, Anna gave the first of three consecutive evening performances of Joan of Arc, at Lincoln's First Christian Church. Many friends had persuaded her to step in at the last minute when Biasco Ibanez, the Spanish poet, was forced to cancel his engagements.

Anna's performance was illustrated with coloured lantern slides, a review stated. Then Anna appeared as Joan through various stages of her life. It was stated her cloak had been in her family for 400 years. At the end, Anna gave an informal talk, in which she said how thankful she was to the people of Lincoln for 'receiving her so kindly'. This proves Anna travelled with all her props, just in case they came in useful.

Anna's performances were introduced by Dr Fred Morrow Fling, the Professor of European History at the University of Nebraska. Fred was a somewhat controversial figure, inasmuch as he had publicly, and strongly, objected to the neutral stand taken by the USA early in the First World War. He, too, became one of Anna's Nebraska State Committee members. Anna was assisted by Alice Howell, Professor of Languages. Alice translated Anna's French dialogue during the performance.

About this time, Jeanne Millerand begins to be mentioned as the Active President of Anna's League/Ligue. This may be due to her husband Alexandre being Prime Minister now.

The Nebraska Chamber of Commerce gave Anna the use of its Secretary to help with the Poppy Days. This Secretary and the Gold Star Mothers, as Anna referred to them at this time, helped Anna plan the state's poppy campaign. By now, Anna had pledged to visit all the schools in any place where she planned a Poppy Day.

That is why the endorsement of any State's Department of Education was so important, because Anna needed permission to visit schools. She would enlighten the children about the suffering of their counterparts in France and ask them to take part in Poppy Days.

Anna personally kept in touch with places after she formed a Committee and/or organised a Poppy Day. The Committee of South Dakota, through the Sioux Falls *Daily Argus-Leader* on 20 January, publicised the receipt of a letter from her.

Anna wrote and thanked people for their work leading up to, and after, their Poppy Days. Anna's letters gave her recipients feedback. South Dakota's letter described how arrangements were going in Nebraska. Anna stated she had Mae Pershing, the State President of Woman's Clubs, and the State Governor on her Nebraska Committee.

Wyoming was the next state. On 28 January, in Cheyenne, Anna attended a special session of the Fifteenth Wyoming legislature. She addressed the senate, asking for assistance in the rehabilitation of France and appealing for a closer relationship between the two countries.

We don't know much about the visit to Wyoming but we do know it shared out its state quota, dependent on a place's population size. Within three days, Casper's *Star Tribune* was alerting readers about a Tri-Color Ball being planned. The Salto Dancing Group held the ball on 26 February, at the Masonic Temple.

An American Legion Post and War Mothers held their dance at the same venue, the previous evening, so as not to clash. These factions were obviously respectful of each other but, at the same time, guarding their individual fundraising goals.

A dance in Wyoming's Salt Creek was held on 10 March. The $75 raised by this dance was handed over to Natrona County's organiser, Welsh-born Mrs Clementina S. Nicolaysen. That week, she forwarded $930 to the League. Clementina had played a big part in Wyoming's war work.

Dances were popular events and Nebraska held them too. Lincoln's American Legion Post No. 3 gave a benefit ball on 11 February for the League, at the auditorium. On 17 February, the League's Lincoln Committee held a Tri-Color Ball at the Lincoln Hotel.

The American Legion was formed in Paris in 1919, on 15 March. The Legion's Women's Auxiliary followed later that year. The first Auxiliary Chapter was the 'Effie B. Kennington Post'. It was formed in Indianapolis, Indiana, on 20 October 1919, and was auxiliary to the 'Robert E. Kennington Post'. Robert was killed at Chery-les-Pouilly, France, on 4 August 1918. Effie was Robert's mother.

Right from the start, the American Legion took Anna's Children's League to its heart. Auxiliary women formed an important part of the female backbone of volunteers who would support Anna in her quest.

Today, this 'Madame E. Guérin' is missing from the history of the American Legion and its Auxiliary, which is a shame because they should be proud of the part members played in this historical affair, I feel.

In her October 1919 to October 1920 report to Paris, Anna told of the 1919/20 winter:

> the organization went on seriously, methodically – but the winter was so long and so hard that the financial part of the work did not give quickly the desired results; and that I was doubly sad because the letters from France told of dire need. At last Spring came and once more I thought that the poppies of Flanders would help us. Dear Red Poppies, red as the pure blood given for humanity, which through the war had covered the battlefields with their brilliant shroud.

By March 1920, Anna was in Colorado. On 9 March, she was guest of honour at the Colorado College, at Pike's Peak, in Colorado Springs. She must have been in Denver beforehand, as the city's Mme Celeste Ollivier Dixon and Mlle Lucienne le Fraper were already her delegates. Both women were French: Celeste a widow and Lucienne a single heiress.

On 10 March, Celeste was in Greeley, and a Poppy Day was held on 10 April. Celeste and Lucienne were in charge. Local French and Latin teacher, Mrs Howard Price, was the poppy girls' chaperone. On that Poppy Day, Greeley became 'a poppy field'. Greeley's quota of $500 was surpassed by over $150.

Celeste and Lucienne also visited Fort Collins. The pair arrived around 22 March and the Poppy Day was held on 27 March, when twenty college girls distributed poppies on the streets. The quota was $500 and the local newspaper had no doubt that the amount was raised.

With no evidence to the contrary, after Pike's Peak, Anna probably spent the rest of March in and around Denver and its environs, promoting her League and networking its high society. One VIP she met was Mrs Leonel Ross Campbell Antony O'Bryan.

Leonel had become the *Denver Post*'s first female reporter. Reportedly, she took the pseudonym of 'Polly Pry' because she could pry information from anyone. She was also known as 'Nell' by some.

She became a stalwart worker for Anna's League. I can imagine why she and Anna became friends. They each married young, divorced, remarried, lived an interesting life, and believed in women's equality. However, Leonel was a more controversial figure. There was even an attempt on her life because of what she wrote. The First World War took each in a different direction and France's After-War Work brought them together.

In the war, Nell was Commissioner of Publicity for the American Red Cross. She visited Austria, Belgium, England, France, Holland, Italy, Germany, Russia, Greece, and Serbia, in her two years' service.

Nell was a valuable asset. She became Anna's advance representative and, from Colorado onwards, visited many states with and without her.

To digress from Poppy Drives for a short while: on 15 March, it was announced in national newspapers that the American Legion's National Commander had received a formal resolution from the Edward B. Rhodes Post, in Tacoma, Washington. This American Legion Post proposed that the poppy be adopted as the American Legion's memorial flower and the Post resolved to inaugurate a movement to secure that.

Five months later, Georgia's American Legion members adopted the poppy as their memorial flower at their State Convention on 18 and 19 August, in Augusta. Reportedly, this was due to Moïna Michael. She had campaigned for the single poppy to be a national memorial flower, after her 'Victory Emblem' (victory torch/poppy) proved 'disappointing' to her. Georgia submitted the same resolution as Tacoma.

These Legion resolutions demonstrate how the Flanders Poppy was becoming more emblematic across the United States of America.

Returning to Colorado: Celeste Dixon and Lucienne le Fraper took the train north, east, and west from Denver. Anna went south, to Pueblo, and branched out west from there. She was in Canon City on 26 March.

Canon City's poppy distribution strategy was to divide the city into ten canvassing districts; each district had two named 'chaperones' for its team of poppy-selling girls; the girls canvassed hard and, by 11.00 am, it was reported that 5,000 poppies had been disposed of and more supplies were called for. Ninety per cent of funds raised went to Paris and 10 per cent went to purchasing the necessary supplies for the Day, such as poppies and badges. Poppy Day was 2 April and approximately $427 was transferred to the Paris committee's bank.

Denver's Poppy Day was held the next day, if 'the day before Easter' is accepted as Easter Saturday. With smaller Poppy Days already held elsewhere, in Julesburg, Loveland, Grand Junction, and so on, Anna described Denver's as 'the first big' one. The weather was bad, there was a blizzard, but Anna said that 'in spite of snow and ice our dear Poppy girls collected several dollars.'

Pueblo's Poppy Day fundraising was so exceptional it was mentioned in a letter of 22 May 1920, from Paris Committee member Madame André Lebon. Pueblo's cheque was delivered and dollars converted to 35,000 francs. At the time, the amount equated to around $2,350. Mme Lebon wrote it would be used to purchase 'Bidart House', if possible. The owners had been written to and Pueblo's Committee Chairman informed of that decision, Mme Lebon was Belgium-born Zinka Paléologue. In the letter, Anna was praised:

> My Dear Madam – I wish to tell you immediately our great satisfaction … We are doing a great deal of good and are doing it at a time when the necessity is great, for these children have suffered much … You may be proud of the wonderful work you are doing. It is in haste we are sending you these words with our affectionate sentiments.

Each article on Pueblo's fundraising included 'Bidart House': the city adopted it. The city specifically asked if its funds could go to it. The generosity of the Pueblo people would not be forgotten by the League and the word 'PUEBLO' was placed above the 'Bidart House' porch.

However, Pueblo's generosity found a karma debt repaid a year later, after it sent the 1921 Poppy Day's monies to Paris. On 3 June, a storm hit and, within two hours, some parts of the city were below ten feet of water. For three days, six inches of rain fell. Anna's Children's League returned Pueblo's money, for the city's own flood relief fund.

Before the end of March, Nell O'Bryan went off to Salt Lake City, in Utah. The amount of information discovered about Anna's campaign is largely dependent on how prolific fundraisers were about publicising their work in local newspapers and, in Utah, they were amongst the best in the States.

Nell O'Bryan had, on 1 April, visited the State Governor Simon Ramberger and applied for the permission and permits to sell poppies on the streets, and had been granted them the same day. She had also visited the First Presidency Superintendent G. N. Child (Latter Day Saints Schools) and the State's Club women, gaining all their cooperation.

Nell must have gone straight off to local newspaper offices as soon as she was given the necessary authority because papers were announcing, on 3 April, Anna's imminent arrival and printing her photograph.

Anna was introduced as a noted lecturer and official delegate of the American and French Children's league, who had been decorated twice by France, and as a person who had assisted in the US Liberty Loan campaigns. The necessity for the Children's League was because France had such a large war debt and the country needed monetary help.

As with every state, the people of Utah were being asked to raise $10,000 and a Poppy Day would be held on 10 April.

On 5 April, Anna arrived at the Hotel Utah, in Salt Lake City, and hit the ground running, with an interview to the *Salt Lake Telegram*. The next day, she spoke 'at several gatherings' including: Woman's Leonard Wood League members; students of the University of Utah and the Latter Day Saints University; and Salt Lake Rotary Club members.

At 8.00 that evening, Anna addressed a special meeting (in French) of Alliance Française members on the Hotel Utah's mezzanine floor. The general public also attended. Ahead of this engagement, Anna was described as the 'Bernhardt of the rostrum'.

In her *Synopsis*, Anna wrote that 'the President of the Mormon' delegated Ogden-based Mrs Georgina Marriott to act as her companion in every town, until the $10,000 state quota was reached.

Georgina was a good church woman. She was on the Board of the Utah State Fair; the Chairman of Ogden's Women's Club; a member of Ogden's Child Culture Club; and Assistant Secretary of the Women's State Republican Committee. During the war, Georgina had been President of the state's Relief Societies organisation. Georgina was an ideal candidate for the post of Anna's Ogden Committee Chairman.

Georgina's husband was Moroni S. Marriott, who was an Ogden Latter Day Saints Bishop and a 'wool grower'. They had married in 1879 and, within the Latter Day Saints culture of polygamy, Georgina had become wife number two. Although the LDS publicly renounced its polygamy ethos in 1890, it has not removed it from its ideology. By the next Poppy Drive, in May 1921, Georgina was the League's Utah State Director.

There is a photograph of Anna standing in the doorway of a sheep-herder wagon, and I believe it is the Marriotts who stand with her.

On 7 April, Anna presided over a Poppy Drive committee meeting and the Utah committee of the American and French Children's League was formed. Later, in order to recruit poppy sellers, she spoke at the East Side High School, the University of Utah, and St Mary's Academy, and finished the day off at the Assembly Hall, Salt Lake City, at 8.00 pm.

The next day, the day before Poppy Day, Anna spoke at the Bryant school. The University of Utah held a Poppy Drive on the campus that contributed $126.24 to the Salt Lake City quota. A 'preliminary' poppy event occurred at noon, when twenty girls distributed poppies for just 20 minutes, for the benefit of Anna's Children's League.

Salt Lake City's Poppy Day dawned. So much had been planned: scouts had sealed many donation boxes, supplied free of charge, from a local box manufacturer; hundreds of girls were ready, including 100 from Mrs Lucy Van Cott, dean of women of the University of Utah, plus High School and

Camp Fire girls; thirty of these girls would 'invade' Bonneville Baseball Park; paper baskets, made by girls, were filled with red paper poppies, from Chicago; the Boy Scouts would replenish poppy stocks on bicycles; Anna would ride on 'an automobile truck amid garlands of poppies' and make street corner speeches, where girls were stationed; there was a Boy Scouts' and school girls' parade at noon, led by the Boy Scout band; and, as a finale, Mayor and Mrs Bock would lead another march.

But the weather was bad and wind so strong that it was described as a 'cyclone'. As a result, the Poppy Drive was only held in the morning. However, just from that short period of poppy distribution, $1,755.99 was able to be cabled to Paris on 12 April. At Hotel Utah, in the afternoon, Anna spoke to the War Mothers of the Service Star Legion instead. The bad weather caused the evening 'French Poppy Ball', due to be held at the Capitol building, to be postponed.

Anna and Nell O'Bryan went north to Ogden on the evening of the Poppy Day. The next morning, Anna spoke at the Third Ward meeting house 'on the condition of French orphaned children'. Georgina Marriott presided at the meeting.

After the Ogden lecture, on the morning of 11 April, Anna and Nell O'Bryan returned to Salt Lake City, to speak at the Latter Day Saints Tabernacle later that day. It had been a quick turnaround for them.

At the Tabernacle, Nell O'Bryan spoke first about the fame of Utah. It was known in Europe as 'the state that led in the intermountain region of America in contributions to the Red Cross during the war.'

Nell spoke about her Red Cross service in the Balkans and elsewhere. She said she had travelled by any means available. In devastated Europe, there was no peace and no rest yet and people had returned to the sites of their homes but had found only ruins and desolation.

Anna spoke next. Anna thanked the people for the generous support they had given her League. She expressed the gratitude of France and paid tribute to the splendid boys of America, who 'turned the tide of the war'. But France still needed America's help and she had every confidence in the generosity of the 'American heart'. She spoke of visiting graves at Chateau Thierry, where 'brave Americans turned the Germans back'. She spoke of speaking to a dying American, who had told her to tell his people 'the boys over there did their best'.

'France is not begging,' Anna said, 'because France is a proud nation,' but she had given all she had. Anna appealed for French children and spoke of the good Salt Lake City's money could do 'over there'. Descriptions of Anna included: eloquent; sincere; straight-forward; and unfeigned, and her speech was 'clear English'; 'with precision'; and with an 'unmistakable French accent'.

President Anthon H. Lund presided at the Tabernacle service. It was described as a mingling of 'gospel doctrine and mercy appeals'. On behalf of the congregation, President Lund said he wanted to assure the visitors that their cause was 'heartily indorsed by this people' and 'an earnest and helpful response' was recommended.

After the Tabernacle talk, several people offered Anna donations, but she said, as always, she did not handle money. Anna asked them to send donations to her Utah State Chairman, Mrs Jeanette Hyde, authorised to receive them, at the Bishop's Building. This was where local women's organisations were based.

Believe it or not, it was back to Ogden for Anna and Nell, another 32-mile train journey, for an evening lecture at the same Third Ward meeting house. The building was crowded and people had to be turned away. Anna and Nell aroused the deepest interest in the case which they represented and a sum of $75 was collected for the needy work, being the first contribution made within Ogden.

The next day, 13 April, Anna visited Ogden High School, the Weber Normal College, and the Sacred Heart Academy. She was promoting her Children's League and also recruiting the young people who would, as a result of her passionate lecturing, volunteer to become Ogden's poppy sellers for Georgina Marriott.

A second Salt Lake City Poppy Drive was arranged for the afternoon of 17 April and shops/banks would not be canvassed again.

Ogden's Poppy Day was organised by Georgina Marriott for the same day. It was described as a 'day of love and affection', with hundreds of women and children on the streets, from morning until late evening. Cadets and scouts also helped. Booths and tables were tended at local stores and hotels. Local schools competed to see which could raise the most funds, each being represented by pupils and teachers alike.

Georgina's Poppy Day was said to have been one of the most pleasing events of the many war services performed in Ogden. Nearly $2,000 was raised for Anna's Children's League.

Salt Lake City's second Poppy Day also took place on 17 April. As planned, it was held in the afternoon only. However, yet another storm came in that day and the 'Ball' was postponed again, until the 24th. As a result, amusingly, it was renamed 'The Poppy Hurricane Ball'.

In the aforementioned letter from Paris, when Madame Lebon mentioned Pueblo, she also wrote that the total amount of money received from Salt

Lake City funded the opening of a dairy to give milk to 'the wasted children of Verdun' and the dairy was called 'Utah'.

Anna spent most of April 1920 in Utah, telling of conditions in France; speaking on the aims of the American and French Children's League; setting up local committees; and asking for the support of the people, especially women and girls, ahead of the Poppy Days/Drives in places such as Brigham City, Logan, Park City, and Provo. Anna was either accompanied by Nell or Georgina.

Anna travelled to these places by train, on the Denver and Rio Grande Western Railway. Of the Poppy Days, Anna recalled Ogden 'did splendidly', as did Brigham City, Provo, Logan, and other towns.

After Anna and Nell spoke in Provo, on 19 April, the *Provo Post* wrote that the 'Poppy Day' would be held on the 24th. The article heartily endorsed it and its last sentence read: 'So we admonish the people of Provo to make the poppy drive here a success.'

On 20 April, Anna spoke at the State Agricultural College's chapel and the High School, in Logan. Georgina was with her. Logan's Poppy Day poppies were red silk, not paper, and nearly $600 was raised.

Anna and Nell, probably with Georgina, returned to Salt Lake City for 'The Poppy Hurricane Ball' on the 24th. Anna and Georgina went into Idaho three days later. Anna gave Georgina the responsibility of Idaho, and the title of State Organiser and delegate.

At the beginning of May, Washington was the next state to welcome Anna. She and Nell O'Bryan ('Polly Pry') booked into the Tacoma Hotel on 5 May. The same day, Anna spoke to students at Tacoma's Annie Wright Seminary. On 6 May, she went to the nearby Camp Lewis to address the army officers and men on her work and take 'the gratitude of France to them for their war deeds'. Seattle was next, where they stayed at the Hotel Washington Annex.

By 10 May, the Governor's permission was obtained; Mayor Hugh M. Caldwell had granted the permit, the public proclamation was issued, and Anna had organised her State Committee. It was announced that Governor Hart, with a group of Seattle men and women, had taken over the arrangements for the Poppy Drive, under Anna's guidance.

The Seattle Poppy Day would be 22 May. Hundreds of pretty girls, wearing badges of the American and French Children's League, would smile and hold out money boxes and the people of Seattle would be asked to do the rest. The girls would wear red caps and streamers (these were probably sashes) and remind people that 'In Flanders fields the poppies grow'. Madame Isabelle Mack was the Poppy Day Secretary for Seattle and State, and this must be where she and Anna first met.

French-born Isabelle was the President of l'Union Française in Seattle. She would become an integral part of Anna's American and French Children's League. More will be written about Isabelle further into this chapter. The Seattle Star, on 18 May, alerted readers that the Alliance Française and the Alliance Alsace-Lorraine planned an artistic parade, including war brides, under Isabelle's direction.

This is where things get shadowy in Seattle because, to date, information from its actual Poppy Day has not been forthcoming. Tacoma and Spokane each had their Children's League Poppy Day on 29 May and it is from Spokane and Anna that more is discovered about Seattle's Poppy Day, rather than from Seattle itself.

Of Seattle, Anna wrote to Hartley Burr Alexander, in Lincoln, Nebraska, that Mrs Buckmaster had come to help her in Seattle (she must have been a mutual friend), $4,700 had been raised, and there were 'not half enough girls'. The *Spokane Chronicle* informed readers that the Spokane Poppy Day raised $3,882, which was 'within $1000 as much as Seattle and almost three times as much as Tacoma'.

Washington State is an example of how empathy towards the poppy was growing: on 6 May 1919, a Poppy Planting Day was held; as noted, Tacoma's Edward B. Rhodes Post had recommended the poppy emblem in March 1920, to American Legion HQ; and, on 25 May 1920, Spokane Legion Auxiliary members held a Poppy Day.

Anna stayed at the Davenport Hotel whilst in Spokane. As usual, she visited schools, where 400 schoolgirls were recruited. On the evening of 23 May, Anna spoke at Spokane's Central Methodist Episcopal Church, the event coming after 'an energetic speaking campaign'.

Newspapers publicised Spokane's Poppy Day well, visually and factually: Poppy HQ was in the Fidelity National Bank's basement; the Drive began between 8.30 and 9.00 am; and Mrs Donna E. Baker, who was in charge, was quoted as saying 'Every penny helps, every dollar means today 15½ francs and 15½ francs buys a lot of bread and milk'. Donna had also campaigned for the Loan and Red Cross, during the war.

Twenty-five marines came to the assistance of the poppy girls during the Poppy Day. They were from Spokane recruiting station. Lieutenant Charles Baylis, the commander of the local station, volunteered the men. The Spokane campaign was run along military grounds: the schoolgirls were an 'army'; the teams were 'corps' of ten girls, led by 'captains'; and the city of Spokane 'surrendered en masse' to the girls as they stood on downtown street corners with baskets of poppies. The girls wore red caps, 'symbolic of the republic of France', and wore red and white sashes inscribed with the words 'Poppies grow in Flanders field.'

For Anna, there was certainly competition in Washington. Spokane's Legion Auxiliary's Poppy Day had raised $2,000 for veterans. However, it was to Anna's credit that her Spokane Poppy Day raised nearly twice that for her French orphans, only four days later. Anna left before the Poppy Day but she wired the organisers, wishing them 'all success'.

Around 27 May, Anna arrived in Portland, Oregon. On that day, she wrote to Hartley Burr Alexander. She wrote she would be going to Boise, Idaho, then Pocatello, then returning to Portland to address the Portland Parent-Teacher Council in the Central Library, about her League, on 4 June.

While Anna spent the few days in Idaho, the *Oregon Daily Journal* printed a short notice, on 30 May. It announced that the Poppy Drive was not endorsed; the National Indorsement League had not given approval; and donations should not be given until it had been investigated.

When Anna wrote to Hartley, she was oblivious of how Oregon plans would go awry. It was rare for suspicions to be raised about the legitimacy of Anna's work and fears were soon allayed because they were unfounded. This was different and Oregon would not be organised. Anna must have been surprised that the state would not be as accepting of the French orphans' plight as the other visited states had been.

Anna wrote to Hartley: 'Please do excuse this business letter I am absolutely worn out.' A sense of tiredness and frustration comes across in her writing: 'I am very tired.'

Hartley had sent Anna a draft of some letter, which she described as 'beautifully worded'. She reiterated her wish to achieve one million francs before she returned to France, which was dependent on successful Poppy Days. Those Days were dependent upon having enough girls. She spoke six to eight times a day to obtain schoolgirls for the Poppy Days.

Anna revealed an emotion which had only surfaced once before, in Omaha, in July 1918: annoyance. Two thousand dollars were outstanding. Perhaps, as each $500 had accumulated, it should have been sent to Hartley. Ladies may have been waiting to send it through altogether. Tardiness meant the dollars-to-francs exchange had been negatively affected.

Uncharacteristically, Anna wrote, 'I am so crossed [sic] with them.' She noted the exchange rate had been 'above 16 now it is hardly 13', and added 'that means we are losing 3000 frs on each thousand or 6000 frs – it is a crime – enough to take care of 6 children a year. For what! For nothing –

only carelessness.' Her annoyance came from a passion for needing the best exchange rate to benefit the French orphans.

Almost as an afterthought, by way of how she worded it, Anna added to her argument by writing she was owed $100 from the expenses fund. Had this $2,000 been sent to France two weeks prior, when the rate was better, Anna would have benefited from 1,600 francs. Now, on 27 May, $100 was worth 1,280 francs. Miss Patsy Epperson was mentioned as having several Poppy Days that week and she would send her money to Hartley. Anna asked him to cable it to Paris, straight away.

Referring to Omaha and her 'annoyance' brings to mind a second issue relating to Anna, leading up to 4 June. Whatever drove people to query Anna's Red Cross credentials in July 1918 had re-emerged as allegations from a 'clique' of Omaha associates of the Fatherless Children of France Fund.

It had all come to a head on the city's Poppy Day, 29 May 1920, which incidentally had been one of delegate Miss Epperson's Poppy Days mentioned in Anna's letter.

Mayor Smith received a letter from prominent social workers a few days before the Poppy Day, accusing Anna of being an 'imposter'. The Poppy Day took place but Patsy Epperson and the local League Chairman, Helene Bixby, arranged a meeting to air the continuing accusations against the Children's League.

On 4 June, the meeting was held at the Hotel Fontenelle, at 1.30 pm. Both women wanted to make a public report about the funds raised by the poppy sale. But, as the local newspaper described them, the rival faction 'Antis' did not appear, although Nebraska State Treasurer, Hartley Burr Alexander, did attend – in case his support was necessary.

Letters from US city mayors and French officials praised 'the phenomenal work done by Madame Guérin in raising funds for the relief of the children of devastated regions of France.' Helene told of attempts by rivals to undermine the Children's League. Examples of Anna's work were given. The meeting adjourned with a hearty endorsement.

So, with Oregon plans thwarted, Anna returned to Idaho and Georgina Marriott. They visited Blackfoot and Rexburg, at least, organising a Poppy Day in each, and then travelled on to Montana.

On 12 June, Anna and Georgina arrived in Butte, Montana. The same day, the two women were guests of Mayor Stodden, at a luncheon at the Thornton Hotel, on East Broadway, where they were staying. After lunch, the mayor took Anna on an 'auto trip over the city, viewing the mines and other points of interest.'

Butte was known as 'The World's Greatest Mining Camp' and 'The Richest Hill on Earth', on account of its rich deposits of gold, silver, copper, lead, and zinc. At the city boundary, the mining area began!

The Thornton Hotel was very convenient because it was on the same street as the Montana Power Company, where Anna made her HQ. It was also where local Red Cross members ran their campaigns from. The Silver Bow County's American Legion assisted in Butte's Poppy Day and its club rooms were in the nearby Public Library, West Broadway.

Anna's campaigns in Butte and neighbouring Anaconda are amongst the best documented, within newspaper coverage. For both campaigns, it helped having the *Butte-Miner* (*Montana Standard*) opposite Butte's Public Library, which housed the American Legion rooms.

On 13 June, Anna travelled to Helena to see State Governor Samuel V. Stewart and Mayor John Dryburg, promote her Children's League, and ask for permission to canvass for State-wide Poppy Days.

Governor Stewart, the American Legion's State Commander, and the Superintendent of Instruction all gave their endorsement. These three individuals, together with the Governor's wife, Mrs Stewart, became part of Anna's Montana State Committee.

Anna met one Miss Genevieve Hamilton Parke, in Helena. They organised a Children's League committee there together. Anna stayed in Helena for two days. Using arrangements Anna made, Genevieve took charge after Anna left. Helena's Mayor, John Dryburg, issued his proclamation on 17 June and Poppy Day would be held on the 19th.

During Helena's Poppy Day, around 200 High School and Camp Fire girls distributed silk poppies, not paper ones. Boy Scouts assisted, as usual, on their bicycles. The Day raised $600.

Genevieve Hamilton Parke organised the Montana Poppy Days in Billings, Livingston, and Great Falls afterwards. Genevieve was with her father, General Hamilton Parke, when he was the military attaché to the American council in Brussels, Belgium. They both had to flee the country when the Germans invaded. Genevieve went on to become a Red Cross volunteer during the war.

News emerged from an interview in Helena. Anna stated that she was impressed with the 'atmosphere of Montana' and she was 'confident that Helena people will help her "young martyrs of the war"'; and she wished for the schools and clubs of the USA to understand the conditions of the devastated areas of France.

Anna concluded: 'Your boys are sleeping in Flanders fields where the poppies are growing once more on their graves. They gave their lives for the country of those children. Can't you give a nickel, a dime, or a dollar to help France revive and save them?'

The article referred to Anna having spoken in forty-two US States, more than 4,000 times. I doubt Anna ever intended to visit Alaska, and Hawaii was not yet a state, leaving forty-eight states. New papers come online all the time and, so far, they have proved Anna lectured in forty. I feel sure I will get them all proved eventually.

On returning to Butte, Anna had planned to speak at an evening meeting, in the American Legion Club Rooms, but the train was late and Georgina had to get the meeting started on her own. She opened with, 'What France has suffered and for what France has suffered we should never forget,' and held the fort until Anna arrived.

Once Anna arrived, she announced Mrs Eloise Smith, Commander of the Silver Bow American Legion Auxiliary (wife of wholesaler Frederick B. Smith), and Mrs Martha Smith (wife of Accountant Cyrenus Hall Smith) would take charge of her Butte Poppy Day, which was to be held on 22 June. They would handle all money and deposit it in a local bank, to send it through to the French government's committee.

In another interview, in Butte, Anna spoke at great length about her League. She was reluctant to talk about herself, changing the subject back to France and the USA. She thought she would enlighten the USA about France, but she was enlightened too. Before arriving in the USA, Anna knew only cowboy stories by Francis Bret Harte and romantic stories of Native Americans, written by James Fenimore Cooper.

Anna was asked if she had met any American boys, 'over there'. She answered she had and gave one amusing anecdote: when she had to travel to Paris 'after an important mission from the front', on one occasion, she had to plead to get onto a 'box car'. It was packed, like sardines, with soldiers, but the men made room for her.

However, as the train began to leave, three American marines needed to get on. No one could move to allow them on but, with no more ado, they jumped through the window of the train and landed on the shoulders of those already on, and wriggled their way down to the floor. When Anna returned to the USA, a young man smiled at her when she was in Minnesota and said, 'Do not you remember me? I was one of three who jumped through the window of the car and nearly smothered you.'

Anna continued to address young women and children about her work. She hoped to enlist 300 into a volunteer corps on the streets of Butte. Anna continued to tug at the heart strings and the newspapers obliged by repeating her messages.

Anna spoke of seeing local children: 'How happy they are, how I wish the children of my country were as carefree as these children are.' After being taken on a visit to Butte's beautiful Columbia Gardens, she said such a place, with its beautiful flowers, should be appreciated because the French children had no such comforts of life. They were nervous wrecks and she hoped to see them 'revived from their miseries',

On 18 June, Anna and Georgina travelled to Anaconda, 24 miles west of Butte. At the Montana Hotel, Anna made a 'stirring appeal' for the French orphans. Both the local broadsheets reviewed her address, with the equivalent of nearly a full column. Anna said 'France needs all of her children. How else can she be revived and re-built? France has stood as a guardian of civilization and by no other means than her children can she be replaced.' If Anaconda women believed it was a world war, then the children of France were the martyrs of the world and it should be considered a privilege to contribute to their relief.

Anna explained the French children were not your usual war orphans. They had lived behind the German lines and were wrecks. Her charity hoped to give them care, fresh air, and food at sanatoriums, to help restore minds and bodies. She described the American soldier as wonderful, adding he had 'the bearing and dash of the Canadian soldier, the courage of the best French and the tenacity of the best English.'

Ahead of Butte's Poppy Day, Tuesday, 22 June, the plea went out for surplus cigar boxes, to collect the money. The Boy Scouts' quest was to find enough of them. Slots were made to take a dollar coin.

The day before, Anna first met with fifteen women involved with Butte's 'Poppy Day', at Gamer's Tea Shop and, at 3.30 pm, she met with 150 women and girls at the American Legion Club Rooms. There, Anna delivered an interesting speech about those living on the battlefields.

Anna eulogised about the scarlet poppy; about millions of soldiers lying in silent graves; about the French seeing the strangest sight, millions of 'the reddest of poppies' blowing to and fro in the wind, all growing between white crosses that stood as silent witnesses.

Poppy Day plans were given: women wearing 'a scarlet and white badge, worn across the breast' bearing the words 'In Flanders' Field, the Poppies Grow' would be given free tram travel; girls would wear 'chic red caps'; the Drive would run from 9.30 am to 6.00 pm; poppies would be carried in wicker baskets; Boy Scouts would be on hand to assist; Anna would address a large crowd at the American Legion dance; and, afterwards, she would go around all the picture houses, of which there were at least twelve, 'making five-minute speeches'.

On Poppy Day, both the *Anaconda Standard* and the *Butte-Miner* newspapers printed a group photograph of girls and women standing on the Public Library steps, in front of the American Legion Silver Bow Post rooms: some girls wore their red caps; some held a poppy; a little girl, standing centre front, held the 'Stars and Stripes' and the 'Tricolore' flags; and Anna Guérin stood prominently in campaign uniform.

Over 200 girls ensured everyone had a tissue-paper poppy on their lapel. $1,537.10 was raised in Butte and Anna was pleased. Anaconda's Poppy Day was the next day: the HQ was in the Montana Hotel; the weather was cold and wet, but apparently that did not stop people from purchasing and wearing the poppies. It was reported, within 15 minutes of leaving the hotel at 9.30 am, that 'Buy a poppy, mister' was the familiar cry heard on the streets. That day raised between $400 and $500.

Anna and Georgina left Butte on 24 June, on the evening train, going to Ogden. During the day, Anna told the *Anaconda Standard* she was sorry to leave Butte; no matter where she went, she would never forget the city or its big-hearted people. In the eleven days in Montana, Anna's Poppy Days appeared in thirty-five articles within the *Anaconda Standard*, the *Montana Standard (Butte-Miner)*, the *Great Falls Tribune*, and the *Independent Record* (of Helena), together with six photographs.

At the end of June, organised League committees received a letter from the League's General Secretary in Paris, Madame Helene Rofer Sciami. She hoped those who had given funds would consider the League had spent them judiciously. The letter documented the work of the American Star/American and French Children's League thus far: at the station of Montescourt (Aisne), food was given; at the Vassar unit (Verdun), money was given to buy a cow; at Senones (Vosges), a milk depot was founded; at Roye (Somme) a maternity home was founded from Delaware funds; at Merville (Nord), Mme Morel was to set up a community near the coast; at Saint-Lawrent-Blangy (Aisne), the reconstruction was helped by the purchase of candles, children's beds, and carriages for Mme de Boigne; at Saint-Quentin and Lergnier (Aisne), and at Fourmies (Nord), beds, baby layettes, and shoes for children were provided; at Arras, provision was made to enable children to be sent to a sanatorium at the coast; contributions were given to Boy Scouts in the devastated regions; at la Bassée (Nord), enough money was given to Mrs Griffen to buy clothing and shoes for the children of that 'unfortunate village'.

Not every beneficiary will be known but here are some others that are:

DISPENSARIES: Bray-sur-Somme; Etival (Vosges); Fargnier (Aisne); Fourmies (Nord); Hénin-Lietard, Arras (Pas-de-Calais);

La Bassée (Nord); Montescourt (Aisne); Nancy (Meurthe-et-Moselle; Saint-Quentin; Sedan (Ardennes); Saint-Quentin.

INSTITUTIONS for Infants: Acy (Aisne); Bray-sur-Somme – Rozière-en-Santerre (Somme); Nouvell Etoile; Reims 'Drop of Milk' – 'Foyer Rémois'; Saint-Quentin (Aisne); Sedan (Ardennes); Société d'Assistance Maternelle et Pouponnière de Saint-Mihiel; Verdun – Saint-Mihiel.

PREVENTORIA: Arbonne (Basses-Pyrénées); Étaples (Pas-de-Calais); Henri Lange Home – Saint-Quentin; Maurice-Pierre Home – Bidart (Basses-Pyrénées); Mautort-Abbeville (Somme); Reims Open-Air School at Villiers-Allerand; Saint-Dié (Vosges); Saint-Jean-Cappelle (Nord); Saint-Pierre-d'Albigny (Savoie); Valloires (Somme); Villers-Allerand (Marne).

After Anna took a few days off in Ogden, perhaps staying with the Marriotts, she took the train west to Sacramento, California, 676 miles away. The train travelled through Nevada but it is not known if she stopped en route. Certainly, nothing yet suggests she did.

A number of reinforcements joined Anna, to cover California: Nell (Leonel) O'Bryan; Celeste O. Dixon; Patsy Epperson; Isabelle Mack; Miss Helen J. Ahern; and Georgina Marriott.

To introduce Helen J. Ahern, she was born in October 1890, in the village of Whitney Point, Buffalo, New York State. Helen was described as a society girl and heiress but, in the war, she worked for the American Red Cross in France, Italy, and Albania. She knew Nell and for Anna, in California, she worked with Nell again. The two of them, after the Californian Drives, went to organise Arizona.

To introduce Isabelle Mack, she was born Isabelle Henrietta Victoria Adolph, on 8 October 1873, in Lille, Nord-Pas-de-Calais, France. She was the second of four children born to German Moritz Heinrich Adolph and his Scottish wife, Isabelle Doig Baxter.

The Baxter family had been big cotton producers and weavers in Dundee, Scotland. In 1839, Isabelle's grandfather, Robert Doig Baxter, was one of two brothers who were asked, by the French government, to set up a cotton weaving industry in northern France. The Baxter brothers chose Lille as their site, because of its comparable climate to Dundee.

When Isabelle was only three years old, her mother died of TB. When her father disappeared to the USA, her maternal Aunt Charlotte took charge of bringing up the four children. As a young woman, Isabelle studied at the Lycee et Fenelon, University de Lille.

In 1890, Charlotte took the family to London. The family was poor, so Isabelle and sister Doris became 'mademoiselles françaises'. From at least 1898, Charlotte lived in Newcastle-upon-Tyne and, that year, Isabelle married auctioneer Charles Mack in the city.

Isabelle and Charles Mack's daughter, Enid Adolph Mack, was born in May 1899 in Newcastle. Six months later, Charles died of meningitis. In 1904, Isabelle's sister Jessie had emigrated to Seattle, USA with her husband. Isabelle and her daughter Enid were invited to join them in 1912.

Enid wrote that her mother Isabelle 'was a very women's equality person'. Isabelle and Anna must have been very compatible. Both were French, the same age, 'mademoiselles françaises', strong advocates of women's liberation, and personally aware of the devastated regions of France. Both shared a common goal to help France.

The lives of Isabelle, Enid, and Jessie, along with Doris (another sister in Lille), became intrinsically linked with Anna and her Children's League. In later life, Isabelle reminisced:

> Having been born in the North of France, in Lille, the ancient capital of 'Flanders', my sister, Jessie E. Spence and I always had a tender heart towards 'La Patrie' [fatherland] – France and French causes. We were in Seattle during the First World War, and active in many Allied and French movements.

Isabelle continued:

> We organized the 'Union Française', planned the reception for Marchal Joffre, organized Bastille Day (July 14, French Independence Day) celebrations and so forth. So it was natural that after the Armistice, we were asked to take part in raising money for French relief ... The Poem 'In Flanders fields the poppies blow, beyond the crosses row on row' was well-known to everyone at that time, so the Poppy became the emblem of our cause.

Accompanying Anna in 1920, Isabelle spoke to an audience:

> I come from Lille. My family has run a large mill there with 12,000 employees but since the war we have done nothing.

We have only 200 men, and can use no more because we can't get the coal. All our buildings are practically useless too. Many of them are still standing but the vibrations from the guns has so weakened the walls that if we wish to use heavy machinery we have to have entirely new buildings. It is a serious question.

In the 1920 Californian Poppy Drives, Isabelle Mack was Anna's delegate in such places as Petaluma, Santa Cruz, Santa Rosa, Stockton, Modesto, and Fresno. Isabelle was always introduced as the President of the Union Française of Seattle, with the Children's League explained. She was found visiting mayors, lecturing, and setting up Poppy Days in California during the months of August, September, and October.

For everyone else on Anna Guérin's team, the Californian Poppy Drives began in July. Anna first visited Sacramento, going to visit State Governor William D. Stephens for his endorsement.

On 8 July, Anna gave an address to the Lions Club. She was introduced as a 'speaker of national fame' and as someone who, whilst touring, had sold more Liberty Loan bonds than any other person. Anna spoke, in a quaint French accent, of charred ruins, which were once villages, fields disfigured by shell holes, half-starved women and children, and brought tears to the eyes of those in the audience.

The review of the speech told of her face 'flushed and eager because of the intensity of her emotions'. Anna was further described as the 'living embodiment of the spirit of Joan of Arc'. The observer wrote about pictures being conjured up in the minds of the audience: 'a wave of horror' passing over the crowd, followed by intense pity, as Anna spoke of the children brought before the Red Cross. It was noted 'more than one man openly showed his emotion'.

Anna spoke of being six weeks in the devastated war-torn areas after the Armistice but, she said, 'Oh! I was aged six years!' She talked about visiting places which been burned to the ground, after people had been driven from their homes. 'I saw there one poor little girl sitting on the edge of a ruined home. "Where is your mama?" I asked. "I do not know, Madame," she said. "She is dead, perhaps. I cannot find her."'

Anna said there were 700,000 widows and one and a half million fatherless children, who were crying out to Americans to give them aid. Her lecture followed the usual campaign theme.

When Anna had finished speaking, the Lions Club Chairman stood up and assured her that if the Club was called upon to give assistance, it would not fail her. The next speaker, Judge Peter J. Shields, said, 'We have been touched and exalted today as perhaps never before. Let us carry the picture Mme. Guérin has given us in our hearts.'

The League began recruiting at least 300 girls. Women from fraternal and patriotic organisations helped the girls when they reported to the St Francis Hotel at 8.30 am on Poppy Day, Bastille Day. Twenty Oak Park Playground girls distributed poppies in 'Joyland' and Oak Park business districts, carrying collection boxes made by boys. The American 'Playground Association' aimed to keep inner-city children healthy.

Sacramento's French colony organised celebrations, which culminated in a large gathering at 'Joyland' amusement park. 'La Marseillaise' was sung and 'In Flanders Fields' was recited. Anna closed the event: 'Your 70,000 boys, with their out-stretched hands, lying as they are together with the tortured women and children of my dear France, are calling upon you, my American friends, my sisters and brothers, to come to the aid of those children who through four years of hardship, torture and violence are left, homeless, parentless and hungry.'

It was to Anna's credit that people were still being generous but her fears of people tiring were evident when the *Sacramento Bee* printed an article on 28 July. It began by giving the Poppy Day as an example of a recent tag day, to help children in devastated France, and went on to give the opinion:

> People, generally, and especially visitors to the cities have become extremely tired of these street demands for money …
> It is annoying to be importuned at every street corner for 'some worthy charity,' to which the importuned, and visitors especially, either do not care to subscribe, or about which they know absolutely nothing.
>
> And among The People generally, there is also a constantly growing determination to confine their donations to American charities and purposes; and as far as possible, even to limit them to local objects. The men and women who have come and are coming to that determination are not ungenerous, but are rather of those who always given freely and who propose to give freely; men and women, however, who believe that 'Charity begins at home' – and that word 'home' does not include every known portion of the habitable globe in which there may be suffering.

But Anna was not going to give up. The day after Poppy Day in Sacramento, Anna spoke to women at the Fairmont Hotel in San Francisco. Nell O'Bryan and Helen Ahern helped Hon. Chairman Mrs Ethel Williard Crocke to organise the Day.

On 9 July, Nell had made a quick visit to Oakland, 8 miles away across San Francisco Bay, to ask the Oakland City Council for permission for a 'bevy of girls' to sell poppies during its Poppy Day on 7 August.

It was in San Francisco that Anna made the aforementioned 22 May Paris letter public. She must have thought publicising the great successes at Pueblo and Salt Lake City would further her cause.

Poppy Day in San Francisco would be held on 26 July. Again, the sellers' Poppy Day badges and banners were inscribed with 'In Flanders Fields the Poppies Grow'. However, this time, the newspapers were promoting paper poppies made in France, 'brilliantly hued'.

The American Legion's Golden Gate Post was one of the Legion posts to place teams of girl sellers at Anna's disposal. Interestingly, in April, that Post was another that had passed resolutions urging the whole organisation to adopt the poppy as its national emblem. Mr Hugh McGinnes, of the Knights of Columbus Employment Bureau (a Catholic fraternal organisation) 'placed' the teams ahead of Poppy Day.

On Poppy Day, at noon, Helen Ahern flew over the city, scattering souvenir copies of 'In Flanders Fields', 'far and wide'. She was flying in one of Earl Cooper's aeroplanes, from the 'Earl Cooper Company'. Earl P. Cooper was a famous racing car driver and a dealer in Curtiss aeroplanes and motor cars. The company's HQ was San Francisco. I would wager Helen took off from Marina Field, in sight of the Golden Gate Bridge.

It was reported that forty teams of women were on the ground, from the same number of organisations. Any woman volunteer without a team was allotted one when they attended the Poppy Day headquarters, on the mezzanine floor of the St Francis Hotel. The claim that 1,000 girls took part in the Drive may be considered rather an exaggeration but there was a reference to a team being twenty-five girls so it must be taken as correct.

The $5,000 raised during the San Francisco Poppy Day was paid directly into William H. Crocker's 'Crocker National Bank'. William's wife Ethel was Hon. Chairman of the city's Poppy Day Committee.

Anna had the last word after Poppy Day, in the *San Francisco Examiner*. The article began 'Did you wear a poppy yesterday?' It stated that most of the city had, from the newsboy to the millionaire, and they had helped swell the League's funds. Anna was quoted as saying: 'Your San Francisco is wonderful. Never have I had so generous an answer.'

On 23 August, we know Anna wrote to Hartley Burr Alexander again, from San Diego. She mentioned her visits to several Californian places, including San Francisco, where she met Samuel Jacques Brun. Samuel was a lawyer of the Consul-General.

Samuel was born in 1857, at Saint-Gilles, Gard, in the ancient province of Languedoc, France. In his time, he wrote three books, including two about the Languedoc region. Samuel arrived in the USA as a young man in 1880 and became a nationalised citizen in 1885.

Anna recruited Samuel to serve as Attorney at Law and Counsellor for her organisation. She wrote he had helped her with by-laws, enabling her to plan the work of 1921. Anna wrote that she would write to every person who was a National Officer or a member of the Advisory Board of Directors and ask for 'their approval, their objections and their suggestions' and their vote. She added, 'It will be their vote.'

It was east across the Bay to Berkeley next, for Anna. Patsy Epperson accompanied her, ahead of forming another League Committee.

Berkeley's Poppy Day was on 29 July. Poppy HQ was at the Hotel Whitecotton, where Anna and Patsy were probably staying. It was on the main thoroughfare through Berkeley's central downtown and very close to the University of California. It was an ideal location.

Anna gave examples from the devastated region of why it was imperative to help French children: when Anna was helping to distribute food to some children, 'One little girl looked on with eager eyes but would not come forward to partake of the food offered. Asked if she were not hungry, she replied "Yes, madame, but it is not my turn to eat. I had bread this morning."' On another occasion, Anna told of two small school children: they 'had to work with their widowed mother in the fields with a day's meal consisting of one piece of bread and a tiny piece of cheese.' 'It is these children we must help,' she said.

Society women, college girls, University students, and nearly every Berkeley women's organisation sold the poppies. The 'Crocker National Bank', again, handled poppy funds raised.

After the Poppy Day, Patsy wrote a letter to the *Berkeley Tribune*'s editor, on behalf of Anna. She wrote that Anna wished to express 'deep appreciation of the generosity' of the people of Berkeley, its Committee, and the *Tribune*, on behalf of herself and the 'little sufferers in France'. Berkeley's Poppy Day raised nearly $8,000.

On 5 August, another East Bay city, Richmond, held a Poppy Day. That morning, Anna met child film star Wesley 'Freckles' Barry. She 'pinned on his coat the first poppy of those made by French children'. Anna had made him 'Special Motion Picture Deputy' of the League and, on the 5th, Anna formally appointed him. Born in LA in 1907, Wesley had been a film star since the age of seven. He pledged to carry out a special Drive for the League among the First National theatres.

Also on Richmond's Poppy Day, Anna addressed an audience at the Standard Oil refinery, spoke at the local cinemas, and other places. The Poppy Day in Richmond raised $760.

Oakland was next for Anna, another East Bay city. Nell O'Bryan and Helen Ahern had done the preliminary work necessary, when she arrived there on 7 August. Anna was present on Poppy Day, to 'supervise'.

Anna either visited Oakland before Poppy Day or was visited by the *Oakland Tribune* because, on 5 August, she was being quoted: 'You bought Liberty Bonds during the war until it hurt. And yet we ask and ask again. These children lean on America and America alone of all the world is in position to aid them. Let your response to the solicitations of our poppy girls on Saturday be most generous.'

Reportedly, bands of girls from San Francisco's French community helped swell the numbers of Community Service girls, all chaperoned by 'lieutenants'. The 'maids and matrons' of Oakland invaded its streets. They were dressed in white, wearing 'In Flanders Fields' sashes, and carrying their baskets of poppies. They accepted money in sealed cigar boxes. One hundred and fifty poppy girls/ladies were posted in the Downtown district.

It was reported that one Mrs Oney Nicely set up a new Poppy Day record, with the amount she collected, because 'she would not conclude an armistice'. To date, it is not known what amount Oakland raised.

Alameda was another East Bay city to hold a Poppy Day on 7 August. The Day raised between $600 and $700. Alameda's monies went to Saint-Quentin, in the Aisne department of France, where garments made by Alameda's Needle-Work Guild were being sent. Mrs Hermann Krusi, who was head of the needle-workers, secured a promise from Anna that this would be carried out. Ida Krusi was also an Alameda Club woman. Her father had been German immigrant, Edward Clawiter, who had arrived in California on a sailing ship, during the Gold Rush.

Both of Ida and Hermann's sons served during the war. One went to France before the USA entered the war. One of his letters home was made public. He made observations about the conditions over there:

> There is hardly a woman to be seen on the streets who is not in mourning. There is no laughter, no whistling, no merriment. It makes me wish the American people were more human and less efficient. When the Americans have lost 10,000,000 men they

will discover that they are human and that there is something in the world besides money.

I wish you would use your influence to make the Americans take a more sensible view of the war and try to make them realize that they must contribute their bit now.

A mother heeded her son's plea, it seems, and the people of Saint-Quentin received the benefits.

On 10 August, Helen Ahern was photographed with flying ace Eddie Rickenbacker and his aeroplane, in Oakland. She was handing him a basket of poppies. Eddie had fought in the war, with 94 Aero Squadron, in France. This particular aeroplane was one of two 'all-metal monoplanes' taking the cargo of poppies down to Los Angeles.

These two planes were two of three that had made history on 29 July, by taking an experimental coast-to-coast aerial mail flight from New York to San Francisco. These two poppy planes remained on the west coast after those flights. After the photoshoot, Helen then went ahead to Santa Cruz and Anna arrived there the next day.

During the evening of 11 August, Anna spoke at New Santa Cruz theatre and the Casino ballroom, in preparation for the Poppy Day there, on the 14th. The next day, she spoke at Native Sons hall and the bandstand on the beach. Stella Finkeldey was Poppy Day Chairman; a teacher, Secretary of the local Red Cross chapter, and a member of the Santa Cruz Native Daughters. The Native Daughters were in charge of Poppy Day, which was 'stimulated' when 'Speed' J. C. Johnson flew over the city, in his Curtiss plane, dropping circulars carrying the poem 'In Flanders Fields'.

Poppies were sold on Santa Cruz streets and from beach stands. The Day raised $407.34 and was considered 'an unqualified success', compared to other similar drives for charitable causes. That day, poppies were also sold in places nearby, including Davenport ($31.97), East Santa Cruz ($15.95), and Capitola ($19.93).

Anna left Santa Cruz ahead of the Poppy Day. It was Los Angeles next, for her. Nell O'Bryan and Helen Ahern had arrived beforehand, to begin arrangements. The Los Angeles Herald printed numerous articles promoting the League, quoting Anna on many occasions: "'Throughout the entire west," said Mme. Guérin, who wears a uniform of French blue with a saucy tam o'shanter to match and whose native French chic and charm cannot be concealed under a uniform of any kind, "our aims and purposes have met with quick sympathy and ready response.'"

Anna was quoted as saying nearly $85,000 was already raised. With Poppy Day held on a Saturday, 15 per cent was held for the 'furtherance of the purposes of the league', 85 per cent was cabled to France on a Monday, and 'on the next day a quota of children who have not known a tight roof or a dry bed since the German invasion of 1914 will be cared for.'

Mrs Charles O. Canfield had consented to be Chairman of the Los Angeles Committee. This was Pearl Rose Canfield (née Shafer). Her paternal heritage was German. Pearl was the second wife of 'Oil Operator' Charles Orville Canfield, whose father was the millionaire oilman and property developer Charles Adelbert Canfield.

The French film director Maurice Tourneur offered the League two silver loving cups: one for the team which secured the largest amount of money, and one for the second largest amount. He was French, born in Paris. His real name was actually Thomas. He was best known for films like *The Last of the Mohicans* and *Treasure Island* (both 1920). One biography suggested he disagreed with where producers were taking film production and, for that reason, he repatriated himself back to France.

The Alexandria Hotel offered the use of Parlor F, on the mezzanine floor, for the Poppy HQ. The Tourneur cups were displayed in its lobby. An appeal went out for 1,000 girls and, by the time Poppy Day arrived, there were five teams and each team held twenty-one girls.

French-born Miss Lucile Roos set her sights on one of the Tourneur silver cups and created her very own team of friends. At the time, it was said, her 'whole heart has been thrown into the work'. However, to date, nothing has emerged about what the LA Poppy Day raised.

Los Angeles, LA or 'La La Land', must have been an interesting city for Anna to visit. She based herself in the Ansonia apartments, at 2205 West Sixth Street. She was there in the city from the evening of 12 August, until the evening of the 16th, prior to departing for Long Beach. It is presumed Anna stayed the week in Long Beach, rather than travelling the 23 miles or so to and from the Ansonia apartments.

Georgina Marriott was Anna's delegate in Long Beach. The well-educated Long Beach Club woman Mrs Florence G. Bixby had been appointed the Chairman of its Poppy Day Committee.

Florence had a very strong philanthropic interest in education and children's welfare. Her husband, Frederick Hathaway Bixby, came from the old pioneering Bixby family, which had developed many parts of California, including Long Beach.

The Long Beach Poppy Day was 21 August, and the Poppy Girls distributed tissue-paper poppies. They stood on different corners in the downtown district, at the entrance of office buildings, and at hotels. They were 'holding up' men of business and pedestrians.

In Long Beach, Anna met with one Miss Julia Ellen Rogers, the Chairman of the Long Beach branch of the Fatherless Children of France. Her branch had operated for four years and, by the time her branch finally closed, at the beginning of April 1922, it had sent $10,000 in subscriptions to France for orphans, from their 257 Long Beach godmothers and godfathers. Julia was a very well-educated lecturer-cum-author. Anna described her as 'very clever'.

Anna's next stop was San Diego. This was just 15 miles from the border with Mexico. Anna probably arrived on 22 August and Patsy Epperson assisted her. The U. S. Grant Hotel became her headquarters.

The first thing on Anna's itinerary was attending the Californian State Convention of the American Legion, taking place from 23–25 August inclusive. It was held in the large industrial building, on the exposition grounds in Balboa Park. At the Convention's opening, State Commander David Prescott Barrows banged the gavel, a hush followed, 'The Star-Spangled Banner' brought veterans to their feet, and, with bowed heads, fallen comrades were remembered. State Governor Stephens welcomed the veterans 'in the name of the State'.

Dr Barrows' day job was President of the University of California, in Berkeley. Initially, he had been a student at the University, then a lecturer, and then, in 1919, he became its ninth President.

Before the war, Barrows was Superintendent of Schools for Manila, in the Philippines and then Director of Education there. At the outbreak of war, he served with the American Commission for Relief, in Belgium. He became a commissioned Major in the US Army, when the USA entered the war, stationed in the Philippines and Serbia. He had only returned to the USA on 8 August, after five weeks in Europe. At the convention, he described what he had seen on French battlefields.

Restoration work was only just beginning. Much of the territory was as it had been left after the battles. He confirmed what Anna would claim, that the American and French Children's League was striving to help to the poor children 'still living in these battle-scarred areas'.

Anna described Dr Barrows as 'clever, nice, powerful' but she felt he did not possess the 'radiance' or the 'splendid soul and big heart' that Hartley Burr Alexander did.

In San Diego, as already mentioned, Anna wrote to Hartley again. She wrote about meeting State Governor Stephens and San Francisco Mayor, James Rolph Jr., who both gave her personal letters. She also mentioned Rear Admiral Roger Welles, in relation to being on the League's National

Committee. He had become the first commander of the new naval base at San Diego. He had sole charge of building and organising the new base. Anna referred to him as Commander of the Légion d'honneur.

Anna wrote of being 'so proud' to have Hartley as National President and about asking her National Officers for guidance about what League workers should be paid. She described Nell O'Bryan as 'very clever, very shrewd' and 'I am willing to see her earn a lot of money if she does the work next year because she has been very faithful to me – but – there is a limit.' Money for salaries had to be considered very carefully.

Anna was only expecting expenses. She wrote: 'I am asking only my expenses (France will give me what they think best).' She wrote of her six trusty stalwarts (Helen, Celeste, Patsy, Isabelle, Georgina, and Nell) vying for her attention: 'I have six ladies working for me – all jealous of the time I give to the other because her percentage after is not so good – four of them older than I am … I must just smile and will what I will and obtain it. It is a little hard – sometimes…'

It is now we learn about Anna's 'big idea':

> My big idea is this one: 'Have the Poppy as the Memorial flower and have the people of America wear a Poppy for Decoration Day – at least for 3 years.' I am going to order 10 millions poppies – silk poppies to the poor women and children of devastated France, get for them the silk etc – and during the week before Decoration day our Committees will see that these Poppies will be sold 5¢ 10¢ anything they like.
>
> I am going to ask here and at the National Convention [of] the American Legion to pass an amendment for that and to order to the League, our League – their poppies for 1 million ½ of their men at 10¢. I am going to ask the same thing to the War Mothers – War Veterans (It is why I stay at their Conventions) And as I shall try and try to have those poppies if 1¢ 1/2 or 2¢ all the benefit will be for the League – to take care of the Children to begin their endowment. I know it can be done – it will be done, my friends, if you help me and sustain me.

Looking back to this time, Anna wrote:

> In San Diego was the American Legion Convention when we arrived there for our Poppy Day. And as I spoke at their State convention the American Legion men told me that I must go

to their National Convention in Cleveland to present the Idea, that it would be surely accepted enthusiastically as it was just a symbol like that the American Legion Organisation was looking for. And they told me to write to Colonel Galbraith who was to run for National President.

Anna knew this Colonel Frederick W. Galbraith and wrote to him with her idea. He wired her, saying he was making a reservation for her in Cleveland. He thought that an annual national Flanders' Poppy Day would be the best memorial to comrades who had given their lives for humanity. Anna felt he was 'with her with all his heart'. She knew he was a great friend of France.

Anna spoke of fatigue again: 'Yes – I am tired and I am looking tired … I am making the sacrifice of my temporary happiness that I must – succeed – for France and America.'

In her last paragraph, Anna remarked that the future was going to be just as tiring for her, though: 'I am going to work very, very hard (that will not change me much – until I shall report to you in order to bring to you an organization naturally organized).'

Anna closed the letter referring to Hartley's wife and mother-in-law: 'Here, for every one especially for Mrs. Griggs and Mrs. Alexander I send only best and most affectionate love – (I was going to put kisses but the gentlemen of the family will object). Yours E. Guérin.'

Returning to San Diego and its environs, dates for the Poppy Days were decided upon. The neighbourhoods of Coronado, Del Mar, La Jolla, and Ocean Beach were amongst those joining San Diego Downtown in having Poppy Days and each had its own committee.

The Daughters of Liberty, American Legion Women's Auxiliary, the Playgrounds Association, the Community Service, the Loung Ladies Institute, the YWCA, and the Boy Scouts all pledged their support and cooperation to Anna's 'worthy cause'. Again, the sellers wore badges inscribed 'In Flanders Fields, the Poppies Grow'. The Southern Trust and Commerce Bank would accept all the money collected.

Poppy Day was initially arranged for 4 September but, for some unknown reason, all bar one was postponed until the 11th. The one was Coronado's Poppy Day and it raised $220.80.

On her last day in San Diego, 8 September, Anna is reported to have given seven addresses. She spoke of her work and of the seventeen states already organised. The next day, she left the city, with all the arranged Poppy Days in the capable hands of the committees.

Anna took the early train north, to Santa Ana. She made a whistlestop round tour of the Orange County cities of Anaheim, Fullerton, and Orange. Back in the evening, she spoke at the Santa Ana American Legion Post No. 131. Utah's Georgina was Anna's delegate again.

Other Poppy Days in California included Burlingame, San Mateo, San Jose, Boulder Creek, Ben Lomond, and Felton (14 August), Petaluma (which raised $365.89), Santa Rosa (28 August), Vallejo ($600–$700, 11 September), Modesto ($263.11), Stockton, Fullerton, Anaheim ($107.60), Orange, Santa Ana (18 September), and Fresno (2 October).

Anna Guérin left Santa Ana on 11 August. Via Los Angeles, she headed east out of California. Her first stop was Des Moines, Iowa, some 1,700 miles away, to address the 'Service Star Legion' convention.

We have an idea of how Anna may have addressed the War Mothers, at the Hotel Fort Des Moines, on 14 August, because a draft speech exists within Dr Hartley B. Alexander's papers. The following extracts total just one-third of this speech. The first paragraph began:

> Madames, it is for me a great, great pleasure to be once more among you. Since your Convention in Baltimore now, nearly a year ago, inspired by you, helped by you everywhere, and pushed by the great love for my Country and for yours, I have been organizing state by state the American and French Children's League called also: 'After War Work.'

Anna continued:

> Madames, when inspired by your Convention of Baltimore, I was praying to see my way to answer the urgent appeal from Northern destroyed France, when I realized that if help was not forth coming soon and steadily for those poor children, they would go many of them – sleeping also under the Poppies of Flanders side by side with their friends the Yankee Boys, whose cold hand had left the torch fall – the answer came to me and there, in Baltimore, we had a week after your departure the first day with poppies – red Poppies of Flanders – color of the pure blood shed by humanity.

Anna explained her League's aims and its virtues. She said the great work of the League was being carried out with the 'maximum of efficiency and the minimum of expenses'. She was organising state after state. In each town, she had the Chairman of the Mothers, or a relative of an ex-soldier, on her Committee. With the help of War Mothers, she was carrying out her Poppy Days – Tag Days – with girls' badges inscribed 'In Flanders Fields the Poppies Grow'.

Speaking more about the League's Poppy Days, Anna pleaded:

> By a magnificent way in its noble simplicity we can carry on and finish the work taking away the sting of the word 'begging' and keeping alive the memory of the sacrificed ones. In memory of those sacrificed ones, I am asking to you – you Mothers, wives, sisters and daughters, you the best part of the nation – to help us finish the work.
>
> It will be an easy task if you would adopt and recognise the Red Poppy as the Memorial Flower to be worn on Decoration Day; if you would ask every one of your members and if possible, your family, to wear a Poppy on Decoration Day and if, as an organization, you would order your Red Poppies to the American and French Children's League which will see that they will reach every one of your chapters three weeks or one month before Decoration Day for the price of 10 ¢ each.

After San Diego, this was the first public exposé of her 'big idea', which would later be called 'Inter-Allied Poppy Day'. She told of her plan to have ten or fifteen million red silk poppies made during the coming winter, by women and children of devastated France. From the 10¢ price, 2–3¢ would be paid to those making the poppies. The remainder would go towards the League's great work – 'to revive these children'.

She said, 'They will make those Memorial Flowers with all their hearts full of gratitude towards America. Each one of those little Red Poppies will bring here a spark of the immortal soul of France: this soul who has always been ready to sacrifice herself for Justice, Liberty and Humanity and also a sparkle of the soul of your boys sleeping in Flanders' fields.'

'Take the Poppies, My Friends,' Anna said, 'your example will be followed by all the Nation. … You can see that if the Poppy becomes the National Memorial Flower of Decoration Day, even at ten cents each, that will allow the American and French Children's League to become the warehouse of all relief French organizations and to put a final end to those drives so hard to put on now that it seems the war is over.'

Anna concluded: 'I beg, you, who have been always in the first line of duty, of sacrifice of service to be the backbone of this sweet, beautiful, magnificent idea which enable us to finish the work of justice – reparation – reconstruction towards France, your sister's country and towards Humanity.' She was pleading for Mothers to keep the poppy as their memorial emblem and continue supporting her. She failed in one quest, when Mothers took the white carnation and red rose instead, but succeeded in keeping their support in all her future Poppy Days.

Anna had carried a basket of poppies and had given a poppy to every delegate. Anna was referred to as 'The poppy girly' and declared to be one of the most popular visitors at the convention.

Indianapolis, Indiana, was next. Anna attended the Encampment of the 'Grand Army of the Republic' and the 'Sons and Daughters of the GAR', held from 19 to 24 August. She needed its permission to use Decoration Day for her 'Poppy Day of the American Legion Men'.

Decoration Day was affiliated to the 'Grand Army of the Republic'. The Day had been established by it after the American Civil War. It was when the graves of that war's dead were decorated throughout the states. Although the first Decoration Day is officially recognised as 5 May 1866, in Waterloo, New York State, it is disputed by some. Other places believe they have a claim, but setting criteria for a 'Day' is complicated.

Many Southern locations, like Augusta, Georgia, decorated graves in April 1866, a month before Waterloo. It is called 'Memorial Day' now, commemorating war dead from all conflicts the USA has been involved in. It is held on the last Monday of May.

The Great Army of the Republic, with its Allied organisations – the Woman's Relief Corps; the Sons of Veterans; the Sons of Veterans' Auxiliary; the Daughters of Veterans; and the Ladies of the GAR – all endorsed Anna's 'big idea'. The Woman's Relief Corps agreed $500 to be used to buy Anna's poppies. These poppies would stay in France and be used to decorate American soldiers' graves 'over there'.

When the Sons of Veterans adopted the poppy as their memorial emblem, the *Indianapolis Star* announced that decision and perfectly expressed why it was logical to do so. It appreciated how much the scarlet blossom had featured in war literature, how American soldiers had written about the poppy, and how much these poppies had impressed the American soldiers. Poppies had become permanently associated with memories of those who had fought during the Great War.

In her *Synopsis*, Anna described her visit to the GAR:

> I spoke to the ENCAMPMENT explaining to them that not only there would be a NATIONAL POPPY DAY each year

ON DECORATION DAY but also that DAY the graves of the Heroes of this last War would be decorated with a wreath of POPPIES while the old graves would be decorated with the flag. That was my Idea and it has been done during many years in many places. The ENCAMPMENT endorsed the Idea and it is with their approval that I arrived at the Convention in Cleveland.

The aforementioned convention at Cleveland, in Ohio, was the American Legion's and it was its second. The convention was held between 27 and 29 September. Anna arrived there, with the invitation from Colonel Frederick W. Galbraith.

Anna first addressed the Committee of forty-eight State Commanders about her 'big idea'. It was accepted unanimously but it had to be put to the convention, for all the delegates to make a vote. Anna wrote:

I was received amongst the guests of Honor they had; MARSHALL PETAIN – ADMIRAL BEATY – GENERAL DIAZ and it was a wonderful Convention. The Flanders' Fields Poppy Idea was adopted first by the Committee of the 48 States Presidents, to whom I spoke presented by Colonel Galbraith, Colonel Parman of Chicago and General Haufman of Oklohama ...

It was accepted unanimously by them, as later on, it was accepted by the Convention from the platform. And when all the speeches by all the Officers, by the President of the GOLD STAR MOTHERS and by the Guest of Honor were over, just before the election was going to take place. General Hoffman came in front and showing me in the logs, near the platform, said: WE CANNOT CLOSE SUCH WONDERFUL MEETING WITHOUT HAVING A FEW WORDS FROM MADAME GUÉRIN – OUR POPPY LADY WHO HAS GIVEN US THE FLANDERS' FIELDS POPPY Symbol in Memoriam for our Heroes.

Anna's own words describe the moment:

Without leaving the loge [private box] I said few words and the ovation I received from that 5000 American men and their guests is a Memory never to be forgotten. After the Convention I was nearly carried on shoulders and Colonel Galbraith and Marshall Petain told me that THE FLANDERS' FIELDS POPPY would make an other lien [link] between France and the U. S.

A long Convention report read: 'Mme. Guérin was given two minutes to tell of her efforts to make the red poppy of France the official flower of the service men of the Allies. Mme Guérin brought tears to the eyes of men who faced unflinchingly the oncoming Hun.' It could be said that during that visit, Anna came of age. She was no longer the 'poppy girly', as the Legionnaires gave her the name of 'The Poppy Lady of France'. Sometimes, she is referred to as 'The Poppy Lady from France'.

The official wording of Resolution No. 83 recorded Georgia as the source but, evidently, an identical idea had been proposed to the National Committee by others, including the earlier nationally publicised formal resolution from Tacoma, on 15 March. With the country's empathy with the poppy and with so many State Commanders knowing or, at least, knowing of Anna and her war work in their country, it was inevitable the poppy would be adopted and support given to Anna's 'big idea'.

It would be publicised, in print, that the poppy was adopted 'after tabling of a similar one presented by the American and French children's league, with which Madame Guérin was associated.'

Immediately afterwards, the nation's newspapers alerted readers to the American Legion's adoption of the poppy as its memorial emblem.

Leading up to the American Legion convention in Cleveland, Chicago had been Anna's League's headquarters. However, during that convention, new alliances were made and arrangements were put in place to move her HQ to Indianapolis instead. Prior to Anna leaving for France in November 1920, changes began to be made.

After the Convention, Anna's American and French Children's League President, Dr Hartley Burr Alexander, wrote to the Director of the National Information Bureau in New York City, asking for the League to be officially recognised by the Bureau. Much historical information was given about the League, Madame Guérin, the 'Fatherless Children of France' charity work that the League would continue, and so on.

In 1941, Anna explained:

After the Convention was over I gave few more lectures to complete the million frs I had promised to the Committee of the Children of Devasted France: in Cleveland, Toledo, Detroit, always making Tags DAYS with the Flanders' Poppies, always

106

continuing to spread the Idea. I was hurrying as it had been decided after the Convention that the first NATIONAL POPPY DAY ON DECORATION DAY would be for the benefit of the CHILDREN OF DEVASTATED FRANCE ...

Whilst in Ohio, Anna visited several places in the state. She also went over state lines into Pennsylvania and Michigan.

On 16 October, Anna and Isabelle Mack were in Indianapolis, to establish the new American and French Children's League HQ. It was home to the American Legion's HQ and its Treasurer, Robert H. Tyndall. Tyndall became Anna's Treasurer and all went ahead to move from Chicago and the former Treasurer, Mrs Frederick Masters.

The *Indianapolis News* published an interview with Anna and Isabelle. Anna was introduced as someone who had given 5,000 lectures in forty-five states. 'We shall not forget' was the League's motto, Anna said. She added 'Indianapolis must be the heart of America, because the American Legion has found it fit for its headquarters, and what is good for the boys must be good for the children.'

Isabelle described conditions in France: no machinery, no coal, $2 for a pound of butter, $1.15 for two pounds of sugar, 600,000 homes destroyed, canals were out of action, and children's health was precarious. She announced the League had declared 10 November as Poppy Day. It meant people could wear a poppy on Armistice Day.

Whereas the procedure had been, after Poppy Days, for a Poppy Day Committee to send its money straight to the League's Paris bank, now money would be sent to Robert Tyndall. He would be a go-between and keep accounts, before the money was wired to France. Robert had been an artillery officer during the First World War and awarded the Distinguished Service Medal, the Croix de guerre, and the Légion d'honneur.

As well as being Treasurer for the American Legion, Robert had also kept the books for the French War Orphan Fund.

The French War Orphan Fund sponsorship began in March 1918, when the American Expeditionary Force's newspaper *Stars and Stripes* opened its campaign with a front-page article with the headline: 'Take as your mascot a French War Orphan.'

Cash began being donated immediately. The Red Cross was designated to administer the fund but, before long, it became overwhelmed with work. By the time the last of the AEF men had left France, not only had 'they left behind their legion of dead' but they also left some 3,444 French orphans who had benefited from this AEF scheme.

After Indianapolis, Anna went off to New York to recruit new National Committee members. In another letter to Hartley, she explained what she had been doing in New York:

> I went to New York where I did start a splendid committee with the help of our Vice-National Chairman Mrs. George Corbin Perine helped by Mrs. Washington (Mrs. M.B.W.) – both from the George Washington's family. The Secretary will be the sister of Mrs. Stein, Mlle. De Mare. Very clever also.

We already know Mrs George Corbin Perine from Baltimore (now President). The Vice-President was Mrs May Bruce Washington (née Brennan) of Manhattan, New York. May was born in Louisville, Kentucky and was married to William L. Washington. He was a banker and direct descendant of the brother of George Washington.

Mlle Marie Edith de Mare was born in Paris. Her parents were well-known French artist/etcher/author Tiburce de Mare and his English-born wife Agnes Louisa (née Healy). Marie was a granddaughter of American historical and portrait painter George P. A. Healy. George had been a photographer at one time, with a studio in Rome.

Marie was a widow. Her husband, Joseph Von Stein, had died in 1919. Denver had remained Marie's home. French culture, like the Scottish one, set great store in the importance of a woman's birth status, hence the 'Mademoiselle' title after being widowed. At this time, Marie had three children: Gustav, 8; Agness, 6; and Jeanne, 2.

All these changes were being made in order to achieve the approval of the Information Bureau. The books had to be signed off in Paris by an auditor and Anna went to Chicago to have the books audited there on 23 October. She had received a report from Général Claude A. L. Legrand, Treasurer in France, and she hoped it would be good enough for the Bureau while it waited for the Paris audit to arrive.

Anna's Treasurer Robert Tyndall had chosen an auditor, George Scott Olive, and he would audit the books every three months. George was a certified public accountant. Anna went back to Indianapolis, after Chicago, to attend a meeting at the Fletcher National Bank, with Messrs. Tyndall and Olive, the lawyer, Mr Nicholas, and 'all the ladies'.

Anna was to 'open the books and fix everything'. Secretary Isabelle Mack would be based in Indianapolis. Isabelle would take the minutes of the meeting and she would send them to Hartley, who was remaining President, for the time being.

Anna suggested that as long as her Poppy Days continued to raise funds, she would not rest and she would continue to worry over them. Anna's Poppy Days continued to be arranged by her local committees in the states that hosted them. For instance, in Montana and South Dakota, Poppy Days were held parallel to the Californian ones in September.

In South Dakota, by mid-September, Poppy Days had raised the following sums: Alexandria ($227.55); Arlington ($91.43); Brookings ($306.66); Deadwood ($107.37); Dell Rapids ($100.44); De Smet ($43.92); Groton ($160.59); Henry ($72.27); Hudson ($90.68); Iroquois ($37.76); Kimball ($72.17); Lake Preston ($39.50); Langford ($100.71); Mt. Pierre ($90.60); Pierpont ($35.36); Rapid City ($127.80); Volga ($96.90); and Winfred ($130).

On 31 October 1920, the Town Hall in Anna's hometown of Vallon received a cheque for 2,500 francs. It was from Anna's League, for the orphans of the town, on the instructions of 'Madame E. Guérin'. Vallon possessed two orphanages: one Protestant, for boys, and one Catholic, for girls. The money was transferred to the commune's Charity Office.

In November, Poppy Days would be held again, with French-made poppies. Cities like Cincinnati, Ohio; Indianapolis, Indiana; and Louisville, Kentucky joined other large cities. Smaller locations also took part. A theme ran through promotional articles: that of including 'In Flanders Fields the poppies grow, between the crosses row on row.' Poppy Days were held before, on, and after 11 November.

On 13 November, Poppy Days were held in Indianapolis, New Castle (Pennsylvania), and Akron (Ohio's Rubber City), raising $2,687, $2,339, and $1,000 respectively; Louisville's Poppy Day was held on the 20th, and raised $2,000. Cincinnati, on the other hand, held its Poppy Day on Armistice Day and raised $10,000. Regardless of dates, Anna and the League were appreciative of any Poppy Day funds.

It was estimated that 100,000 poppies were distributed in Cincinnati. Incidentally, Cincinnati was where Col. Fred Galbraith, the National Commander of the American Legion, had his home. The delegates had voted Col. Galbraith in as their second National Commander. He became Anna's ally, but fate would be unkind and end the alliance.

'Nell' O'Bryan and Helen Ahern organised Kentucky. This included aforementioned Louisville, where Anna joined them in November. They had organised Arizona previously, arriving there on 11 September. Arizona was a great campaign for these American Red Cross women.

Phoenix is a prime example of their large drives. They described the conditions they had seen in France, whilst working for the American Red

Cross. They told of four million homeless; 2,400 cities, towns, and villages were dust; and there were cities in the devastated region, six times as large as Phoenix, where not a fragment of wall was left standing. The French government was helpless because of the magnitude of its task.

They had stood at Verdun last February, which was a heap of stone and brick: 'everywhere a desolation so complete, so overwhelming, that you are lost in amazement that anyone could have remained alive.'

In Phoenix, Nell spoke to dozens of girls and hoped that they would volunteer to sell poppies for the children of France. She would be glad to have them enrol to help on Poppy Day, by standing on street corners and selling replica scarlet poppies, like those 'that grow in Flanders fields'.

Nell and Helen spoke to many audiences, at meetings such as that of the Kiwanis. It was a club originating in Detroit, in 1917, and is now international – its ethos was and is to proudly serve the needs of children.

A unique event took place at Tally's Open-Air Arena, Phoenix. It was a large charity 'Boxing Carnival', a 'real fistic treat'. The event took place on the evening of 21 September. It was the idea of boxers Jimmy Curley and Billy McCann, Nell's friends. Tally offered his Arena for free and Matchmaker Benjamin H. McAhren offered to help too.

Jimmy Curley was James Supples, from Buffalo, New York. He was also known as 'Kid Curley' or James 'Curley' Supples. Billy McCann was a lightweight, based in Phoenix at the time. Curley and McCann promised to get others together and many well-known boxers took part. Local singers agreed to take part in the programme. Services were given free. Seats were 50/75 cents and $1. Every cent went to the League.

Reportedly, there were 100 girls selling poppies in Phoenix and almost everyone wore a poppy by the end of the day. On 18 September, Mesa, Glendale, Peoria, and Phoenix ($1,000) held Poppy Days.

Nell and Helen went on to Tucson to organise a Poppy Day there, on 25 September. Poppy HQ was the Santa Rita Hotel, where Nell and Helen stayed. Tucson's Day raised $300.31. Bisbee followed, with the two women arriving on the 28th, to organise a Poppy Day on 6 October. The Copper Queen Hotel was Poppy HQ. Poppy Day began at 8.00 am and everyone kept going until after 10.00 pm. Bisbee's Day raised nearly $500. Who knows where else the women went in Arizona?

Coming full circle, Nell and Helen went on to organise Kentucky. On 10 November, Anna arrived in Louisville to make a rendezvous. With Nell, Anna attended a meeting of the Women's Club. They promoted the League and asked for assistance in their Poppy Day. The next day, Armistice Day, Anna spoke at the Louisville Girls' High School.

Armistice Day was commemorated all over the states. The papers were full of the programmes, poppy references, and 'In Flanders Fields' poems. Individual American Legion Posts held Poppy Days too.

After Louisville, Anna returned to Indianapolis to supervise its Poppy Day alongside Isabelle Mack, on 13 November. The usual promotions had been undertaken in schools, to recruit 400 girls, and in clubs, but now the American Legion was 100 per cent behind the poppy. If anyone doubted the strength of empathy towards the poppy as a remembrance emblem, the evidence just kept coming.

From Indianapolis, Anna went to New York. On 20 November, after twenty months of campaigning, Anna was ready to return to France. Before she set sail, she went to see how she could have her boxes of poppies taken out from the pier without paying any custom duty.

Anna found a broker who told her he would do the work for her very cheaply. The broker sent one of his men with her, to see the head of the Customs Service of New York. He informed her that the League had to request a 'special privilege' in Washington DC. Anna decided she would ask her National Chairman to apply on her behalf.

Anna left New York on the *Touraine*. She was accompanied by Marie de Mare (Stein). The miles Anna had travelled during those months can only be estimated. It is evident it was more than 21,000 miles.

Anna returned to France to report to the French Committee of La Ligue des Enfants de France et d'Amérique, in Paris. On 9 December, with Marie de Mare, Anna went to the Élysée Palace, the official residence of the President of the French Republic, to report to Madame Millerand, the Committee and guests. She wanted to return to France having raised one million francs and she had come close to achieving it.

Madame Jeanne Millerand followed the campaign through letters from Anna, State Governors, and other influential Americans. One reply to Anna proves Jeanne Millerand's appreciation:

> We thank you infinitely and all those who are helping you in your Flanders' Fields Poppy Days … I pray you to tell to all those you are soliciting their help how urgent and immense is our task of rehabilitation. Express to them our gratitude for the fraternity they are showing indefatigably towards our Country. Let the Flanders' Fields poppy be the voice of the poor children

111

of the Devastated France where only the Poppies are blooming
amongst the ruins ...

Much detail is discovered about La Ligue's first annual report (October
1919–October 1920) from Anna's 1941 *Synopsis*, and pages 11–16 inclusive
of the February 1921 edition of *Le Semeur*, which was the Literary Review
published under the patronage of the Ministry of Foreign Affairs and the
Alliance Française.

'AMERICAN STAR – American and French Children's League –
The After-War Work' was the *Le Semeur* title. The French National
Committee members were listed first, then American National Committee
members. 'Madame E. Guérin (Officier d'Instruction Publique)' was listed
as 'Official Delegate to the United States and Founder'. The League's aims
and beneficiaries followed.

The year ending October 1920 showed 926,296.03 francs had been
raised by Anna's League. Outstanding monies were to be carried over into
the next year's account. That included amounts raised latterly in States like
Ohio, South Dakota, Indiana, and Kentucky. The fluctuating dollar-to-franc
exchange rate makes it difficult to assess and compare amounts but, surely,
Anna must have raised her quest of one million francs.

Before speaking to the Assembly, Anna and Marie explained to members
of the Committee that they must have at least five million silk poppies made
in France. They needed this amount to be ready for shipping next April,
for the first National Flanders Poppy Day would be held in the USA, on
Decoration Day, 30 May 1921.

However, there was one enormous obstacle standing in the way of Anna's
request for poppies for her 'Inter-Allied Poppy Day' plan. La Ligue was not
able to fund it!

The Committee told her La Ligue's statutes were 'irrevocable: every
cent sent from the U.S. was to be used for the welfare of the poor children
and only for that.' Not one cent of Anna's 'million Francs could be used for
the fabrication of the Poppies, even in view of the large sum of money that
the Poppy day would bring to the poor children'.

From that time, Anna enlightens: 'As Originator of the Poppy's Idea,
and the sponsor and knowing how philanthropic this Idea could become,
I ordered, on my own responsibility not 5 but 3,000,000 of silk poppies.'

Anna began her Paris speech as follows:

Ladies and Gentlemen: I shall not apologize for coming before
you as those soldiers who, after a long campaign, return with

112

a shabby uniform – but with hope and strength because 'over here' they felt that Victory was – approaching ... I am here in the same condition. After 20 months of struggle, at last I see the full success of our great work of Justice, Humanity, Fraternity and Remembrance. This great hope makes me forget all: My shabby uniform, my physical and moral fatigue – I am happy, bringing to you wonderful tidings from all our friends and supporters in the United States.

Continuing, Anna spoke about the USA and its attitude towards the League:

The United States, marvellous country, whose immensity, power, energy and richness would overpower you if, at each step, you did not feel its big heart throbbing with generosity, a great mind full of wonderful ideals for Humanity – France being considered a very loved part of Humanity ... Do not judge the United States without having been there, do not judge before knowing them as I do, for then you will understand why I love them so dearly, why I hope so much from this young, strong nation who loves France like an older sister, wounded and worthy of the most tender care.

Anna spoke of 'unfortunate experiences, due to misunderstanding generally'. These known misunderstandings have, of course, already been documented. Anna blamed some German propaganda, which caused 'a feeling of disaffection towards France'.

Anna said she had to deny many false reports and foolish stories. But, she said, 'sincerity soon got the better of distrust; in their Commercial Clubs, in their Women's Clubs, sympathy, admiration was expressed not merely by applause but by donations and help.'

Anna also spoke about her love for the American schools and students: 'But I do love especially the school children, the students of High Schools and Universities, all this generous new generation which seems to me the best part of America, from whom we can expect great things.'

At this point, Anna talked about her tour of Minnesota's Iron Range. She spoke of the poppy becoming immortalised in the poem 'In Flanders Fields' and recited it. She followed it by Moïna Michael's poem, which she called admirable.

Anna generously stated: 'Those two poems were my inspiration for the "Poppy Days". Yes, the red poppy would finish the work – it would be the national emblem, the international one, that would allow the American and French Children's League to carry on the work of Justice, Humanity and Remembrance.'

She added: 'The Poppy idea was growing, and I realized that since we were forgetting too soon those sleeping in Flanders fields, the "poppy" should become a symbol and be the memorial flower.'

Anna told of attending the conventions of the Service Star Legion, Great Army of the Republic, Sons of the Veterans, Daughters of the Veterans, Auxiliary of the Sons of the Veterans, Ladies of the Grand Army, and Women of the Relief Corps.

Anna had asked them all to adopt the resolution:

> Be it resolved that every member, if possible, and his (or her) family shall wear a silk poppy on Decoration Day in memory of those who gave their lives for Humanity ... Everywhere the resolution was adopted with emotion ... The same Resolution was adopted also by the American Legion at its National Convention in Cleveland.

Anna spoke of how important it was to have the American Legion's support. It was, she said, the 'backbone of the country' and estimated, with one and a half million Legionnaires, together with their Auxiliaries (wives, mothers, sisters, daughters), they must total several million. At this point, though, perhaps she found herself wondering whether three million poppies would be enough for the drives in the United States.

We learn of the emotion Anna felt when the American Legion adopted the resolution: 'my joy was so deep that tears filled my eyes and I could hardly contain my emotion when they asked me for a speech in their Convention Hall. They called me "the Poppy Lady from France" ... I do not wish a more glorious title than this one.'

In French, 'de' means both 'from' and 'of', which may account for Anna being quoted as both 'from France' and/or 'of France'.

Knowing La Ligue could not help her buy poppies, Anna spoke of being

> confronted with the tremendous work of having the millions of poppies made and furnishing the money to pay for them. We shall accomplish a 'miracle' and have as many poppies ready as possible for next May – but the obtaining of funds now is not only urgent, but it is a question of life for our League – the After-War Work.

It is worth publishing much of Anna's report because it shows how much she appreciated everyone who helped her in her endeavours. Anna's closing words express the sincere love and gratitude she felt for the USA:

> In closing this report I wish to express my deep gratitude to all who helped me, every one of the officers of our State Committees, every child and student of the schools who joined in the work, every one of the devoted national organizers who, indefatigably have sewn, in spite of all difficulties, the beautiful seed of the 'Poppies', and who will go on carrying the work for God, for France, for Humanity.

By this time, through her fundraising, Anna had formed a strong and positive impression of the country. She genuinely expressed great admiration for the USA and its customs. The 'freedom of life' and the 'vigorous life' of that country appealed to her. Comparing the French way of life, she declared the American way was the right way. She stated the French way was 'too delicate, too refined'.

Marie de Mare sailed from Le Havre on 18 December, arriving in New York on 29 December. Anna remained in France and was there when 1921 dawned. It would be natural for Anna, after giving her report in Paris, to go and spend some time with her daughters, perhaps.

In early January, organised US State committees were receiving letters of thanks, along with New Year good wishes, from Madame André Lebon in Paris, on behalf of Madame Millerand. It was not possible for the Paris Committee to contact every committee in a state, so specific committees in the state capitals were singled out. Capitals such as Baltimore, Maryland; Butte, Montana; and Sioux Falls, South Dakota published their contact within local newspapers.

How long Anna relaxed, if she did, is not known. Certainly, she was back working on 19 January, when she wrote letters from France to the War Mothers, Mothers of Baltimore, Service Star Legion, clubs, Grand Army of the Republic, Commanders of the American Legion, and other Allied organisations.

Hartley Burr Alexander's papers enlighten once again about Anna's work, in a letter written by Anna to him. Part of the letter reads: 'I am now in France superintending the making of millions of red silk poppies (to be sold at 10 cents each) by the widows and daughters of French soldiers.' Continuing, Anna felt respective members would consider it 'a sacred and loyal obligation to wear the Poppy of Flanders Fields' on 30 May, on 1921's Memorial Day.

I have been asked, several times, if I know where the poppies were made, but I cannot say. I can speculate, given what little evidence exists. Anna told the Paris Committee at the Élysée Palace that orphanages must make her poppies and the League made donations to many institutions that could commit to helping in this way.

When Anna first shared her 'big idea' in August 1920 with Hartley, she wrote about millions of poppies, the poor women and children of devastated France, and 'get for them the silk etc'.

The city of Lille may have been one location where poppies were made and, perhaps, it was a central hub. Isabelle Mack's sister Doris (Mrs Henry E. Walker) lived there and, certainly, the League had other links to Lille, because some of its children went to 'Bidart House'.

Also supporting Lille playing a part in poppy manufacture was the fact that Isabelle's other sister Jessie, now a widow, was in Lille during February 1921, on behalf of the Children's League. It is not known how long Jessie was in Lille, staying with Doris, but she left Le Havre on 26 February, returning to the USA with a cargo of poppies.

I can imagine that any family who had received aid from Anna's League would be willing to reciprocate in any way possible. Receiving a wage would make it an easy decision. I surmise that Anna had a sense, right from the beginning, of how production could be organised and, as with the development of Poppy Days, practical experience meant operations would evolve with time.

Groups of women and children would have been organised in many communes; the fabric, with all other necessary materials, delivered to a central point; and, in their rough temporary accommodation, poppy making would be carried out. No doubt, they would all work and earn on a piece-work basis, paid according to the amount each produced.

While Anna was 'superintending' in France, Isabelle Mack was working hard in Indianapolis. Perhaps via the Associated Press, she was circulating articles which newspapers printed all over the United States.

The articles declared that 'Memorial Day will be "Poppy Day".' Poppies were made by women and children of devastated France, sold by the American and French Children's League, would cost 10 cents each, would benefit both French and American orphans, and must be ordered from Madame Isabelle Mack, 238 East Tenth Street, Indianapolis, Indiana, 'before February 28, so delivery may be made in ample time'.

The *American Legion Weekly* of 4 February carried a feature under the auspices of both the Legion and Children's League. It covered most of page 19 and contained what I feel is one of the best images of Anna.

Its message from Paris to American Legion Post Commanders and to Presidents of all Units of the Women's Auxiliary began:

> I, Madame E. Guérin, whom you called, at your last national convention in Cleveland, 'The Poppy Lady of France,' am unable to write to you all individually as I would like to do, so I am using the best available means I know of for placing my message before you – your own official publication.

Anna duplicated the wording of the American Legion's 1920 resolutions, verbatim, which had culminated in the Legion's adoption of the poppy as its emblem and its commitment that it would urge everyone to wear a red poppy on Memorial Day, every year.

The message from Anna told of widows and daughters of fallen Frenchmen making poppies for the American and French Children's League, of which, she stated, 'I am the founder and director'; an office being opened in Indianapolis; the League's treasurer being the same treasurer as the American Legion, Robert H. Tyndall; and quoted the two lines 'In Flanders fields, the poppies grow. Among the crosses – row on row.' It asked for orders to be in as early as possible and a coupon was included that could be completed and sent off to Isabelle Mack.

Anna arrived back in New York on 17 February, on SS *Chicago*, from Le Havre, accompanied by her daughter Raymonde Rabanit and her sister Juliette 'Yette' Boulle.

In her 1941 *Synopsis*, Anna wrote of arriving back in New York with '3 millions poppies', 'ordered on her own responsibility'.

Anna wrote about the high Customs duties but she had gone to the Customs Court as the 'Originator of the Idea explaining the purpose of this coming campaign in such a way that the Government refunded me $12,000 of duties'. Anna added that the Court sent the refund to 'Mme E. Guérin the Founder of the National Flanders' Fields Poppy Days' and said the judgement was recorded thus at the Customs Court.

The three women were heading to 2057 Kenilworth Avenue, Chicago, the home of Margaret Masters, who had been the League's Business Manager/ Treasurer before the American Legion's Robert H. Tyndall.

At a guess, I can imagine Anna was probably tying up loose ends, collecting documents, thanking Margaret, and saying 'au revoir'. Anna, together with Raymonde and Juliette, then headed for Indianapolis.

The publicity campaign had been continued by Isabelle Mack. Writing to Hartley again, Anna expressed she was 'much delighted' and 'astonished' to see the 'beautiful work' Isabelle had accomplished.

On its own, the *American Legion Weekly* advertisement would reach a readership of 750,000. Isabelle also sent letters to all American Legion State Commanders, Chambers of Commerce, and Presidents of patriotic societies such as the War Mothers.

In fact, Isabelle had sent out about 3,000 letters on Anna's behalf, promoting the League's Poppy Drives. Replies and orders were coming in fast, including one reply from the National Chairman of the Federation of Women's Clubs, stating there were 6,000 clubs ready to order.

As splendid as Anna thought Isabelle's work was, she had brought Raymonde and her sister Yette to be trained to help with the administrative work. Anna had written to Hartley: 'Mrs. Mack is too splendid [an] organiser not to be in the field and two or three French ladies ... are coming to the rescue.' The third French lady was Blanche Berneron.

Blanche was a widow. Born in Paris, she was listed as a 'Clerk' when she arrived in the USA in 1916. After staying for a few months, Blanche returned again to the USA in August 1919, going to San Francisco. Perhaps Anna met Blanche during San Francisco's Poppy Drive in 1920. Whatever the truth of it, Blanche would come to regard Anna and Yette as sisters.

Of the letters Anna sent out to Women's Clubs and War Mothers, some branches published their copies in local newspapers. The American Legion and its Women's Auxiliary also began a systematic distribution of articles across the states. They all told of their particular organisation's adoption of the Flanders Poppy as a memorial emblem; the wish that every man, woman, and child would wear a poppy on Memorial or Decoration Day; and mentioned either Madame E. Guérin, as the Poppy Lady of France, or the American and French Children's League.

Anna's Headquarters was at 238 East 10th Street, Indianapolis. She and her staff worked closely with the American Legion HQ, at the nearby World War Memorial Plaza. National President Col. Frederick W. Galbraith, National Adjutant Major Col. Lemuel Bolles and Treasurer Col. Robert H. Tyndall gave 'all the help possible'.

Anna's East 10th Street HQ was the home of Frenchman Dr Edouard Julien Duboise. Edouard was a very skilled man: physician, surgeon, city bacteriologist, and a Federal Health Service Inspector. He was born in 1867, in the Paris suburb of Vincennes. He arrived in the USA in 1893. Like Isabelle Mack, Edouard must have had a tender heart for La Patrie too.

Aged 50, he had enlisted and returned to France as a medical officer with the 42nd division of the United States Army.

He was cited for his 'magnificent example of bravery'. In the line, 'under violent bombardment', he gave treatment to American and French wounded on three days in July 1918, in Champagne. On a sad note, Edouard's son René, with his first wife Marie Dore, was killed at Verdun in 1917. René had enlisted into the French Army in 1914 and was also cited for bravery in action like his father, twice.

Raymonde and Yette were in charge of the East 10th Street office sometimes, when Isabelle gave occasional lectures in Pennsylvania, New Jersey, and the District of Columbia, for which she was responsible.

Yette had been given responsibility for lecturing in Nebraska. Even Isabelle's daughter Enid helped a little, by canvassing her university. Enid was studying at Barnard College, at Columbia University in New York City, and was Chairman of its Poppy Day Committee.

By the time the poppy ordering deadline of 28 February arrived, the operation was outgrowing Edouard's home. It was too small to be the American Legion's main office so the headquarters of the League would soon change, as would the Children's League itself.

These changes were the result of decisions made due to Hartley applying to have the League 'Incorporated' in October 1920. A Mr Dennis, a Baltimore lawyer, was also involved with the application.

The only officers' names put forward for this were: Mme E. Guérin, Founder of the American and French Children's League in the US; Mr Hartley B. Alexander, of Nebraska, President; Mrs George Corbin Perine (Tyler Perine), National Chairman; Mrs M. B. Washington, National Vice-Chairman; and Mr. Robert H. Tyndall, National Treasurer.

There was much to be decided and documented for the by-laws. For instance, what percentage, from all money collected, would be kept in the United States to cover League expenses, and so on.

The provision of 15 per cent had been agreed for the work: 10 per cent to pay all the workers and 5 per cent for general expenses. Anna did not think it could be any less for that year. That would not mean the League would use the full general expenses amount, but she thought the League would have to use the full 10 per cent for the workers because of all the organising that had to be done, in a short amount of time. She felt they were already behind.

Robert Tyndall told Anna he hoped the application would be agreed soon. He said that in the by-laws it must be well documented that the National Chairman must ask the Treasurer (him, in this case) to pay cheques or must delegate someone to do that. Requests could be done by letter, though – it was not necessary to do that personally.

Tyndall advised that the National Chairman should be located near the National Vice-Chairman. Thus, Mrs Tyler Perine had to choose between being based in Baltimore or New York. New York triumphed. That may have influenced Anna to move her headquarters to larger premises in New York. The Indianapolis office continued to be manned, because its address was accepting orders.

I cannot imagine how many discussions Anna had to have with all manner of people. There would be many with League officers but also with Frederick W. Galbraith Jr. of Cincinnati. Prior to becoming, and as, the American Legion National Commander, Frederick had assisted Anna in her quest to gain the Legion's support. He invited and presented her to the Legion's Convention, in 1920, and wholly supported her 'Inter-Allied Poppy Day' idea. Having been unanimously elected as the second National Commander, he was a great ally.

Even at this point, before Decoration/Memorial Poppy Days, Galbraith and Guérin were discussing how to proceed. Anna's 'big idea' had grown, and it was decided that she could organise all the Allied countries. Anna would go first to Canada. In her *Synopsis*, Anna wrote that 'he would follow after to organise them as the FIDAC'.

Galbraith was interested in developing the FIDAC, la Fédération Interalliée des Anciens Combattants (the Association of the Veterans of All the Allies), which had been founded in November 1920, in Paris.

The ethos of FIDAC was quoted as using the 'friendship born on the field of battle to dissipate any difficulties which may arise from time to time between the allied nations.' It ceased to exist in 1940.

Anna wrote in 1941: 'Colonel Galbraith gave me a letter for the National President of the Canadian Veterans introducing Mme E. Guérin – Originator of the National Poppy's Days.'

The National Poppy Drive, Anna wrote, 'was taking a tremendous development' and, either before or after a move to New York, the Drive was put 'in the hands of a very important Corporation used to make such National Drives'. The move probably occurred during March.

Initially I thought the Corporation might be Ward, Hill, Pierce & Wells, Inc. which was a philanthropic company, with a reputation for running large money-raising campaigns for charities. It had run successful Drives for the American Red Cross during the war.

Anna's New York base was in rented office space at 1 Madison Avenue. Interestingly, Ward, Hill, Pierce & Wells, Inc. was in the same building, so it was a strong contender. However, this was not the agency.

Above: The school where Anna Alix Boulle studied. L'école Superior, Largentière, Ardèche, France. *Johnson Collection*

Right: Anna Alix Boulle. February 1896, Ironbridge, Shropshire, England. *J. BOULLE Collection*

136. - MADAGASCAR. - TAMATAVE - Cases indigènes du Quartier de la Pointe Hastie

Couadou, phot., Toulon-sur-Mer

Above: Indigenous huts, Pointe Hastie district of Tamatave, Madagascar. *Johnson Collection*

Below left: Anna's daughters Renée and Raymonde Rabanit, 1905. *GUIBAL-BOULLE Family*

Below right: Anna, impersonating Jeanne d'Arc praying. *Johnson Collection*

JEANNE d'ARC priant   Mme Guérin

MARIE-ANTOINETTE à Trianon

Mme E. Guérin

Above left: Anna, impersonating Marie Antoinette. *Johnson Collection*

Above right: A signed family photograph of Anna, in costume. *THOUARD-BOULLE Family*

Right: Anna, impersonating Jeanne d'Arc spinning. *Johnson Collection*

JEANNE d'ARC filant

Mme E. Guérin

Joséphine de Bauharnais

Une Marquise Louis XIV

Mme E. Guérin

Joséphine BONAPARTE à la Malmaison

Above left: Anna, impersonating Joséphine de Beauharnais, wife of Napoléon. *Terry McCully Collection*

Above right: Anna, impersonating the Marquise Louis XIV. *Johnson Collection*

Left: Anna, impersonating Joséphine Bonaparte à la Malmaison. *Terry McCully Collection*

Mme E. Guérin

Charlotte CORDAY

Above left: Anna, impersonating [Marie-Anne] Charlotte Corday, a personality of the French Revolution. *Johnson Collection*

Above right: Advertisement for Patriotic Lectures on the Guérin and Oliveau tour. *Vicksburg Evening Post (of Mississippi, USA), February 7, 1918. Newspapers.com/Ancestry*

Right: Anna, 'The Spirit of France Incarnate', wearing her campaigning uniform. *The Lincoln Star (of Nebraska, USA). July 7, 1918. Newspapers.com/Ancestry*

Above: Rue du Vieux Marche-aux-Poulets, Lille, France, after October 1914 bombardment. *Johnson Collection*

Below: Place du Cantin, Lens, France. Before and after the War. *Johnson Collection*

MME. EUGENE GUÉRIN.

Above: A 1918 'United in Liberty's Cause' badge, distributed by Anna Guérin in Nebraska. *Johnson Collection*

Right: Anna 'Speaks Here Tonight in Interest of Loan'. *The Star Press (of Muncie, Indiana, USA). May 1, 1919. Newspapers. com/Ancestry*

Anna, centre right, with leaders of the War Mothers/Service Star Legion. *The Baltimore Sun (of Baltimore, Maryland, USA). October 19, 1919. Newspapers.com/Ancestry*

Above left: 'MME. GUERIN WORKER FOR FRANCE SINCE WAR STARTED'. *The Anaconda Standard (of Anaconda, Montana, USA). June 17, 1920. Newspapers.com/ Ancestry*

Above right: Anna, standing on a sheep herder wagon, c.1920. Probably in Utah. *GUIBAL-BOULLE Family*

Below: Anna, with poppy sellers outside the Montana Power Company Building, Butte, Montana, USA. *The Anaconda Standard (of Montana, USA). June 23, 1920. Newspapers. com/Ancestry*

ANACONDA, MONTANA, WEDNESDAY MORNING, JUNE 23, 1920.

SCENES DURING THE SALE OF POPPIES IN BUTTE

LITTLE SALESWOMEN STARTING TO WORK.
Mme. Guerin passing out the baskets of poppies and money boxes to girl volunteers in front of the Montana Power Company building.

CATCHING A PAIR FROM CITY HALL
Left to right—Mme. Guerin, John S. Wulf, Jacob Oliver and Miss Alice Jackson.

Above: Anna Guérin
'CATCHING A PAIR FROM
CITY HALL', Butte, Montana.
*The Anaconda Standard (of
Montana, USA). June 23, 1920.
Newspapers.com/Ancestry.*

Right: Anna, 'POPPIES TO BE
BADGE OF AID'. Girls could win
a cup for selling the most poppies.
*The San Francisco Examiner
(of California). August 6, 1920.
Newspapers.com/Ancestry*

GIRLS TO AID WAR ORPHANS

Beatrice Sibbet   Gladvs Realy.   Edna Caten.

POPPIES TO BE BADGE OF AID

Above: Anna hands poppies to Leonel O'Bryan ('Polly Pry'). c1920. Location is unknown.
The Denver Public Library, Special Collections, Denver, Colorado, USA. License: 324

Below: Victims of War at Bidart House, Bidart, France – funded by Anna's Children's League.
History Nebraska Photograph Collection, Lincoln, Nebraska, USA. Licence RG4028-11

Above: An American-Franco Children's League badge. c.1921 or 1922. *Johnson Collection*

Right: Anna Guérin at the American Legion Convention in Cleveland, Ohio. September 1920. American Legion Weekly Post-Convention issue, October 15, 1920. *Johnson Collection*

AMONG THOSE PRESENT AT CLEVELAND

Above left: Anna with a veteran of the Grand Army of the Republic. September 1920. Indianapolis, USA. *History Nebraska Photograph Collection, Lincoln, Nebraska, USA. Licence RG4028-09*

Above right: 'The Poppy Lady Brings Flowers'. New Castle Herald, Pennsylvania, USA 5 May 1921, p.14. *Newspapers.com/ Ancestry*

Women and children making poppies. Location in France and date unknown. *Quick March Journal, April 10, 1923, p.18. Auckland Libraries, New Zealand*

Mothers and children at Moyenmoutier, Vosges, France, c.1920. *Hartley Burr Alexander Archive, History Nebraska. Under Licence from History Nebraska Lincoln RG4028-12*

Above: Mothers and children at 'Bidart House', Bidart, France, c.1920. *Hartley Burr Alexander Archive, History Nebraska. Under Licence from Nebraska State Historical Society RG4028-13*

Below: Anna met the women of the Independent Order of the Daughters of the Empire (I.O.D.E.) and Great War Veterans' Association Auxiliary in Winnipeg, Manitoba, in October 1921. *The Winnipeg Tribune (of Winnipeg, Manitoba, Canada). October 10, 1921*

Representative Women Arrange Poppy Sale

POPPY DAY'S BEGINNING IN CANADA

Above: Anna, pictured with officers of Canada's Great War Veterans' Association. 1921. *Service: The Story of the Canadian Legion 1925 to 1960 by Clifford H. Bowering*

Below: 1923. Poppy ladies at an unknown location in Great Britain. *Johnson Collection*

Above: 1934. Decorated
Remembrance window.
Uxbridge, West London.
Johnson Collection

Right: A French poppy.
*'Made by the women and
children of the devastated
areas of France'*. It was
distributed on Great
Britain's streets on
'Remembrance Day',
11 November 1921. French
women and children
benefitted, as did the British
World War I veterans.
*'Remember The Dead, Help
The Living'. Andy Chaloner
Collection*

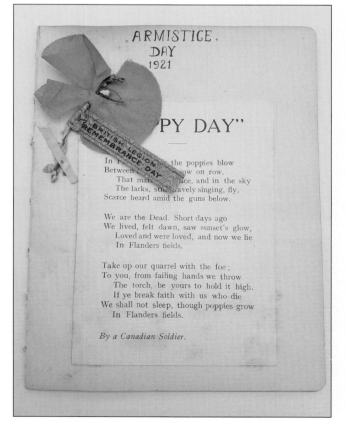

. ARMISTICE .
DAY
1921

"PY DAY"

In [...] the poppies blow
Between [...] row on row,
   That mark [...] ce, and in the sky
   The larks, sti[...] avely singing, fly,
Scarce heard amid the guns below.

We are the Dead. Short days ago
We lived, felt dawn, saw sunset's glow,
   Loved and were loved, and now we lie
   In Flanders fields.

Take up our quarrel with the foe;
To you, from failing hands we throw
   The torch, be yours to hold it high.
   If ye break faith with us who die
We shall not sleep, though poppies grow
   In Flanders fields.

By a Canadian Soldier.

Above left: Poppy Ladies in New Zealand's First Poppy Drive in April 1922, ahead of Anzac Day. *Quick March Journal, April 10, 1923, p. 18. Auckland Libraries, New Zealand*

Above right: Anna Alix Boulle. A photograph of a mature 'Poppy Lady'. *GUIBAL-BOULLE Family*

The plaques unveiled in Vallon-Pont-d'Arc, Ardèche, on 8 March 2022. Anna Alix Boulle's birth place (left) and Anna Alix Boulle's burial place (bottom). *BOULLE Collection*

Anna wrote 'Mr. Jenkins was put in charge' and a Roger Jenkins worked for the publicity agency of Bronson Batchelor Inc., on the thirty-ninth floor of New York's Metropolitan Life Tower.

Jenkins sent out thousands of pamphlets stating: 'Mme E. Guérin – Originator and sponsor of the National Flanders' Fields' Poppy's Days has brought back from France millions of silk Flanders Poppies etc.' Jenkins, Batchelor, and Anna would soon find themselves sued!

On 3 March, Anna spoke again to War Mothers at Baltimore. She reminded the women it was with them she first shared her poppy plan. A draft speech suggests how Anna spoke of Poppy Days:

> Those days have been glorious days in the towns where they have been held. The Mayors having made for them a special proclamation. Towards the evening when you see everyone wearing a Red Poppy for which he has given what he liked – it seems like if the souls of those Boys, of those Men sleeping in Flanders fields are all over the town, smiling, blessing the town which is finishing the work of reconstruction reparation.

Anna wore 'a one-piece frock with black accordion pleated skirt and bodice of French blue, with cord-trimmed eyelets of black and blue; a Russian fur-top coat, with sable collar; a turban covered with the chenille-embroidered taupe veils, now so popular, and tall laced boots of patent leather and gray suede.' Gone was her campaigning uniform, for the moment anyway. Anna returned to New York the next morning.

On 10 March, Isabelle's sister Jessie arrived back in the USA, from Lille, France. The *Indianapolis Star* headlined her arrival: '2,000,000 MORE "FLANDERS POPPIES" REACH AMERICA. Mme. Spence, Who Was in Charge of Shipment, Arrives in City.' The article reminded readers of the American Legion's adoption of the poppy.

There were three poppy designs: a 10-cent Memorial Day poppy; a 15-cent Corsage poppy, for balls and dinners; and a 25-cent Decorative poppy (five for $1) for banquets, ceremonials, and so on. It was stated the Memorial poppy cost 5 cents to make so the League gained 5 cents. Any amount over that could be kept and used locally, for agreed upon causes. It appears it was a 'sale or return' agreement.

French-made poppies had a green cloth tag, representing a leaf. Each tag carried these words: 'DECORATION DAY 1921 – POPPY LADY FROM FRANCE' and was adorned with stylised poppy outlines.

But still more poppies were needed. Anna had brought as much of her own money from France as she could, in order to help 'the work' by lending it, and it was her money that purchased these extra poppies.

Anna wrote: 'I ordered – on my own responsibility, 3 millions more of those silk poppies, as we were running short, to Angelo Alpi Co. in New-York.' Anna's artificial flower maker was Alpi and Company, owned by Italian brothers Angelo and Pietro Alpi. Flowers were manufactured in a Houston Street factory and by out-workers.

Alpi employed more than 200 workers. They were mostly Italian immigrant women who worked together, away from the factory. This working practice was a common Italian tradition for women who had to care for a home and children, as well as take employment.

Perhaps making fun of herself, Anna wrote to Hartley: 'Don't laugh and don't think I am Frenchy when I say to you that I am already planning to order 5,000,000 more of poppies, which would make the 10,000,000 they are speaking of in the enclosed clipping.' Such a clipping could have been any of the many printed.

Campaigns took advantage of every opportunity: in New York, the Legion and League Committees held a St Valentine Poppy Ball on 14 February. It was described as 'a gorgeous pageant of color'.

Debutants vied to be the local 'Poppy Girl'. She was not a regular poppy-selling volunteer but someone chosen to be the visual figurehead, promoting the Poppy Drive in local newspapers. Miss Carolyn Woolsey Ferriday beat several debutants to claim the New York crown. She was described as 'one of the young women of fine American ancestry who willingly consented to peddle the Memorial Day poppies.'

Women's Clubs and civic and patriotic bodies received letters from the 'Poppy Lady of France'. Every person was asked to wear a poppy on 30 May, Memorial Day. Groups and newspapers used their initiative, making unique and personal pleas to readers to further the cause.

The *Oregon Statesman*, of Salem, Oregon, asked:

> Will you wear a red poppy on Memorial day? A red poppy, made by the widows and daughters of French soldiers, close to the battlefields in France? ... for all the Aubrey Jones in the world should Salem folk pin the crimson flower of Flanders Field over their hearts on Memorial day ... For all the Ernest Eckerlens, Wayne Jacksons, Milton Koormans and Captain William Smiths – in some of our hearts, 'rank on rank they filed' as we saluted their flag, flying half-mast over the town they loved.

Stories like Salem's help us understand why a community had so much empathy for the poppy emblem. Those names were not statistics to the people of Salem, they were their 'boys'. They were killed 'over there' on the French battlefields of Chateau Thierry and Meuse-Argonne. They were lying there still, under poppies. Aubrey was singled out, specifically, because he was cited for bravery at least three times.

Aubrey was 23 years old when he was killed 'in a daring charge' on 26 October 1918 at Meuse-Argonne. His family chose to have his body repatriated and he arrived in Salem on 20 October 1921. About 1,000 people attended his Military Funeral, four days later.

Emotions were still raw in communities. Red poppy emblems had become synonymous with those emotions. People, especially women, could channel sorrows for lost loved ones by helping in the Poppy Drives. A poppy on a lapel would be a symbol of remembrance but would help French orphans, who were suffering where their 'boys' died.

As the *Oregon Statesman* article quoted: 'If ye break faith with us who die, We shall not sleep, though poppies grow, On Flanders fields.'

During March, and into April, near-identical promotional articles were printed within American newspapers, instigated by the American Legion:

> An appeal has been made to National Headquarters of the American Legion by officers of the American and French Children's League to aid the league in its distribution of several millions of poppies, which the women of France had made to be worn on Memorial Day. The poppies will be sold in all parts of the United States and the proceeds will be used for French and American war orphans.

The National Information Bureau's potential endorsement would impact Anna and her American and French Children's League. The Bureau would endorse the Children's League but only with certain provisos. The American and French Children's League must have a wider scope and be more aligned with its Paris-based committee of La Ligue Americaine Française des Enfants.

Anna wrote: 'To please the Bureau I have nothing to do on the work to raise the money, I am just the founder of the work and the official delegate of the French Committee.' As National Chairman, Tyler Perine would appoint everybody and sign letters of appointment and contracts. The words 'nothing to do on the work' surely must only refer to official administrative work because Anna was still allowed to campaign.

Anna confided:

> I am already half rewarded in seeing those hundreds
> of letters in which the Poppy Lady from France will be
> liked from one end of country to the other. Of course, the
> American people will never like me as much as I do them.
> Endorsement or not I feel sure now that in working the
> poppies will be taken with enthusiasm by the people. The
> Bureau is not America.

There seems a hint of sadness within the last quote, that an adoration that
Anna felt she possessed, felt she had earned, in America could be diluted by
Bureau constraints. It was revealing, when Anna stated that 'the American
people will never like me as much as I do them', but it was a prophecy that
would hold true in the future, with some.

The National Information Bureau was an organisation that only endorsed
'worthy charitable enterprises'. It protected the public and assisted in the
'conservation and proper distribution of the charitable resources'. It had
been called the National Investigation Bureau but had been reorganised and
launched under its new name in 1919.

The National Information Bureau had three purposes: (1) to establish
some 'reasonable standards of administration and work with national social
and philanthropic agencies' and endorse charities that met these; (2) 'The
protection of the public from imposition'; and (3) to assist, as far as possible,
'national agencies in their efforts to adapt their programs and their work',
and assist 'the communities in which they are engaged'.

Minimum requirements were established and the Bureau would
'observe, most carefully the spirit of co-operation rather than the spirit of
domination'. To continue, the Children's League had to have the credibility
the National Information Bureau endorsement offered.

The 'wider scope' would be achieved by creating a reorganised League:
along Bureau lines, being realigned with the French Committee, and by
the old League metamorphosing into a new one, under a new President,
the Right Rev. Herbert Shipman. The League would officially emerge
on 27 April 1921, under its first title of the American-Franco Children's
League. More of that, and the ensuing troubles, later. Meanwhile, everybody
continued campaigning.

There were other national circulations of articles, which included one
where the 'Poppy Lady of France', Madame E. Guérin, was 'asking' the
American women to wear the poppy of Flanders Field on 30 May.

The Chamber of Commerce was publicising the fact that the American and French Children's League had written letters asking all businesses to 'decorate their windows with poppies, significant of Flanders fields, as well as the American flag'. It would be done in memory of those who 'sleep in Flanders fields'. Chamber branches would help to handle and distribute stocks of poppies.

During the months of campaigning leading up to Memorial Day on 30 May, thousands of newspapers printed 'In Flanders Fields'. One article about John McCrae's poem and pinning a poppy on every heart concluded, 'the beautiful sentiment involved has captured every heart, and the general public is only too willing to take this means of silently expressing its gratitude and devotion to "those who lived, felt dawn, saw sunset glow, loved and were loved, and lie in Flanders Fields."'

Montgomery, Alabama, planned a Poppy Drop. Aviators from the city's aviation repair depot would drop a poppy for every Montgomery man who had made the supreme sacrifice during the war.

Alongside one article, announcing the Poppy Drop, were 'The Two Great Poems of Memorial Day – The Appeal of the Dead, and Answer of the Living': 'In Flanders Fields' was printed above the previously mentioned poem by Charles Burleigh Galbreath, 'An Answer'. Both poems were firing the imagination.

Nebraska's *Lincoln Journal Star* waxed lyrical about the poppy, on 25 March, in a lengthy article: 'It has been enshrined in poetry. It is interwoven in all our fancies. Its color splashes the dull gray of some of our saddest memories. Its brilliance shines like a star in our night.'

The Lincoln article wrote about Memorial Day and the recollection of the Civil War fading but, after the Great War, 'we are called upon to rededicate Memorial day ... Memorial day this year comes with a richer significance because the picture of that great sacrifice is still undimmed and many a broken heart is yet unhealed.'

It reported on the children in war-torn France and ordered readers to buy one of the Children's League's silken poppies: 'buy a dozen, and then buy some more to give away. And wear one.' The article also suggested if its readers could not 'pluck a living poppy, nor buy one, make one out of red cloth or paper and join in this vast communion service of humanity to commemorate the men who flung their lives away for freedom as splendidly as ever any heroes of history or legend.'

Anna was doing nowhere near the amount of travelling that the previous years had dictated. Lectures were selective. One was on 12 April, when she addressed the first Convention of the American Legion's Women's Auxiliary, in Columbus, Ohio. Her speech was entitled 'A Message from France'. The Women's Auxiliary had already taken the poppy as its memorial flower, like the American Legion men.

Throughout April and into May, newspapers across the United States printed an identical article, with the headline '"The Poppy Lady" Brings Flowers from Flanders Field for Memorial Day'. Every article was accompanied by the same photograph of Anna, although her name was printed as 'Anne'. She looked young in it but, probably, it was not that old an image. As Anna admitted, campaigning had aged her.

'The Poppy Lady of France has come to America again!' it began. That suggested she had literally just arrived, but it made for good publicity. The article carried the usual sentiments but, this time, described the poppy as 'this blood hued blossom, immortalised in poetry'.

It told how France would cover the 'graves of American soldiers with poppies, while every patriotic man, woman and child over here will wear a poppy to show that the "brave dead have not died in vain."' This promise would be kept in every commune where an American soldier lay. It was Anna's idea and her promise was kept.

Tensions were emerging in the League, though. On 27 April, at the Waldorf, the transition took place from the old League into the new American-Franco Children's League. This caused a division. In reality, it was a mutiny on a small scale, but it had the greatest of impacts.

Some members from the old League, including Mrs Mercedes McAllister Smith, the League's New York State Chairman, were not prepared to move across to the new League.

Evidence suggests that the National Chairman, Mrs Tyler Perine, was part of this group too initially, as it was reported that she endeavoured to continue with the old League. It is difficult to say if there was one ringleader but, certainly, Mercedes McAllister Smith received the most publicity within the newspaper accounts.

Robert Tyndall stated that the old American and French Children's League transferred all rights, titles, and interests to the American-Franco Children's League. Evidently, it was the chief reason for the dispute.

The American-Franco Children's League insisted that the American and French Children's League dissolved itself on 27 April, but the latter contested 'it did nothing of the sort'. The old League carried on and even succeeded in having US President Harding accept the role of its Honorary President. President Harding's acceptance of the role, and his surprise endorsement, did complicate matters somewhat.

Newspapers announced the new League 'captured' the old League's HQ at 1 Madison Avenue. Perhaps that was not as dramatic as it sounds, unless the mutineers had been locked down there. This old group ran its separate poppy campaign under the auspices of the old American and French Children's League name, working out of Mercedes McAllister Smith's New York home at 234 Central Park West, New York City. Where its raised funds were to be directed to is not known.

With the dissenting McAllister Smith/Perine group operating under the old name, alongside the new American-Franco Children's League, the situation must have been very confusing to the public.

As in such transitional situations, the old League's Treasurer, Robert H. Tyndall, resigned from it but was reappointed as Treasurer of the new League. In the same vein, it was necessary for Hartley Burr Alexander to relinquish his position as President of the old League.

Hartley Burr Alexander's resignation was not missed by the media and the event was headlined as 'Alexander Resigns'. However, it had been previously decided that he would be appointed joint Vice-President, along with Irene du Pont, within the new League. As Hartley had confided to the NI Bureau, officers were 'desirous of complying'.

The *New York Times* hit the news-stands on 12 May with the headline: 'RIVAL SOCIETIES IN WAR OF POPPIES. Privilege of Selling Flowers to Commemorate American Dead in France in Dispute. TWO LEAGUES ASSERT RIGHT. Mme. Millerand, Wife of French President, Head of Parent Organization.'

Other New York newspapers picked up on the story quickly and none held back, sensationalising the situation. In Lincoln, Nebraska, the *Journal Star* and *Nebraska State Journal* followed the dispute, calling it a 'squabble', but they reported in a more sympathetic manner. The *State Journal* called the New York response an 'ebullition' and printed several articles, over time, all supportive of Anna.

Both duplicated, and commented on, a Waldorf Hotel interview with Anna appearing in the *New York Evening Post*. They felt Anna was made fun of, when her interview was phonetically written. The following extracts give an idea of the article's mocking theme:

'I 'ave been made so sad,' Madame asserted. 'My big 'eart 'as been broke.' Zee 'Poppy Lady' eez desolee. She 'as work' so 'art. She 'as 'ad zee bee-u-tiful idea. She 'as wish to remembair zee dead. An' she 'as wish to remembair zee poo leetle childrens of ze region rouge. She 'as feeneesh 'er works ...

Madame then insisted that the reporter write down the following statement as she dictated it: 'Say, please. Zat Mme. Guérin says zat for vair' am-por-tan' raisons zee Americain an' French Children's league, as 'er work was called lately, would not be indorse' by see nationale information bureau of New York, which ees, as every one knows, a nationale institution …

Zis new reorganization, which is backed, as we shall see, by zee more prominent names internationally known in our two countries, is zee only one recognized by zee Frainch commitay an' zee nationale information bureau …

Mme. Guérin is vair 'appy to say zat she gave 'er resignassion of all activitays and responsigilitarys, putting zem in zee 'ands of zis responsible commitay, of which zee Rev. Dr. Shipman, D. D., is active president …

Mme. Guérin is prepare' to return to France to bring to zee Frainch commitay zee news 'ow sympathetically zee bee-u-tiful idea of zee poppies 'as been receive'.

The *Nebraska State Journal* accused New York reporters of mischief and being

unpleasantly flippant in dealing with Mme. Guérin, the 'poppy lady.' They have evidently marked her down as fair game, for their treatment of her speech amounts to a caricature. Mme. Guérin does have an accent, a very fascinating accent …

They make it strictly stage French. As a matter of fact she has been over here collecting money long enough to have acquired a reasonable mastery of England [sic].

It further remarked, 'the people in Lincoln who knew Madame Guérin best are considerably exercised over what they call the unfairness of the treatment given her in this matter.'

It clarified her credentials as 'sound'. Even though, it said, some people had been critical of her when she first arrived in Nebraska, being endorsed by a group of Oklahoma oil millionaires. However, those critics were 'disarmed' because she handled no money personally.

More quotes surfaced, between Anna and the interviewer:

'I have done my work an' I am 'appy,' Madame explained.

The suggestion that she had taken the American public for 'a good thing' was denied by Madame with indignation.

'Eeet ees not so,' Madame said.

'The idea of the Flanders poppy 'as been vair' bee-u-tiful. The work 'as been heroique superbe.'

Madame rolled her eyes.

The reporter remained unmoved and Madame said:

'Oh you do 'ave confidence in me, 'ave you not. Why zey call me zee Poppy Lady. An' zee state of Nebraskar she adopt me.

'Yes, she adop' me altogezzer.'

'How was that Madame?' the reporter inquired.

'Eet was at a gr-rand meeting at Lin-koln. Zee maire 'e preside. We raze so much money for zee Lee-bairty loan zat zee maire 'e turn to me 'an 'e say 'Madame, zzee state of Nebraskar she adop' you.'

Significant others felt they needed to comment on events too: Mr Lemuel Bolles, National Adjutant of the American Legion at Indianapolis, sent the following statement to all Legion departments: 'The national information bureau has indorsed the American-Franco Children's League, which is the successor to the American and French children's league, inc., which was directed by Mme. Guérin. This is sufficient proof to warrant our undivided support of the poppy project.'

Hartley Burr Alexander made a public statement, in the wake of Mrs Tyler Perine stating he remained with her League.

> Upon receipt of word that the reorganization was necessary I resigned as president of the American and French children's league …
>
> Apparently Mrs. Perine is endeavoring to continue it. If she is using my name, it is not only without my consent, but contrary to word which I have addressed to her. I am not president of this league, and I not responsible for its present activities.

Hartley emphasised the credibility of Nebraska's link with Anna:

> Madame Guérin has never received a cent of money collected in Nebraska. Money so collected has been sent directly to the French committee, of which the wife of the president

of France, Madame Millerande, is president. Nearly seven thousand dollars has been sent from Nebraska, and is receipted for by the Paris treasurer.

In New York, it was soon reported that Mrs Tyler Perine had been seen hurriedly leaving the city, for Baltimore.

A statement was issued on Mrs Tyler Perine's behalf by her counsel J. W. Fuller Thompson, of 355 Madison Avenue, New York: 'The American and French children's league wishes to state emphatically and definitely that it has not merged, and has no intention of merging, with any other organization whatsoever. It is carrying on its present campaign with unremitting vigor.'

Her statement continued that, when the current campaign was over, her League would redouble its efforts to prepare for 1922.

Tyler Perine deemed it cowardly 'to the trust imposed in it by the public, which has loyally supported it, were it to turn over its contributions, property, and organization to any corporation or body of men regarding whose merits and ability it knows nothing.'

It is stating the obvious to say some old League members were upset with change and, perhaps, with new Committee members. I doubt if there was any objection to Robert Tyndall as Treasurer again, nor the indefatigable Marie Speakman as Secretary and, no doubt, Irene du Pont and Hartley were accepted, but others may have been regarded as interlopers.

The 'others' were those named in the *American Legion Weekly* of 20 May. New League Committee Members needed to have international reputations and most fitted the criteria.

Mrs Martha W. Bacon was a charity patroness. During the war, she helped organise the American Hospital Corps in Paris, for which she was awarded the Légion d'honneur. She was socially prominent and very active in various philanthropic and cultural organisations. Her late husband, Robert, had served as a member of General Pershing's staff.

Joseph Hodges Choate Jr. was a well-known New York lawyer. His late father had been a famous American lawyer who served as the US Ambassador to Great Britain, under Presidents William McKinley and Theodore Roosevelt. The family was known for its philanthropy. One of Joseph H. Choate Jr.'s famous quotes was: 'You cannot live without lawyers, and certainly cannot die without them.'

Colonel Arthur Little was Chairman of the Board of J. J. Little and Ives, a printing company based in Manhattan. He was a First World War hero, having been wounded and decorated several times.

Maurice Leon was a French-born New York lawyer, a colleague of Joseph Choate. He was a writer on international topics. In the USA, Maurice was an international counsel who had represented the French government and had strong connections with it.

Brigadier General William Jones Nicholson commanded the US 157th Infantry Brigade during the First World War. Under his command, the Brigade had captured Montfaucon d'Argonne on 27 September 1918. He had been awarded the Légion d'honneur, Croix de Guerre, and the Distinguished Service Cross, for his war service.

The Rt. Rev. Shipman was Rector of New York's fashionable Church of the Heavenly Rest. The Shipmans were members of the smartest set in New York. Unlike many clergymen of the time, Herbert did not denounce the up-and-coming trend of divorce.

Once the National Information Bureau announced the American-Franco Children's League was the only charity authorised to sell poppies, there could be no viable future for the old League group, but it and Mercedes carried on regardless. President Harding's endorsement was transferred away from it and to the new League.

Administratively speaking, Anna was not connected to either League. It was reported, however, that she and La Ligue Americaine Française des Enfants committee in Paris lined up with the new American-Franco Children's League, as did the American Legion and other supporting bodies. Anna remained official Delegate and figurehead, as the founder.

There was also another dimension to this controversy: that of Mercedes being rumoured to be a mysterious and notorious French adventuress, namely the 'Duchesse de Villande', who had, under an alias, served a sentence in a French prison for swindling, in 1906.

It was reported that both the American and French governments became involved. In essence, that was because President Harding and Madame Millerand had been caught up in the whole rebellion.

It was alleged the French government had reported Mercedes to the National Information Bureau, and the Secret Services of both France and the United States were investigating this rumour. This would result in more controversy later in the year.

This turmoil must have been the last thing Anna and the American-Franco Children's League wanted, or needed, in the run-up to Memorial Day – with all the Poppy Days arranged in every state during Memorial Week. But the campaign had to go on and it had been going on during the whole controversy.

A pin badge survives from either this campaign or 1922. It depicts an eagle with outstretched wings, holding an olive branch in its beak. In the USA, this image symbolises the country's desire for peace.

The eagle holds an American 'Stars and Stripes' flag and a French 'Tricolore' flag. This must signify that same desire for peace, with unity and a continued friendship between the two countries: part of the ethos of Anna's League. 'AMERICAN-FRANCO' is printed above the eagle and flags imagery, and 'CHILDREN'S LEAGUE' is printed below them.

The badge cannot be accurately dated but it is doubtful it originates from the time when the Children's League was first carrying the 'American-Franco' prefix, in 1919.

And so preparations carried on ahead of Memorial Day. American Legion veterans and auxiliaries embraced Anna's 'big idea'. Legion Posts voted on whether to allow veterans to wear the poppy emblem on their uniforms and authorisation was given. The veterans would 'wear blood red poppies on their lapels to honor the dead' and urge civilians to do the same, as well as aiding French orphans.

Temporary Regional Poppy headquarters were created, which distributed supplies. For instance, HQ for the Southern States was 516 Peters Building, Atlanta, Georgia. It supplied Georgia and eight other states: Alabama, Arkansas, Florida, Kentucky, Louisiana, North Carolina, South Carolina, and Tennessee. Each state, in turn, had county, city, and town headquarters and, thereafter, borough outposts.

May 28 was designated the League's official day for Drives, but communities could decide which day or days to hold their Poppy Day Drives on and mayors publicly proclaimed their permissions. As with other Poppy Drives, women and chaperoned girls were assigned streets and areas to canvass businesses and passers-by. The objective was for every American to have a poppy on their lapel on 30 May.

If any place was running right up to the wire, without poppies or without someone to take charge of a Poppy Day Drive, the League gave notice that 'an order sent in by telegram at the expense of the American-Franco children's league, will bring a supply of poppies at once.'

In Lancaster, Pennsylvania, American Legion Rooms' headquarters received its poppies only the night before its three-day Drive began the next day, 27 May. Lancaster had 100 poppy sellers, including thirty-seven schoolgirls, fifteen Salvation Army women 'guards', and a delegation from the Dames of Malta Puritan Sisterhood (a Roman Catholic order). Fifty Boy Scouts took poppies from house to house.

Taken from an edition of the military's *Stars and Stripes* paper, near-identical articles appeared before and on Memorial or Decoration Day. They described Madame Anna E. Guérin, 'The Poppy Lady of France', as the inspiration for wearing the poppy for remembrance.

Quoting Anna, articles described an event she had spoken of, one that took place near the American cemetery at Romagne. After the Armistice, she had stood near the cemetery and watched children picking poppies. They made 'crude' poppy wreaths for the American graves.

> Does that not prove to the Americans that we in France will never forget your dead? Although they were Americans, they died for France, and because of that we have enshrined them with our own poilus. I saw that the frail blood-red flowers could be made the strongest binding link between our two countries.

Anna said they were the first poppies of the spring (1919), and 'their crimson petals stood out in startling prominence'.

On 27 May, Washington DC's 1921 Poppy Drive was opened by, it was reported, Miss Beatrice Evelyn Wilson. She pinned the capital's first poppy on President Harding's lapel, in his White House office.

Beatrice was photographed selling a poppy to General Pershing. One particular image was published in newspapers, including in Canada, after Memorial Day. The image always carried identical text: 'GENERAL PERSHING BUYING A FLANDERS POPPY TO AID LITTLE WAR ZONE VICTIMS ... General Pershing was much interested in the success in [sic] the American Legion's poppy sale week.'

Of course, it has to be remembered that Anna had met General Pershing over in France and she knew two of his sisters, who were involved with her Children's League in Nebraska. Pershing knew well the devastated regions of France, having served there. All in all, Pershing certainly would have much empathy with the Drive.

And so, on 30 May 1921, Memorial Day arrived and Anna's 'Inter-Allied Poppy Day' idea was embraced. Americans either wore one of Anna's French-made poppies or one of the Alpi ones. This was the world's first national Poppy Day and it was organised by Anna's American-Franco Children's League, with the assistance of others.

As in past years, the graves of veterans in American cemeteries, both men and women, had been decorated with 'Stars and Stripes' flags and floral tributes for 'Decoration Day'.

There were now veterans' graves linked to three wars America had taken part in, from the Civil, Spanish, and First World War. Veterans of all three wars were amongst those paying their respects at services.

In Massachusetts, at Boston's Forest Hills Cemetery, Governor Cox stated in his speech:

> We make no distinction between those [veterans] who died in battle and those who passed away in time of peace ... The Nation should be grateful to those who defend her and the people should appreciate those men who are ready to lay aside all material consideration and take arms for the country's defense.

The Poppy Drives had been carried out as they always had been: women and girls visited railway stations at times when trains were due to arrive; newspapers named female team captains and the streets they were responsible for; shops, businesses, and commercial plants were all canvassed; and Boy Scouts were usually there helping. Of course, men played their part, but women and girls were the campaign's backbone.

It is believed Anna went north into Canada immediately after the Memorial Day commemorations. On the evening of 1 June, Anna was addressing a meeting of the Catholic Women's League of Canada at the Knights of Columbus Hall, in Toronto. She was also in the city to speak to the convention of the National Chapter Imperial Order Daughters of the Empire, the IODE, held between 30 May and 4 June.

Anna had always planned to go to Port Arthur (now Thunder Bay), in Ontario, to speak to veterans of the Great War Veterans Association, at the beginning of July. She would take with her American Legion National Commander Galbraith's letter of recommendation. But fate dealt a cruel blow and Galbraith was killed in Indianapolis.

On 9 June, Frederick W. Galbraith, the 'Fighting Colonel of the Fighting First' in France, had been a passenger in a car which left the road and plunged down a 16-foot embankment. Two passengers, Henry Ryan and Milton J. Foreman, were only scratched and bruised, but Frederick W. Galbraith was pinned under the car and pronounced dead at the scene.

Anna makes no mention of attending Galbraith's funeral, on 11 June, in Cincinnati. She may have interrupted the campaign in Canada to attend it, because she was definitely back in the USA later in the month.

It was reported that an 'endless procession of mourning of men, women and children' passed the body of Colonel Galbraith, as it lay in state in the rotunda of Cincinnati's Music Hall. Every one of the 4,000 seats was taken in the auditorium, where the funeral service took place. Galbraith's body was taken on a gun carriage, through Cincinnati, to the Spring Grove Cemetery. President Harding offered Mrs Galbraith and family an Arlington Cemetery burial but it was not accepted.

Amongst the hundreds of floral tributes was one which attracted particular attention. It was one of palms, bound with the 'Tricolore' flag of France. It was a tribute from citizens of Chateau Thierry. It carried a card with the inscription, 'To one of our bravest liberators.' In Congress, the death was mentioned, with an expression of grief and sorrow.

Until 20 June, perhaps Anna may have enjoyed some rest and relaxation. However, on that day, she was addressing a meeting of the American Legion Delaware Post No. 1, at St Andrew's Parish House in Wilmington. She spoke of the American Legion's aid to France and thanked the Post for its help in the Poppy Drive the previous month. She said Delaware was the only state to over-sell its quota and she presented a silk 'Tricolore' flag to the Post, as a token of her esteem.

Anna told of the American soldier only seeing France 'during the most trying days of her life as a nation and could not fairly judge the country by what he had seen ... France will never forget what you have done. Her soldiers, who were your comrades, testify to your courage, and their praise can be summed up by saying that you were wonderful fighters,' Anna said, adding that Americans would always find a warm welcome in France.

In her *Synopsis*, Anna wrote:

> (Colonel Galbraith had been killed in an automobile accident by now) Colonel Bolles and all my friends gathered around me to ask what was to be done ... I said That WE WERE TO FOLLOW THE IDEA OF COLONEL GALBRAITH: CARRY THE FLANDERS POPPIES TO ALL THE ALLIED COUNTRIES, organise for them, for the benefit of their Veterans organisations and in MEMORIAM of their Heroes, a National POPPY DAY each year on Armistice Day (as the other countries had no DECORATION DAY), and continue them in the U. S.

Thus, Anna Guérin returned to Canada and the next chapters will follow her on her quest beyond the USA.

However, the poppy story in America does not stop here. Trouble was afoot for the Inter-Allied Poppy Day and Anna had to rush back to the United States in October.

Anna left Canada on 26 October, after meeting with women of the Imperial Order Daughters of the Empire (IODE) and the Great War Veterans' Association (GWVA) Women's Auxiliary, in Winnipeg. She made her way to Kansas City, Missouri.

Anna would have known Kansas City well, from her successful Red Cross Drive Days in the summer of 1918. She went to attend the third American Legion Convention, being held from 31 October to 2 November. Many 'world famous heroes' were to be the guests of honour: Marshall Foch (France); Earl Beatty (Great Britain); General Diaz (Italy); General Jacques (Belgium); and General John J. Pershing (USA).

Anna had been invited once again because of her status, but she was also there to fight for the poppy because the American Legion was to vote on whether to substitute it with the daisy.

Complaints had been received against the poppy being the American Legion's memorial flower. It was due to it not being a native flower and only available in artificial form. The consensus was that a daisy was always accessible. But there was no Col. Galbraith to support Anna.

Sympathy for him and his family aside, that he should lose his life so prematurely, his death changed the Poppy Day's history. Anna's fears were realised. The Legion reneged on the decision it made at the 1920 Convention to adopt the poppy as its memorial flower. The American daisy replaced the French poppy. As National Commander, would Galbraith have swayed the Legionnaires' vote?

Moïna Michael, of the 1918 poem, was in Kansas City too. Her 1919 'Victory Emblem', of a victory torch and poppy, was history now. She was fighting for the single poppy bloom too. In a February 1922 letter to Moïna, Anna recalled how she tried unsuccessfully to find Moïna in her hotel during the Convention. Anna described the quest they both followed to have 'Flanders Field Poppy recognised as the Memorial Flower of the Great War' as 'our great idea of us'. They belonged to an ever-growing movement to have the poppy recognised as a memorial emblem.

In that same letter, Anna commented on the decisions made about the poppy and daisy. She expressed how worried she had been because she knew how very important it was to have both the American Legion and its Auxiliary women adopt the Flanders Poppy as their memorial flower and, subsequently, support her Flanders Field Poppy Days.

In her *Synopsis*, Anna referred to attending this Convention and the decisions made:

> I went to the National Convention of the American Legion,
> in Kansas, where I had been invited as Marechal Foch was

to be there. In Kansas City THE AMERICAN LEGION AUXILIARY was formed and while the American Legion Auxiliary was adopting the Flanders' Poppy as Symbol, at the Convention of the American Legion they had repudiated it to take the DAISY.

Yes, the Women's Auxiliary had adopted the poppy as its memorial flower, but Anna needed the support of the Auxiliary for another National Poppy Day in 1922, to further help the French women and children.

That being so, Anna spoke to the Auxiliary's Executive Committee and proposed the following: she and the Auxiliary, together with help from other patriotic organisations, could make 1922's Decoration Day a National Poppy Day again; the Women's Auxiliary's headquarters could buy in the French-made poppies for 4 cents; headquarters could sell the poppies across the USA, for 4½ cents, giving it a small profit; each town could keep anything over the cost price, for its own particular relief work; and it could create a very large profit for every local Auxiliary Charity Committee, considering 10 cents was asked for the 1921 poppies.

The Executive Committee members told her they would make a decision at their Annual Meeting in January 1922 and asked her to wait until then for an answer. Anna told them 'Yes,' sure they would see the good in her idea. Apparently, Legion National Adjutant, Lemuel Bolles, was enthusiastic about it, and intimated to the Auxiliary that the daisy being the Legion's flower should have no bearing on their decision.

For Armistice Day, American-Franco Children's League poppies were sold in the USA as usual. League committees organised, with Legion members' support. Amongst the people, faith was not waning if Des Moines, Iowa, could muster 800 men and women to help.

Anna returned to Canada. However, she left behind trouble brewing in New York. On 22 December, Mrs Mercedes McAllister Smith began making headlines again. She was suing seven significant people.

The significant seven were: the Right Rev. Herbert Shipman (Bishop Suffragan of the Diocese of New York); Maurice Leon (member of law firm Evarts, Choate, Sherman & Leon, writer, representative of the French Government during the war); George W. Burleigh (Judge Advocate-General of the New York National Guard); Bronson Batchelor (of Bronson Batchelor Inc., publicity agency); Roger Jenkins (officer of the Bronson Batchelor Inc. agency); Barry N. Smith (Head of the National Information Bureau); and Madame Anna Guérin.

Mercedes was alleging conspiracy on the part of these seven, 'to slander and blacken her reputation by representing her as a notorious French

137

courtesan [and therefore] Mrs. Marion McAllister Smith, formerly Miss Mercedes Hearn, member of a prominent Texas family, has brought suit against them in New York city.' She was asking for $200,000 in damages.

From 27 December, more detailed articles began to be printed, including the headline: 'Society Beauty, Ex-Actress, Charges Bishop Slandered Her.' Before marriage to Marion Smith of Rhode Island, she was an actress under the stage name of Mercedes Leigh.

Now, Mercedes McAllister Smith was going to the Supreme Court, alleging Barry Smith told her the French government had reported her to the National Bureau of Information as the notorious adventuress Duchesse de Villanda, convicted of a crime in 1906.

Rumours began circulating after the American-Franco Children's League revolt, before the 1921 Memorial Day. Mercedes M. Smith stated President Harding had withdrawn his support for her plan to raise funds for French war orphans and 'her work was interfered with in other ways'. She declared her social position had suffered as a result. Her supporters stated: 'when the case is brought to trial evidence will be introduced that will startle the entire country.'

Referring back to the American Legion Auxiliary's decision not to organise Flanders Poppy Day with Anna's French poppies, Anna wrote to Moïna Michael that she left Kansas City 'full of hope', leaving to take the National Inter-Allied Poppy Day to the other allied countries.

The Legion's Women's Auxiliary National Executive Committee meeting took place in Indianapolis, Indiana, from 10 to 22 January. Prior to the meeting, a letter was sent out to attending delegates. It asked for a survey to be carried out, in relation to the American Legion Women's Auxiliary taking over the French poppy as its memorial flower. This would mean the American Legion's Auxiliary committing to organising the Poppy Days, with Anna's French-made poppies.

The Committee requested the number of poppies the departments thought they could dispose of. Dependent on both these responses, if the majority were in favour, the Auxiliary would make this an annual national work. It stated that Madame Guérin was waiting for the decision.

Anna learned of the Auxiliary's decision on 23 January. Possibly for the first time, in all her fundraising years, Anna was experiencing passive women. Their sympathies were still with the Flanders Poppy and wanted to continue with Poppy Days, just not with Anna's French poppies.

Anna declared: 'My deception [disappointment] was great on the 23rd January to hear that the American Legion Auxiliary had not taken the Idea to sponsor for themselves, the National Poppy Day of the U.S.'

In hindsight, this was the latest step toward Anna's prophecy, 'the American people will never like me as much as I do them', becoming true.

When the American Legion documents its history, within accounts of the Remembrance Poppy, the reneging on the Flanders Poppy as its memorial flower and replacing it with the daisy is conspicuous by its absence. Similarly, the name 'Madame E. Guérin' is missing.

By erasing Anna, the American Legion erases the notable part it played in those formative Poppy Day years. In that era, Legion men and women did so much to support Anna and, when they pledged support for her in 1920, they helped make her Inter-Allied Poppy Day 'big idea' a reality. In the absence of any recognition, I feel their part is missing too.

Anna would not be deterred, though. She believed all the country would be with her, for her, and with her 'idea', regardless. She went to the Veterans of Foreign Wars of the United States organisation. The VFW was an older, smaller, and poorer organisation. They agreed the same terms as were offered by Anna to the Legion's Auxiliary.

The Veterans of Foreign Wars was America's oldest major veterans' association, being founded in 1898/1899, by servicemen of the Spanish American War. Its Auxiliary was founded in 1914 and it goes without saying that its ladies backed Poppy Day. The War Mothers were backing it too. Again, they formed an important part of the campaign.

Ironically, some Legion Auxiliary women assisted too. However, the National American Legion Auxiliary President publicly stated the Auxiliary was not sponsoring this National Poppy Day, linked to the Veterans of Foreign Wars. She asked that 'in the case of any auxiliary cooperating with other bodies in the sale of poppies, the auxiliary communicate first with the national organization.'

The impact of split loyalties should not be underestimated. Any Legion women working with other bodies, namely the VFW, could be perceived as fraternising with the enemy. If a Legion Auxiliary member was also a War Mother, it was a difficult choice to make.

Anna's ever-faithful sister Yette and friend Blanche assisted in the organisation of the 1922 VFW poppy campaign once they arrived back in New York on 5 February from Havana. They had successfully taken Anna's Inter-Allied Poppy Day idea to Cuba.

Other Allied countries had taken up Anna's Inter-Allied Poppy Day idea by January 1922. Thus, the VFW advertised its nationwide Drive as being consistent with all the Allied countries; the idea of 'The Poppy Lady of France'; and the means of raising funds for both American disabled veterans and the homeless children in France.

It was now, on 9 February, that Anna wrote her long letter to Moïna Michael. Anna was in Canada, where she was settling the Poppy Day finances for her League, but she gave her address as c/o Mr N. S. Hall, *Foreign Service* Editor, 32 Union Square, New York City. *Foreign Service* was the VFW official publication.

The letter began 'My dear Miss Michael', and Anna asked that her long silence and poor typewriting be excused. The reason being that nearly seven years of war work meant her nerves were unable to stand writing long letters anymore – and she had loved to write.

Anna waxed lyrical about Poppy Days: 'our great idea of us, I mean by that: To see the Flanders Field Poppy recognised as the Memorial Flower of the Great War' and her successes in that regard. She wrote that she would soon be finished in Canada, and she would go to New York 'to make the plans for the [VFW] Campaign'.

Anna asked Moïna for authorisation to have her 'splendid' 'Answer' poem published beside John McCrae's 'In Flanders Fields'. She thought both poems could be on all publicity matter, including posters. I have not discovered the VFW promoting its 1922 Poppy Day with these two poems. However, I did find 'In Flanders Fields' paired with Lilliard's poem 'America's Answer'.

Moïna was asked if she could find a person who would take charge of organising the State of Georgia. Anna elaborated by stating the person would receive a payment (10 per cent of sales). She gave an example: 100,000 small poppies (4½ cents each) = $4,500; 20,000 large (12½ cents each) = $2,500; plus, say, $500 for wreaths = total $7,500. Thus, 10 per cent would result in a payment of $750.00.

Details of cost prices/profit margins for poppies were given: small silk (having pin and badge) – 4½ cents, not to be sold for less than 10 cents in streets and 5 cents in schools; large – 12½ cents, no less than 25 cents; small wreaths, windows – 70 cents, $1.00; wreaths, graves – $1.75, $3.50; wreaths, monuments – $3.00, $5.00.

Anna stated it would make a great profit for the local charities. The profit would not be sent to France, it was a question of giving work to the poor French women and paying them for it.

This would keep the memory of the 'Souvenir of France all over the world' and that memory or souvenir 'will bloom once more every year in every town of the Allied countries'.

Then, Anna asked if Moïna could do the work in Georgia. Anna stated there would be three full uninterrupted months for the campaigning, and local VFW committees were doing so well that no unsold poppies would be returned because they would pay for all of them, rather than return any, and keep them for next year.

Anna planned to add, to the stationery, all the names of the countries that had taken and kept the 'idea'. She planned to also add the names of the countries that were holding a Poppy Day in 1922. The stationery would be sent out free of charge, together with the sashes and badges for the poppy-selling girls. Anna said she hoped to send delegates to these three countries: Argentina, Brazil, and Portugal.

Anna wrote: 'For me, as for you, those Poppies are the inheritance towards the Dead to carry on the work of Justice and Rehabilitation towards the real sufferers left behind the War; the people of the battle fields and in all the Allied countries; the disabled or the un-employed.'

Anna concluded by apologising again for the bad typing and her long silence because she had been in Canada, England, and 'all over France'. As soon as she knew the VFW campaign plans were organised, Anna said she would return to France 'to push the making of the poppies', because she was afraid there would not be enough.

Anna finished by hoping to receive Moïna's answer the next week and she was sending her 'great admiration with the expressions of my best sentiments. Most sincerely yours, E. Guérin Poppy Lady of France.'

I have not seen any evidence suggesting Moïna obliged Anna in the Georgia VFW campaign. Being a member of the American Legion Auxiliary, Moïna's allegiance was not with the VFW or the War Mothers. I have not discovered her name associated with this work in promotional newspaper articles. Atlanta may have held the only 'Poppy Drive' in Georgia. It raised a healthy $2,300.

Anna's 'care-of' address of 32 Union Square, New York was also where the headquarters of the Veterans of Foreign Wars organisation was based. Like the League's HQ at 1 Madison Avenue, NY, it was a building of rented offices. Veterans of Foreign Wars veteran, Walter Irving Joyce, one-time Commander-in-Chief of the VFW, owned the building and he allowed the organisation to use office space within it, rent-free. Walter was a veteran of the Spanish American War.

Of course, New York was the home city of Mercedes M. Smith and, on 25 February, she appeared in the *New York Tribune* under the headline: 'Mrs. Smith Must Tell Who Heard Slander.' Supreme Court Justice Bijur had, the day before, directed her 'to furnish a bill of particulars in her $200,000 slander suit against several defendants'.

'Mrs. Smith has charged that these persons were in a conspiracy to discredit her patriotic work and to injure and destroy her good name.'

Mercedes' counsel told Judge Bijur 'that it was impossible for his client to give the names of all the persons who heard the statements'. Justice Bijur directed her to 'furnish such particulars'.

Anna did not waste many words on Mrs Mercedes McAllister in her *Synopsis*: 'Here, I do not speak about the law suit that a Mrs. Mac Allister [sic] … made' but Anna did make the point that, in the Court, 'they called me Mme E. Guérin, the Originator of the National Poppy Days in the U. S. and Allied Countries.' The case was thrown out ten months later. Anna remarked 'she lost naturally'.

The VFW promoted its campaign very well. But these promotions raised hackles within the American Legion and its Auxiliary, given that they were running Poppy Days as well as Daisy Days.

For instance, in Massachusetts, a state-wide Daisy Drive was held on 24–25 February, in aid of 'the wounded'. In Alliance, Nebraska, the Auxiliary would hold Daisy Days on 27 and 29 May. The daisies were sold for ten cents each, the same amount as Anna's poppies. The proceeds from Alliance went to buy the local Legion Post a flag.

Evidently, an air of competitiveness existed between the Veterans and the Legionnaires over Poppy Days. There may have been a longstanding rivalry, just under the surface, between the two veteran groups but, if that was the case, Poppy Days brought it to the surface.

Newspapers gave insights into the feud between the two veterans' organisations. On 11 April, the headline in the *Bridgeport Telegram* of Connecticut read 'VETERANS CLASH OVER POPPY SALE'. The American Legion, on the attack, declared it originated the idea the year before and 'Vets are butting in'. The defending VFW announced that, by purchasing its poppies, the public would not only be helping the VFW but providing sustenance for women in war-torn France.

What the article omitted to state was that the common denominator between the two organisations was 'The Poppy Lady of France', Anna Guérin. The Legion had a point. Anna had taken her 'Inter-Allied Poppy Day' idea to it first but it alone had allowed the VFW to 'butt in'.

Another example of tensions was initiated by the Legion's Auxiliary in Texas. The State President announced the state-wide Poppy Drive would have to be on 27 April, due to the fact it could not have its usual Memorial Day campaign. Because, she added, 'a permit for Memorial day had already been granted to another organization.'

The Texan Legion Auxiliary stressed it had no connection with the other poppy sale. It considered the sale of the crimson poppy 'too sacred a trust to be for any purpose other than the welfare of the disabled ex-service men', adding, 'The proceeds of this sale will be used to carry on the work for disabled ex-service men in Texas. No part of this money will go out of the State of Texas' – meaning out to France.

The Auxiliary President was also at pains to make it clear it was 'in no way connected or affiliated with the so-called American-Franco Children's league or with Mme. E. Guérin or her agents'. Ouch...

It is wondered if some Auxiliaries were striving to display a position of superiority by making certain statements, when perhaps the true feeling was insecurity. At this time, perhaps the Legion and its Auxiliary had come to feel remorse after reneging on the Flanders Poppy and Anna's 1922 Poppy Drive: inviting the Veterans of Foreign Wars in.

Ironically, the Legion adopting the daisy was what forced Anna to seek help from the Veterans of Foreign Wars in the first place. I feel, as an outsider, it was only natural if the Legion felt jealous about what Anna, the War Mothers, and the VFW were achieving.

Proof of regret came at the American Legion's Fourth Convention in New Orleans, held 16–20 October 1922, when the poppy was reinstated as its memorial flower. In the *American Legion Weekly* edition of 10 November, one of the noted 'Keynote Policies', on page 9, was 'Re-adopted the French poppy as the Legion's official flower'.

Thus, a longstanding poppy rivalry between Legionnaires and Veterans began. The American Legion had missed its chance to become the first veterans' group in the USA to organise a nationwide Poppy Drive. Legionnaires had handed that honour to the Veterans of Foreign Wars and the Veterans could hold and be proud of that title forever.

Official 'Poppy Day' was Saturday, 27 May 1922. Local clergymen were asked to designate 28 May as 'Poppy Sunday' and, in most states and cities, the governors and mayors were asked to consider 22–29 May as 'Poppy Week'. Windows were decorated for the week and some were described in newspapers.

Windows at VFW Poppy Headquarters, at 1333 O Street, Lincoln, Nebraska, were set out: in one, there was a replica soldier's grave, with a white cross; a 'dog' or ID tag was nailed to the cross, with an American helmet hung on it, and the grave was strewn with poppies. The other window was adorned with poppy wreaths, poppies, and American flags.

The American Legion was not the only competition Anna and the VFW encountered in this poppy campaign. In New York, there was a third group, the Senior League, and Mercedes M. Smith was a member of it.

The Senior League wanted to run a Poppy Drive too. The *New York Daily News* and *Tribune* reported on the 'fight'.

The initial conflict was when both the Veterans of Foreign Wars and the American Legion (Auxiliaries), in New York, objected when the Senior League applied for a permit to carry out its Drive. So Commissioner Coler, of the Department of Public Welfare, refused the permit.

An indignant group of Senior League members, including Mercedes, called on the mayor to protest. The group was dubbed 'society women' and they asked why they had been discriminated against and Mayor Hylan over-ruled Coler's decision and granted the permit. Thus, in New York, there were three groups selling poppies at the same time.

Commissioner Coler updated his views and stated he had written to the VFW State Commander, requesting that the organisation 'disregard their plan to purchase the poppies made by French people and place their order with American concerns'. He would personally defend the organisation, he stated, and assume responsibility for any damages, should it face litigation for refusing to pay for French poppies.

Coler believed the poppies from France to be more commercial than charitable. The VFW National Commander was indignant at that insinuation, stating, 'We have nothing to do with any commercial undertaking.' Coler also asked all groups to 'refrain from enlisting the services of women for this purpose'. However, women still sold them!

Contrastingly printed adjacent to the Commissioner's public criticism was the announcement of President Harding's endorsement of the Veterans of Foreign Wars campaign. In his letter, to Adjutant General Rueul W. Elton, Harding's message began: 'I find myself heartily in sympathy with the purposes of the Veterans of Foreign Wars, and the American War Mothers in their request that the people at large shall wear on Memorial Day a poppy, the interallied memorial flower.'

Reportedly, the Senior League had enlisted 300 girls, purchased 500 sashes and badges, reminiscent of Anna's League strategy, and they would sell 150,000 poppies made by disabled veterans from the local 'Dugout' workshop. Also reminiscent of Anna's strategy, the poppies would be sold at 10 cents and profits given to the 'Dugout'.

The negative campaigning increased and the three New York poppy campaigns evolved into a nasty squabble; it was an eternal triangle but without the love. Allegations were made, which were all repudiated.

The Senior League claimed VFW poppies had never seen France but were made in sweatshops on the City's east side. The VFW said the League was paying sellers $5 a day, which was refuted until the Veterans stated they had proof. Then, it was admitted some had been paid.

The VFW accused the Senior League of causing the 'Dugout' to cancel a verbal contract with the VFW for its poppies, perhaps to top up Anna's supply or to placate the Commissioner, and having three VFW veterans wrongly arrested for illegally selling poppies.

New York's Senior League stated its poppies were American and veteran-made but the Legion's poppies were foreign. New York's Legion retorted that its poppies were American-made, but not veteran-made. However, elsewhere in the USA, there were veteran-made poppies.

The situation reached a point where New York Commissioner Coler threatened to abolish the sales entirely. However, the American Legion and VFW agreed on this: the intrusion by the Senior League, this non-veteran group, had greatly hampered the two veterans' New York campaigns.

Anna was away from all this aggravation, though. She left New York on 23 March, returning to France to 'push' manufacture of the poppies. Two high-ranking Veterans also retreated, on 20 May. The VFW Adjutant General Reuel William Elton and Aide-de-Camp Robert Smith Cain sailed on the White Star ocean liner *Majestic*.

The two Veterans were photographed in their military uniforms, standing on the deck of the *Majestic*. They held a 4ft-tall poppy wreath, to be placed on the tomb of the Unknown Soldier, at the Arc de Triomphe in Paris. They were part of the Veterans of Foreign Wars delegation, which included the VFW Commander-in-Chief Robert G. Woodside. They had been invited to France by l'Union Nationale des Combattants, a French veterans' organisation.

The Veterans of Foreign Wars were there to take part in Memorial Day commemorations in Paris. Representatives of many organisations took part, including the American Legion, American Women's Club, French Legion, and Anna's American-Franco Children's League.

Anna recorded that part of her Poppy Day history:

> as at the Headquarters of the American Legion they had not yet been able to straighten between the Poppy and the Daisy. I carried the Idea and the POPPIES to the VETERANS OF FOREIGN WARS ORGANIZATION in New York ... A very small and poor organization at that time, and the National Poppy Day of 1922 was a great success for the Veterans of Foreign Wars, such a success that their Officers went to Paris with me to deposit a wreath of large Poppies on the Unknown Soldier's grave under the ARC de TRIOMPHE. A banquet was

given to them and they received the Legion of Honor, at my
table, as the banquet was given by me.

On Memorial Day, the *Brooklyn Citizen* noted President Harding was
wearing a red silk replica on his lapel. It was one of the VFW French
Flanders Poppies, from the first veterans' nationwide Poppy Drive. Again,
an American President wore one of Anna's poppies.

The article noted Flanders Poppy Day had been observed in forty-four
states. It had been 'fostered' in the USA, to make the poppy the 'Inter-Allied
Memorial Flower'. It was said the Veterans of Foreign Wars had shipped
2,585,000 poppies all over the United States, from its VFW National
Headquarters, Alaska being the furthest north.

Some accounts state the American-Franco Children's League was
dissolved 'early in 1922' but none are substantiated. That said, I have not
discovered any contemporary mention of the League after 1922.

However, Anna continued to supply French-made poppies beyond
1922 and one of the League officers of France, Madame Lebon, was still
communicating in her role in November 1923.

An American-Franco Children's League report, believed to have been
printed mid-1922 (after profits from most of the first Inter-Allied Poppy
Days were in), documents the diversity of causes benefiting from the funds
raised by Anna and her Children's League. The report began by stating the
'Diamond State' of Delaware was first to send money in 1919 and, by 1922,
the Allied nations had 'added their gifts' too.

The report described the following beneficiaries in more detail: Bidart
Home; Henri Lange Home, Saint-Quentin; Valloire Preventorium; Lying-
In/Maternity Hospital, Roye; a school, Villers-Allerand; a Milk Station at
Bray-sur-Somme; Vassar Unit at Verdun; an Infants' Home at Saint-Mihiel;
Sister Gabrielle at Clermont-en-Argonne; a Milk Station at Reims; aid to
the inhabitants of Lassigny; more cow houses at Senones; a Preventorium
at Étaples; and a Rest Home at Mautort-Abbeville. Here, a little of the
descriptions are shared about some of the beneficiaries:

The Henri Lange Home was described as sitting on a high plateau,
just 3 kilometres from Saint-Quentin, Aisne. It had an orchard, kitchen
garden, and a poultry yard. The Home had shower-baths, central heating,
and electricity. When the weather was fine, the classes were held outside.
Initially, the Home was only intended for twenty-five children but it soon
had to be extended. In 1922, it was housing sixty children aged 4 to 13.

The Preventorium at Valloires, on the Somme, was at the Abbaye. It
housed fifty boys and girls, aged from 3 to 9. When weather was fine, from

around April to October, classes were held in the cloisters or surrounding woods, alternating with gardening and singing. Teachers provided a primary education to the children.

Roye Lying-In Hospital has been mentioned before. Anna's Children's League had helped to establish a maternity Lying-In Hospital in huts, in the midst of the ruins. On 11 July 1921, Marshall Joffre laid the first stone of a permanent hospital, which replaced huts. The report stated that the original 'Delaware Ward' would be transferred over to that building. In 1922, more than seventy women had been received there.

Villers-Allerand Open-Air School, near Reims, Marne, was created on a beautiful 15-acre estate. Since opening it had taken in a total of 1,345 children and Anna's Children's League had funded 350. The boys did simple gardening and girls did needlework. The children were taught good manners and cleanliness. The health of the children improved enormously during their stay of two to three months. One wing had been named after Anna's 'American-Franco Children's League'.

A Milk Station was set up in Reims. It was given a huge grant by Anna's Children's League. One was set up at Bray-sur-Somme, run by Nurse Louise Marais d'Arc. She lived in a ruined house, 'giving her life to helping the little ones'. She visited nineteen surrounding villages, by almost impossible roads. She helped all the mothers and babies.

The 'Vassar Unit' at Verdun, Meuse, run by Miss Elsa Butler, for the American Red Cross, was given a few extra cows by Anna's Children's League. In 1920, Verdun still entirely lacked milk.

Madame Fragassi, who kept a cow herd at Senones, Vosges, was given 40,000 francs by the Children's League, to help fund her cows and cow houses. The big cow house was named after the League.

This 1922 report stated that large sums of money, received from poppy sales of the Allied veterans on the 1921 anniversary of the Armistice, were added to those raised in the USA and totalled 1,279,373 Frs. 55.

France was in need of just as much aid after the war as it was during it. After the war, the devastated region had been divided into four areas – red, green, yellow, and blue. The red area, 'Zone Rouge', was the worst and was described as stretching between Lille and Bapaume. The region had to be cleared and levelled before reconstruction could begin. It had looked 'unreclaimable' but, with help, the people were reclaiming it.

After 1922's Memorial Day, the poppy and daisy confusion existing among the public was aired. The American Legion and its Auxiliaries had unwittingly perpetuated this to some extent: the Legion adopting the daisy and its Auxiliary keeping the poppy. It must have been confusing in some places, when Auxiliary units held both a 'Poppy Day' and a 'Daisy Day'.

It has been suggested that Anna caused difficulties by bringing her French poppies to the United States of America and that her poppies were competing against veterans, who were making them in government hospitals for one cent. However, I did not find any one-cent poppies until 1922.

From a newspaper in Minnesota, we learn that there were 60,000 veterans in US government hospitals at that time. These veterans were making poppies for one cent each; their materials cost one cent per poppy, and poppies were sold to Legion Auxiliary units for two cents. In Minnesota, it had been agreed that each Auxiliary unit would keep its proceeds but only use them for sick and disabled soldiers.

The American Legion had to try to source as many poppies as possible in-house. But, because of the high demand generated by Anna, recovering veterans and Auxiliaries could never make enough poppies. Commercially made poppies had to try to fill the void. It also purchased some of Anna's French-made poppies in 1923 and 1924 but at least the cost price of Anna Guérin's poppies went to a charitable cause.

Writing with hindsight, Anna's *Synopsis* disclosed:

> In fact of this success of the VETERANS OF THE FOREIGN WARS at the next Convention of the American Legion the Flanders Fields Poppy was readopted and the American Legion asked to me to have 2 millions of silk Poppies made in France for them. What I did, I brought them in March 1923, but already the Flanders Poppies had been commercialised and it is why the NATIONAL POPPIES DAYS have never had the tremendous success that they have had in the ENGLISH EMPIRE.

There were Poppy Days on Armistice Day, 1922, but I cannot say if any of the poppies distributed were made in France. For example, on the islands of Hawaii, the poppies had been made in the Veterans' Hospital in Rochester, Minnesota, and in Altoona, Pennsylvania, they were made by the American Red Cross.

In Texas, they were American: Legion Auxiliary women sold blue and gold poppies, the Legion colours. The proceeds were split between hospital work and soldiers' relief. In Atlanta, Georgia, American church organisations made them and sold them to the Legion Auxiliary's Poppy

Committee. Church profits went to soldiers' relief work and Auxiliary profits went to disabled men in Atlanta and relief in France, where the men of Atlanta fought.

In Binghamton, New York, the *Press and Sun Bulletin* wrote about how the Veterans of Foreign Wars 'beat the Legionaires to it by rescuing the poppy from oblivion' after officially adopting the daisy. But now that the Legion men had 'called back' the poppy, the VFW men were 'hopeful that better co-operation and a fuller spirit of "camaraderie" may be brought about'.

It was now 1923 and, as stated in her *Synopsis* extract above, Anna was involved with the Legion again, through its Poppy orders.

Leading up to 1923's Poppy Drive, articles mentioned that both the Legion and the VFW had purchased poppies made in France. It was noted the VFW experienced some problems obtaining as many poppies as it needed in 1922. That must have been restricted to the odd place because it was also noted the VFW had a rare surplus of poppies from 1922, which was carried over to the 1923 campaign.

If there was any issue, it was not enough to deter the Veterans from ordering from Anna again. For the balance, the VFW ordered from artificial flower manufacturers in New York City.

The VFW initiated a tag for the poppies, bearing the words: 'Honor the Dead by Helping the Living – Made by the Poppy Ladies of France', which, the organisation felt, best expressed the sentiment of the poppy. The public could choose between French or American-made poppies. Again, French poppies were distributed for the familiar 10 cents each. It appears to have been the same 'sale or return' arrangement.

It was during this 1923 campaign that the VFW explored an idea that would result in the VFW 'Buddy' Poppy being patented. It would be made by disabled and needy veterans, who were paid for their work as a practical means of providing assistance for these comrades.

In 1923, the American Legion's French poppies were accompanied by a gummed sticker, which had to be stuck to every poppy sold. It bore the official Legion emblem, to 'safeguard' the organisation. This, it was stated, was to insure its 'loyal members and friends that the Legion is unitedly behind the promotion of this sale on or near Memorial Day'.

Explaining further, both Legion Posts and Auxiliaries were 'unitedly behind the proposition'. No doubt, that was a reference back to 1922's campaign, when loyalties were divided between the daisy and poppy.

However, the USA continued to say 'au revoir' to Anna. Utah is a good example of how. Salt Lake City's Legion Auxiliary women had been so good to Anna in 1920 but, for weeks, they had been making their own 'flaming beauties' to sell at their own Poppy Day, on 26 May.

The City's Tribune mentioned Anna, who

> first brought the thought of Poppy Day to America. She came here with an appeal to Americans to help France complete the wonderful work they had helped to accomplish, by assisting in the rehabilitation of that country. She asked that Americans sell poppies on one day of each of three years and to donate the proceeds of those sales to France. Those three years now are past.

In Salt Lake City, in 1923, funds raised from its Poppy Day would solely benefit America. Proceeds would be used 'for the same good cause for which they were needed in France'. However, Salt Lake City's VFW Auxiliary women held their Poppy Drive along national lines.

Now it was 1924 and Poppy Lady Anna Guérin was still involved with the United States, with the American Legion's Poppy Drives.

As she had done the year before, Anna arrived in the USA in March. She landed in New York on 4 March, having left Le Havre on 23 February with a cargo of poppies.

Anna was now 46 years old and had been campaigning and raising funds for France and other First World War humanitarian causes for nearly nine and a half years.

By April, it was reported that the first consignment of poppies was at the Legion's National Headquarters. The HQ had orders for 100,000 French silken replica poppies and they were being filled in rotation.

The Veterans of Foreign Wars organisation had said 'au revoir' to Anna after its 1923 Poppy Drives. Within its history, the VFW states it registered the name 'Buddy Poppy' in February 1924 with the US Patent Office. The decision was made at its 24th National Encampment, in Norfolk, Virginia, between 27 and 31 August 1923.

On 20 May 1924, before Memorial Day, a certificate was issued to the VFW, granting it the trademark rights to the word 'Buddy'. Disabled veterans had already been making VFW poppies.

Since that Memorial Day, 'Buddy' Poppies have been distributed by the VFW throughout the USA. The days of the French-made poppies were over for the VFW, but not the loyalty and respect that the organisation still shows for Poppy Lady Madame Anna Guérin – as the 'originator' of the Poppy Day and as an important part of its history.

Onwards, the Legion HQ continued to outsource. For instance, in 1925, 3,000,000 poppies were made by disabled veterans but over 3,000,000 were commercially manufactured poppies.

On 21 February 1925, the Legion in Massachusetts held a state-wide Poppy Day – with at least 300,000 poppies from Anna. It was in dire need of replenishing its Welfare Fund. Each poppy's green paper slip read: 'POPPY LADY OF FRANCE' on one side and 'IN MEMORIAM' on the other. They were made by the orphans in the 'still devastated regions of France'. There was no 'middleman's profit', as Anna supplied them direct – 'purely from benevolence and without a cent of profit'.

In 1927, the Legion HQ declared only its Auxiliary could distribute poppies and only poppies made by 'needy and disabled' ex-service men and women, or by Legion/Auxiliary units, could be sold. Each red four-petal crêpe-paper poppy bore an official Legion/Auxiliary sticker.

The state of Pennsylvania stands out, because it created its own official state poppy. During the years 1927 to 1934, the State of Pennsylvania's American Legion (and its Auxiliary) produced a particular type of tagged Remembrance Poppy.

The Pennsylvanian American Legion tags read: 'IN MEMORIAM. Made by Disabled Veterans in Hospitals' on one side, and 'OFFICIAL PENNSYLVANIA POPPY THE AMERICAN LEGION AND AMERICAN LEGION AUXILIARY' on the other. It must have received official permission from HQ.

The Pennsylvanian poppies were identical in style and size to the ones Anna supplied to the USA in 1921. They were identical to the extent that any specimen could be, given that they were each handmade and many pairs of hands made them. Pennsylvanian poppies had two layers of fabric, though, rather than one, and their tags were paper, not cloth.

Likewise, Pennsylvanian poppies compare favourably to the French-made 1921 ones that graced the streets of Great Britain. It is deduced that the Legion Auxiliary must have used the French poppy as a template.

I am lucky enough to own a few American Remembrance Poppies and two of them are these Pennsylvanian examples. One is scarlet and the other pink. As to the pink one, surely its original colour was scarlet. I cannot believe the Auxiliary would have made pink poppies. It may have been subjected to something called 'fume fading'. Sunlight would have faded one side only, but this fabric is pink on both sides.

Today, the official American Legion poppy design is a longstanding one: four petals in red crêpe paper and every poppy sold bears the official Legion/Auxiliary tag. It is a throwback to the Legion's 1927 decision.

Some would have it believed that this 'Poppy Lady of France', Madame E. Guérin, caused difficulties with her poppies in the USA but, personally, I do not think she did. She stepped on no one's toes.

I think American veteran organisations and Anna mutually benefited from associating with each other. I feel it was because of Anna's resourcefulness, her inspiring character, and her leadership that the American Legion and the Veterans of Foreign Wars felt confident enough to go it alone eventually.

It was inevitable that the United States of America would, at some point, say 'see you later, Madame Guérin'.

Chapter 7

Canada, Newfoundland, and the Poppy

Given Canadian John McCrae's contribution to Anna Guérin's work, by way of her integrating his 'In Flanders Fields' poem within her speeches, it was only fitting that Canada played a pivotal role in the acceptance of the poppy emblem within Empire countries. Canada did this well. Topography played a role but, that aside, the British dominion became the first country of the British Empire (now the Commonwealth) to adopt Anna's 'big idea' and it set an important precedent for all to follow.

Similar to the worries aired about real poppies in the USA, some in Canada were not keen either. Made so well-known by McCrae's poem, there was an alternative view, other than the poignant sentimentality of commemorating the fallen. In February 1919, the Hon. George S. Henry, Canada's Minister of Agriculture, was commenting on suggestions made to have poppies growing at war memorials. In Ontario, there had been efforts made to bring over seeds of the Flanders poppies from Europe.

The Minister had asked Ontario's Agricultural College for a report. There had already been varieties of poppies introduced into Canadian gardens but, thus far, they had not posed a problem to cultivated fields. Professor John Percival, of the Wye Agriculture College in England, was consulted. He said, given that seeds lay dormant for years, were so tiny, and had 'considerable vitality', the poppy might become a troublesome weed if it were introduced 'wholesale' by patriotic organisations. He thought planting trees might be a suitable alternative instead.

As in the USA, Poppy Days were occurring in Canada before Anna arrived but, as in America, they occurred intermittently. Women of the Imperial Order Daughters of the Empire (IODE), in Winnipeg, Ottawa, and Saskatoon initiated all those discovered.

The IODE was initially 'The Daughters of the Empire', with junior branches called 'Children of the Empire'. Margaret Polson Murray, of Montreal, advocated its creation in January 1900. She wrote, in an open letter, of the war in South Africa creating an enthusiastic patriotism that was 'bubbling over'. She added: 'Our soldiers have gone. More are going. Those of us at home here are attending to their needs.'

Margaret had been helping American women fit out a hospital ship and she asked why Canadian women could not 'place themselves in the front rank of colonial patriotism? Why not arise as the daughters of the Empire – the women (if not the soldiers) of the Queen?' She invited sisters in Australasia to do the same. The Empire's blood was strong.

Her object was 'to make a great golden chain of patriotism across the country, bringing the women and children into touch with each other by means of small clubs called "Chapters".' Each chapter would have its own badge and flag, meeting once a month in a member's home.

Today, the IODE carries out educational and philanthropic work throughout Canada and issues awards, bursaries, and scholarships.

In Winnipeg, the Soldiers' Memorial Chapter held a Poppy Day on Armistice Day, 1920. It raised $1,027.26 for the Chapter's work with soldiers' graves. Canada did not repatriate its First World War fallen. Any military graves within Canada from that era belonged to those who died whilst in service at home: by accident, from disease (for instance the influenza pandemic), en route home from the Front, or post-arrival.

In Ottawa, in March 1921, the Perley Home's Women's Auxiliary raised $3,220.28 in a two-day Poppy Drive, to help buy an elevator there. Poppies were sold on streets and at theatres. The Home's Auxiliary President, Mrs A. J. Freiman, became one of Ottawa's best-known philanthropic workers and features strongly in Canada's poppy history.

In Saskatoon, Saskatchewan, it was the IODE Festiburt Chapter that was advocating the poppy. Just as Anna did, appeals for 'taggers' appeared in the newspaper beforehand. On 21 May, the Chapter ladies held a Poppy Day, to benefit the National War Memorial fund.

For Canada's 'Decoration Day', 5 June, the Public Parks Board was authorised to supply tributes to be placed on all war graves and Winnipeg IODE Chapters planned to decorate these graves with red poppies and Canadian flags. Two months before, the Winnipeg Chapters had held their 9th Annual Meeting at Fort Garry Hotel, Winnipeg.

At this meeting, it was decided to send a resolution to the National Chapter of the Imperial Order Daughters of the Empire, asking it to adopt a 'Poppy Day' as part of Armistice Day. Funds raised all over Canada could go to the National War Memorial in Ottawa.

Thus, it was an empathic Canada that Anna Guérin arrived in, after the US 'Memorial Day' Poppy Drive. She hoped to organise a Canadian version of her League, 'The Canadian-Franco Children's League', and ask Canadians to adopt her 'Inter-Allied Poppy Day' idea.

I often wonder how much Canadians knew about her before she arrived; probably not much at all. The *Toronto Star*, on 3 June, reported that 'The Poppy Lady of France' had arrived on a 'special mission to speak to the conventions of the National Chapter, I.O.D.E. and the Catholic Women's League of Canada on behalf of the women and children of the war devastated areas of her own country, "the real martyrs of the war."'

On the evening of 1 June, Anna addressed the Catholic Women's League of Canada at the Knights of Columbus Hall, in Toronto. This was the Catholic Women's first annual convention and, the next day, the *Toronto Daily Star* included a paragraph about Anna's part in it. Anna was introduced as Madame Guérin, from the Franco-Canadian Children's League of France. She had brought two million poppies to Canada.

Anna spoke to the IODE at its National Conference in Toronto, during the first week of June. She put forward the same resolution as the Winnipeg women, to make Armistice Day a permanent 'Poppy Day'.

Anna made a 'touching appeal' for women and children of war-torn France and urged the wearing of the scarlet Flanders Poppies on Armistice Day, which would be made by them. She added, 'In memory of your boys and our boys who sleep side by side in Flanders field.'

During ensuing discussions, it was noted that Winnipeg's resolution 'did not call for poppies made in France'. Some members protested that 'soldiers had told them red poppies had too painful associations for them to want to see them again'. The maple leaf was suggested as the best emblem, and it was decided to ask the Chapters for their verdicts.

It is believed Anna also spoke to Great War Veterans' Association's Auxiliary during this visit. These meetings were laying the groundwork, prior to approaching the GWVA veterans with her 'Inter-Allied Poppy Day' idea: her donor-recognition replica poppy to be worn, nationwide, for Armistice Day. It would be a visual pledge. Canadian veterans would benefit from anything above the price purchased from Anna.

The Great War Veterans Association was the largest veteran organisation in Canada. Anna could go before its veterans confident in the knowledge that these women's groups would help distribute her French silk poppies, if they endorsed her 'Inter-Allied Poppy Day' idea.

As she had always done in her campaigning days in the USA, Anna was back wearing her 'Blue Devils uniform', wearing a scarlet poppy and medals on her jacket. It all set her apart from the crowd.

Anna's arrival caused a problem that kept cropping up. A Toronto spinster, Mary Ellen 'Belle' Guerin, was raising funds for her 'Franco-Canadian Orphanages Society' orphans in France. Articles referred to her as 'Madame', 'Mlle', or 'Miss'.

Some articles were clearly referring to the single Guerin lady but were calling her 'Madame'. It was confusing to many. As a result, each woman found it necessary to distance themselves from each other. Each feared donations would go to the wrong woman.

An acquaintance pointed out a significant fact that might explain misunderstandings between 'Mme' Guerin and 'Mlle' Guerin: there was a French tradition whereby a 'Mademoiselle', approximately over 35 years old, could be given a courtesy title of 'Madame'. Interestingly, in 2012, the 'Mademoiselle' title was officially abolished in France.

Later in June, Anna made a brief visit back to the USA. She may or may not have attended Colonel Galbraith's funeral, on 11 June, in Cincinnati, but she was found in Delaware on 20 June.

By 4 July, Anna had returned to Canada. She was in Port Arthur (now Thunder Bay), Ontario, to attend the GWVA Special Conference. The City of Port Arthur gave a luncheon at the Prince Arthur Hotel, which was attended by the GWVA veterans and Anna.

On that day, Port Arthur's *News Chronicle* announced over thirty delegates would be attending the Conference, which included a man from each province. Anna, noted as 'Madam de Guérin, France' was specifically mentioned as attending too.

Anna gave an interview with the *News Chronicle* that day, at noon. She stated that John McCrae's 'In Flanders Fields' verses, in translated form, were read in every school in France.

'On Armistice Day', she said, 'when red poppies will be distributed throughout Canada, French children will lay wreaths of the bright flowers on the graves in France of 55,000 Canadians.'

She stated her mission was to cooperate, in an unofficial manner, with the Graves Registration Department for wreaths of flowers to be placed on Canadians' graves in France, on Armistice Day. They would be 'little tokens of intimate and personal remembrances'.

She was in Port Arthur to ask the GWVA Dominion Executive Committee members for their cooperation in making Armistice Day a 'Poppy Day'. The scarlet poppies, made by the women and children of France, would benefit '450,000 children in France, and the veterans of Canada. She hopes to make it an annual movement.'

The Executive Committee suspended its business of the afternoon session to welcome Anna. She addressed the veterans, outlining her proposal to observe Armistice Day as 'Poppy Day', in memory of the fallen, and asked them to sanction it.

For 4 July, the Minutes of the Conference record:

> Madame Guérin gave an interesting account of her activities on behalf of the French Children's League of Paris, and solicited the support of the Great War Veterans' Association in Canada. Madame Guérin was assured by the Chair that most earnest consideration would be given her proposal, following which the regular order of business was resumed.

We know the late Colonel Galbraith had given her a letter of recommendation, introducing her as the 'Originator of the National Poppy Day'. It appears Anna spoke to the Veterans again on 5 July.

For that morning, the Minutes record:

> Proposal Madame Guérin re Poppy Day: Following a motion suspending the regular order of business, Madame E. Guérin, 'The Poppy Lady of France,' was presented to the Conference and invited to outline her suggestion as to the adoption of the Poppy as a National Emblem to be worn on Armistice Day, in memory of fallen Comrades.

In the afternoon, a motion was moved by the Secretary Treasurer, Comrade William E. Turley, of Toronto, and seconded by Comrade H. F. Hamilton, of Lawrencetown, Nova Scotia, to approve Anna's proposal 'that citizens of this Dominion of Canada accept the poppy as its flower of remembrance, and recommend that the Poppy be worn on the anniversary of Armistice Day'. The motion was carried.

For the morning of the 6th, the Minutes record: 'Poppy Day: The regular order of business was suspended to permit Madame E. Guérin to present her credentials to the conference. Madame Guérin took advantage of this opportunity and placed before the Conference, for examination, all documents regarding her mission.' These credentials must have included her letter from the late Colonel Galbraith.

It was moved by Comrade David Loughman (*The Veteran* ex-editor), seconded by Comrade Harvie J. Staunton, of Peterborough, Ontario, and carried, that 'a hearty note of thanks' be extended to Madame Guérin 'for her patient and lucid explanation of the proposed activities in aid of the Children of the devastated areas of France'.

The GWVA Dominion Executive Committee announced its decision on 6 July and, in doing so, Canadian veterans were first of the British Empire to accept Anna's 'Inter-Allied Poppy Day' scheme.

As a precaution, it was moved by Comrade Turley and seconded by Comrade George W. Whitman, Stellarton, Nova Scotia, that the evidence Anna submitted be placed before the French Consul, in Ottawa, in order to receive clarification that her claims were genuine. If it were necessary, the President of France would be cabled to achieve confirmation.

To commemorate the 70th anniversary of the July 1921 event, the Port Arthur Branch No. 5, Manitoba and Northwestern Command, Royal Canadian Legion, unveiled a plaque in Prince Arthur Hotel's lobby.

On 4 July 2021, another plaque was unveiled by the same Royal Canadian Legion Port Arthur Branch, to commemorate the centenary of that meeting. Both plaques now hang in the Prince Arthur Hotel:

IN COMMEMORATION OF THE ONE HUNDREDTH ANNIVERSARY OF THE BLOOD RED POPPY AS A SYMBOL OF REMEMBERANCE TO WAR VETERANS AND THOSE WHO GAVE THEIR LIVES FOR FREEDOM AND TRUTH DURING WORLD WAR ONE. MADAME GUERIN, THE POPPY LADY OF FRANCE FIRST PROPOSED THAT A POPPY DAY BE HELD IN CANADA AT A NATIONAL CONFERENCE OF THE GREAT WAR VETERANS ASSOCIATION DURING THEIR MEETING AT THE PRINCE ARTHUR HOTEL, PORT ARTHUR, ONTARIO 4TH JULY, 1921. THE FIRST POPPY CAMPAIGN HELD IN CANADA, 11TH NOVEMBER, 1921 PORT ARTHUR BRANCH No. 5, MANITOBA AND NORTHWESTERN ONTARIO COMMAND, ROYAL CANADIAN LEGION. 4TH JULY, 2021.

The cities of Port Arthur and Fort William now form Thunder Bay, 'City of the Poppy'. Its location is at the head of Lake Superior. A docudrama, *Where the Poppies Grow*, premiered there, on 4 November 2018. It featured Anna Guérin meeting the GWVA men.

This drama commemorated the centenary of the end of the Great War and was produced by Kelly Saxberg (MA, BA) and Ron Harpelle (PhD, MA, BA), of Lakehead University. A colleague of Ron and Kelly, Lieut. Colonel David Ratz, PhD, MA, BA, is thanked and duly acknowledged for clarifying facts and dates surrounding this momentous Port Arthur GWVA meeting.

In one *News Chronicle* article, readers were told all about Anna's life up until that point, most of which has appeared in this book already. In this article, though, the only mention appears of Anna receiving her l'Officier de l'Instruction Publique medal from the French Ambassador in London, although photographs prove she was awarded it.

Of Anna's lecturing talent, the article compared her to two famous French stage actresses, Sarah Bernhardt and, a generation later, Yvette Guilbert, who was also a film actress and orator.

On 6 July, Anna returned to Toronto. The *Toronto Star* printed an article on the 5th, which brought up the Mlle and Mme saga again. The heading read 'TAKES FIRM STAND AGAINST OVERLAPPING'. The article highlighted the resolutions passed by an annual meeting of 'Mademoiselle Guerin's Franco-Canadian Orphanages Society'.

The Society would write to organisations all over Canada, drawing attention to its work of the past four or five years. That would include orphanages in France and aid given to children in the devastated regions and to blind French veterans. It would point out 'any new organization seeking funds in Canada for French war orphans is unnecessary'.

The Society thought overlapping was inevitable, if the two groups were seeking funds for the same work. It was noted that there had been confusion already, because the League's promoter was 'Madame Anna E. Guérin' and the Society's founder and organiser was 'Mlle. M. Guerin, whose work is widely known in Canada'.

It was only natural that Mlle Guerin was worried about her newly arrived namesake. But Anna, sent by the French government, was not doing the same work, only trying to reach those who had slipped through the net and were not receiving help from anyone else. Although not publicised, both women had raised funds for the Secours Nationale. In reality, they were on the same side.

At this time, Winnipeg women were busy making poppies again. They made several thousand, ahead of another Poppy Day on 27 July. It raised $1,009.55 to help furnish new club rooms for ex-service men.

Here it can be explained how Canada played a part in promoting Anna's 'big idea' to, at least, the Australian veterans of the Returned Sailors and Soldiers' Imperial League. At a guess, this took place soon after GWVA veterans formally adopted Anna's idea on 6 July because the Australian veterans adopted it too, within a month.

The *Brisbane Telegraph* of Queensland, Australia confirmed the part Canada's veterans played in the Australian veterans' acceptance of Anna's 'big idea', in its edition of 5 August 1921. The RSSIL annual congress statement was published and this is relevant to Canada:

> SOLDIERS' CONGRESS ... THE POPPY. It was decided; to accept a Canadian suggestion that the red poppy, so conspicuous on the fields of France, should be adopted as an international emblem on armistice day, and it was mentioned that a French lady – would visit Australia, bringing with her silk emblems manufactured by women in the devastated areas of France and Belgium.

The Australians immediately replied by cablegram, requesting 'this lady's credentials'. The GWVA cabled in reply that the French Ambassador at Washington verified the personnel and enterprise of the Guérin Committee.

If Canada's GWVA veterans recommended Anna's 'Inter-Allied Poppy Day' to Australian veterans, did they send cablegrams to other Allied nations? No evidence has been discovered to support that, either in Canada or elsewhere.

It would not be Anna, but a Scottish-born nationalised American, reportedly familiar with Australians, who left Canada for 'down under'.

In Toronto, Anna stayed at the Queen's Hotel. One Col. Samuel A. Moffat met with her there. The Colonel had been a US Red Cross Commissioner during the First World War.

A letter from Anna Guérin formed part of his passport application. Written on a separate sheet of 'The American-Franco Children's League Inc' (over 'LA LIGUE AMERICAINE FRANÇAISE DES ENFANTS. FOUNDED BY MME. E. GUÉRIN') headed paper, to the New York Passport Office, 'Madame E. Guérin' wrote:

> Gentlemen: With reference to the application of Mr. S. A. Moffat for passport to Australia, I wish to state that Mr. Moffat has been employed by La Ligue Americaine Française Des Enfants to organize its work in Australia.
>
> Mr. Moffat during the last four months has been representing the League in the United States.
>
> Anything you can do to expedite this passport, so that Mr. Moffat may leave from Vancouver not later than August 6, will be greatly appreciated.

Very truly yours, Madame E. Guérin. Official Delegate of
La Ligue Americaine Française Des Enfants. Queen's Hotel,
Toronto, Ontario.

Samuel Moffat sailed from Vancouver, British Columbia, Canada, as
planned – his first stop was New Zealand. He would move back and forth
between New Zealand and Australia, incorporating a quick visit to veterans
in South Africa, en route to England: 'I was sending Colonel Moffat to
South Africa (Natal), to Australia and New-Zealand.'

On the afternoon of 31 July 1921, still in Ontario, Anna spoke at a GWVA
Memorial Service at Rivercourt Park in Todmorden, for that district's
fallen comrades. It was held by the local GWVA branch. A telegram from
St Catherine's, Ontario, gave an insight. Anna was dubbed 'EVANGEL OF
THE POPPY' and said:

'I wish to tell you that the graves of your loved ones in France
are gratefully and lovingly cared for. Now and evermore the
name of Canada is written, not only at Ypres, at the Somme,
at Vimy Ridge, but in the hearts of every ally the name of
Canada is inscribed, and not more so than in the heart of
France.'

Madame Guérin is in Canada and is touring all the
Dominions of the British empire, as well as the old country,
to establish the wearing of a red poppy on armistice day, as a
remembrance of the fallen.

By now, Anna had her sister Yette and friend Blanche in Toronto with her.
The two arrived at the Queen's Hotel, Toronto on 15 July, after visiting
GWVA Secretary, William 'Bill' Edward Turley, to discuss transport
arrangements for the memorial poppies.

The *Toronto Star* notified readers of Yette and Blanche's arrival with
'WOMEN FROM PARIS, FRANCE, HERE TO SELL POPPIES'. It told
how they were there to organise the sale of poppies and were likely to make
their headquarters at 41 Isabella Street.

Around 19 August, Anna set sail for England, to take her 'Poppy Day'
campaign to the British Legion. Meanwhile, Yette and Blanche continued
Anna's campaign in Canada. They prepared for a Poppy Day at the Toronto
Exhibition, on the first 'Warriors' Day', 27 August.

On 26 August, the *Toronto Daily Star* stated the sale of poppies was a
joint venture between the Distress Fund of the GWVA and the Children's

League of France. Additionally, it tried to clarify the Mme/Mlle Guerin confusion issue, but it may have failed in that.

The article pointed out that 'Madame Guérin' of the Children's League was not connected with the Franco-Canadian Orphanage Society's 'Madame Guerin', who had been a resident of Toronto for a number of years and who had established the Society, with support from friends and schoolchildren in Ontario.

On Warriors' Day, thousands of veterans gathered at Trinity Park, Toronto. Old uniforms were worn but, it was reported, they were pressed and the buttons were shining. The GWVA Ladies Auxiliary sold small red poppy tags for 10 cents and larger poppies for 25 cents.

From around 19 September, Canadian newspapers printed the same article, under their own specific headings. The roll-out came from the GWVA, probably because it was the GWVA asking people to adopt the custom of wearing a poppy on Armistice Day. There would be three benefits: first, the creation of a memorial poppy on Armistice Day, when the memory of those who fell in the Great War would be revered; secondly, profits from poppy sales would provide relief funds for the unemployed, during the coming winter; and thirdly, purchases from 'the French war orphans' helped with their relief.

The articles explained the idea was initiated by Madame Guérin of the 'French Children's League', in the USA, in 1920. The GWVA had adopted it and its branches were acting as poppy distributing centres.

With Yette supervising in Toronto, Blanche went to the Ritz Carlton Hotel in Montreal on 22 September. She attended a meeting in the Green Room there. It was called by Lady Williams-Taylor and Mrs Rosaire Tribaudeau, to discuss Poppy Day. They were members of the Disabled Soldiers' Employment Association, which was handling the poppy campaign in Quebec. Additionally, the women were co-presidents of 'L'Aide a la France', which had been begun at the beginning of the war to send aid to the 'invaded districts' of France.

On 27 September, GWVA veterans received a wire from Anna in Europe and announced its receipt in newspapers. Anna stated the British had adopted her scheme. She added, 'already complete success is assured by the manner in which the campaign is being receiving by the people generally'.

The GWVA took advantage of the release to repeat the benefits of the poppy campaign and to mention that Canada's campaign would take place a few days before 11 November, in order for every person to be wearing a Flanders Poppy on Armistice Day.

Another meeting had been held at the Ritz Carlton, in Montreal, on 29 September. The *Montreal Herald* described how the French and

English-speaking communities collaborated in the city, and organising the Poppy Day campaign was a good example. The city was described as 'the meeting ground of the two races'. Lady Williams-Taylor, heading the campaign, was 'supported by the leading ladies of both races'.

Lady Williams-Taylor, a friend of Queen Mary and a proficient French speaker, had done more than anyone to promote good feelings between English- and French-speaking communities in Montreal. Now, in Montreal, she was the 'heart and soul in the Red Poppy Day movement'.

Having sailed to England to see the men of the British Legion, and gone to France, with a Legion delegate to confirm her credentials, Anna may have visited Belgium and Italy afterwards. Anna set sail from Liverpool, on 1 October, on the ship Celtic.

She arrived back in America on 10 October and in Canada the day after. Her last address was 'c/o American Express Co., 84 Queen Street, London'. It was one of two addresses the company had in London, as part of its worldwide general shipping, banking, and travel business. Anna was a lecturer 'in transit', going to join Yette at the 'Kent Building, Toronto, Ontario. c/o Great War Veterans, Toronto'.

On 11 October, the *Ottawa Journal* announced the appointment of the Poppy Day 'organization convener' in the city. Mrs A. J. Freiman had been chosen at a preliminary organisational meeting of various women's organisations and the GWVA executive, on 6 October. We know Mrs Freiman from the Perley Home Women's Auxiliary.

Mrs Freiman was born Lillian Bilsky, in Ontario, to Russian-Jewish pawnbroker Moses Bilsky and his German wife Pauline Reich. Her father was poor but known for his kindness and charity. Lillian followed in her father's footsteps, feeding the hungry and befriending the stranger.

Lillian had been a book-keeper before marrying Lithuanian-born merchant and philanthropist Archibald Jacob Freiman, who had founded Ottawa's largest department store on Rideau Street.

When the Great War broke out, Lillian set up sewing machines at her home and organised a Red Cross sewing circle to send blankets and clothing to soldiers and sailors overseas. In 1918, this circle became the IODE Disraeli Chapter. Interested in the ex-servicemen's welfare, she helped to form the GWVA and was the first woman to be an honorary life member of the Royal Canadian Legion.

King George V awarded Lillian the Order of the British Empire in 1934 in recognition of her charity work. In 1935, Lillian received the King George V Silver Jubilee Medal and, in 1936, she was one of 100 people to receive a French medal, struck for the unveiling of the Vimy Memorial. Lillian was linked to National Poppy Days for nineteen years.

When Lillian died in November 1940, a journalist who knew her well called her 'the most charitable woman in the Dominion of Canada' and, it was written, her death was bound to leave a void in Jewish life. She died in Montreal, but her funeral took place in Ottawa and was said to have been one of the most impressive Ottawa had seen.

Canada's Prime Minister, Canadian Senators, and Members of the Canadian Parliament were among those who attended Lillian's funeral. Veterans were wheeled in their chairs; they hobbled on crutches and threw poppies on her grave. Lillian will be mentioned again further on.

From 17 to 22 October, the GWVA veterans held their Fifth Annual Dominion Convention. Again, the veterans gathered at the Prince Arthur Hotel, in Port Arthur. The *Toronto Star*, on 10 October, suggested Anna would attend and she did.

A press release, which came out of Port Arthur, informed of Anna's arrival in the city. It recorded Anna as stating she was delighted with how the campaign was being received:

> She says, 'Of course I knew that you Canadians would be the first ones over the top. After checking up all the poppy campaigns held in the Allied countries, you have obtained proportionately the greatest result. Hundreds of letters have been received at the Dominion headquarters of the G.W.V.A. in Ottawa, all showing the great enthusiasm with which the National Poppy Day has been taken up by every province.'

Less than a fortnight after arriving back in Canada, Anna visited Regina, Saskatchewan, on 24 October. She addressed the students of the Collegiate Institute and provincial Normal School, under the auspices of the GWVA. She was introduced as 'Originator of the international "Flanders Poppy" campaign, Madame E. Guérin, known in all the Allied countries as the "Poppy Lady of France."'

Regina's *Leader Post* mentioned Anna had given more than 6,000 lectures since October 1914. Apart from the usual noting of Anna's two 'Officier' medals, a new one was mentioned: Officier du Nicham, for war work. Anna was encouraging pupils in every school to sell at least two or three poppies each. The school selling the largest number of poppies, in proportion to the number of students, would be awarded a French flag. Booths were going to sell poppies in department stores, the Post Office, in hotels, and 'other strategic points'. Poppies, bouquets, crosses, and wreaths were all available to acquire.

It was stated veterans pledged to assist in each Armistice Day campaign and there was enlightenment about the Great War Veterans' Association's acceptance of Anna's 'big idea' in the *Calgary Herald*:

> While there is no room to doubt that the cause is a worthy one, and while the G.W.V.A., earnestly desires to help these [women and children of the devastated areas of France] in every way possible, it is nevertheless apparent that public opinion in Canada would be opposed to the transmission of any large sum of money to France in the face of the existing distress there.
>
> The G.W.V.A., therefore, decided to amend Madame Guérin's proposal so as to permit individual branches to secure funds for local relief purposes, while at the same time contributing to relief work in France. The amended suggestion is that branches participating in the poppy campaign for November 11, should order the number of poppies considered necessary, and at the conclusion of the campaign forward to headquarters only the amount necessary to pay for the poppies actually sold.

The cost of poppies went to France, the surplus to Canada.

One account gave the cost price of lapel poppies as 6 cents, but others stated half the 10-cent street price would go to Canada. Poppies would be transported around Canada free of charge. Alberta's *Calgary Herald* gave other prices of poppies: a 'natural' sized poppy, as it was called, would cost 10 cents each and upwards; the large size 25 cents and upwards; and bouquets, crosses, and wreaths $2.50 to $35 each.

Anna then went on to Winnipeg, in Manitoba. Arrangements were going well all over Canada. Manitoba's Winnipeg is a great example of this. To give one example, the women of the IODE Princess Patricia Chapter were meeting at their Regent's home to make poppies to swell the stocks of French-made supplies, and demand was forecast as high.

Around this time, the *Ottawa Journal* was headlining with 'HEAVY DEMAND FOR POPPIES'. It stated the GWVA regional commands were 'clamouring for more poppies to sell on Poppy Day, November 11, than headquarters in Toronto can supply' and it continued, 'The G.W.V.A. is now absolutely convinced that the sale of these poppies on Armistice Day will be a phenomenal success.'

165

The *Winnipeg Tribune*, on 24 October, stated it was believed 200,000 silk poppies 'made by French children of the devastated areas of France' could be sold in Manitoba on its Poppy Day, 11 November. 'More than 7,000 advertising cards, together with descriptive matter, will be forwarded soon to the 275 organized districts of the province.'

The next day, Anna was actually in Winnipeg to attend the annual general meeting of the Winnipeg branch of the GWVA. It was held during the evening, in the club rooms of the London block, on Main Street. There was a large attendance, which included the Ladies' Auxiliary.

Anna addressed the meeting, stating that 2,400 towns and villages had been destroyed and people were still living in cellars and dugouts. She made a strong plea on behalf of the women and children. Addressing the Winnipeg Auxiliary, Anna said:

> Ladies, when you go out to make the day a success, remember that those boys here and those who are 'over there,' were going over the top, not once, but perhaps several times a week, to give their blood and perhaps their lives. I am not preaching charity, but I am preaching help, as I should do for the sake of the men who have brought honor to your country, glory to your flag and peace to the world.

At this meeting, the Manitoba lodge No. 24, Knights of Pythias, gave a donation of $25 towards the 'Poppy Day' campaign.

On the 26th, Anna was the guest at a luncheon given by the ladies of Imperial Order Daughters of the Empire and the GWVA Women's Auxiliary, at the Fort Garry Hotel. It was announced she had brought 1,500,000 more poppies from France.

A Canadian expressed the view to me that Winnipeg is seen as a very patriotic city. It seems more so than Toronto or others from southern Ontario. A higher percentage of Westerners enlisted in the Canadian Expeditionary Force and Winnipeg's Peace Day celebrations, in July 1919, were the largest and most elaborate in Canada.

Perhaps there is something in the genes because, even in 1909, the *Winnipeg Tribune* headlined an article: '"TAG DAY" A TRIBUTE TO THE ORGANIZING ABILITY OF THE WOMEN OF WINNIPEG'. For a long time, Winnipeg women had been a force to be reckoned with.

For there to have already been Poppy Days in Canada, albeit not very often, for the Winnipeg Chapters to have suggested a permanent Armistice Day Poppy Day before Anna's physical appearance in Canada, and for there to have been some preference for the maple leaf, Anna has to be praised for her success in Canada.

After the luncheon and having her photograph taken with women of Winnipeg's GWVA Women's Auxiliary and IODE, Anna left the city in the evening. She expressed disappointment at only being able to remain in the city for a few hours, before she was obliged to leave for Kansas City, Missouri, USA.

Anna left Winnipeg to attend the American Legion's third convention, being held from 31 October to 2 November. She joined top Allied military men. She must have left Kansas City in a quandary: despondent, because the American Legion had adopted the daisy, but ever hopeful, albeit pointlessly, that its Auxiliary would continue to support her Poppy Days. No doubt, the Canadian campaign boosted her mood.

At the beginning of November, Winnipeg's newspapers continued to be proactive with words about deeds. On Armistice Day, the graves of more than 300 soldiers from Manitoba, buried in France, would be decorated by representatives of Anna's Children's League there and over 100 Memorial Rolls, adorning Winnipeg churches and schools, would be decorated with sprays of silk poppies.

The *Winnipeg Tribune* wrote that 'the human side of the "Poppy Day"' was being demonstrated on a daily basis, by the next of kin purchasing a wreath or spray to decorate graves and rolls. They were also being used to decorate photographs of relatives who paid the supreme sacrifice.

Winnipeg's GWVA President, Mr Percy George Rumer, announced, 'The red Flanders poppy will be adopted by war veteran organizations of Canada as the national memorial flower.'

A press release out of Ottawa on 1 November, from GWVA's Dominion command officials, announced that Baron Byng of Vimy, Governor-General of Canada, had consented to be patron of the Poppy Day campaign. One newspaper named Lady Byng as patron too.

Ottawa's plans were going well. For instance, one meeting that Lillian Freiman organised, at the GWVA rooms, was attended by nearly all the city's women's organisations, including: the GWVA Ladies Auxiliary of the West End branch; IODE; Catholic Women's League; Fédération des Femmes Canadiennes françaises; War Widows; Halycon Club; Veterans' Women's Association; Catholic Girls' Clubs; Local Council of Women; and the Girl Guides.

Ottawa's Poppy Day was set for Saturday 5 November and the morning of 7 November, the latter being Canada's Thanksgiving Day. The Poppy Day HQ was in the Union Bank Building on Sparks Street.

Some of those involved with Ottawa's campaign were named as: Lady Borden, Lady Laurier and Mrs Arthur Meighen, Patrons; Mrs A. J. Freiman, General Convener; sale of wreaths and floral decorations, Mrs W. E. Hodgins, Convener; tag day arrangements, Mrs J. A. Wilson, Convener; headquarters, Madame de Salaberry, Convener; Secretary, Matron-in-Chief Macdonald; treasurer, Madame Marchand; distribution, Mrs A. M. Dechene, Convener; sales room, Canadian National Railway ticket office, Catholic Women's League; HQ staff; the Girl Guides. There were many more conveners for the various wards in the city.

Ottawa's first street sale took place on 5 November, as planned. The city was the first to open the poppy campaign, with many other places holding their Poppy Days on Armistice Day.

The *Ottawa Journal* wrote 'POPPY TAGGERS STAND IN SLUSH TO AID ORPHANS'. It was reported that hundreds of girls had stood on slushy streets from before 7.00 am until 5.00 pm and asked people to 'Buy a poppy' for the orphans and women in France and dependent soldiers' families in Ottawa. Most women and men entered their offices wearing a poppy. The *Journal* stated that newsboys to civil servants all wore a poppy.

Girl Guides, not Boy Scouts, were mentioned as being kept busy 'answering calls for more tags and the demand was brisk in nearly every section of the city'. The Poppy Day Committee's ambition was to see every man, woman, and child wearing a poppy on Armistice Day, just as it was always the ambition of Anna whenever there was a Poppy Day.

The cause that the article promoted was 'to assist the dependants of the brave Poilus who gave up their lives in the Great War and provide a fund for relief among local returned men'.

On Monday, Thanksgiving Day, poppies were sold from 7.00 am until 2.00 pm. In Canada, the Thanksgiving Day dates had fluctuated, and been debated, for years. It would not be resolved until 31 January 1957, when State Secretary, Roch Pinard, announced that Thanksgiving Day would be set at the second Monday every October.

However, in 1921, Thanksgiving Day and Armistice Day were jointly commemorated on 7 November across Canada. The event had been passed that year, at the last session of the Canadian Parliament: 'the observation of both Thanksgiving Day and Armistice Day has been fixed for the Monday nearest to the memorable date'.

In Ottawa, on 7 November, the service was held on Parliament Hill and Anna was one of the VIPs. Announcing her arrival in the city, the *Ottawa Journal* referred to her as: 'MME. E. GUÉRIN, the founder and promoter of the Inter-Allied movement of the Memorial Poppy Day'. Anna was present in the Commemoration Service's VIP enclosure, with Lord and Lady Byng and significant others.

It was reported that, during that morning's Poppy Drive in Ottawa, there were 44,000 poppies distributed, which was considered a very large percentage for a population of 110,000.

The *Ottawa Citizen* stated that $7,000 had been raised in the city, in total, of which 40 per cent would be going to the GWVA relief committee and 60 per cent to Anna's Children's League. That confirms a cost price of 6 cents per poppy, if sold for 10 cents.

The next day, 8 November, the city's *Evening Journal* reported on the 'Impressive Service on Parliament Hill'. The article covered one and a half full length columns and Anna was mentioned as being amongst the host of very important people.

The enclosure was positioned at the top of the steps leading to the main entrance of the Parliament building. Mr R. B. Maxwell was representing the GWVA Dominion Command and 'Madame Guérin of France representing the orphaned children of France'. Others in the group included Sir James Lougheed, Speaker of the House of Commons, and Captain Hose, representing the Navy.

> A bitter wind swept across Parliament Hill but the sun broke through the clouds, shone brightly on the white cenotaph and gave a little warmth to the gathering of 4,000 people, who stood on the cold ground throughout the solemn ceremony. Particularly impressive was the two minutes' silence in memory of the heroic dead.

'God Save the King' was played, which opened the ceremony, and many had difficulty holding back their tears 'as they thought of the brave sacrifices of the vast army of splendid young men'.

> Men who had fought and come back, mothers and widows of those who had made the supreme sacrifice, and little children of the public schools met together on Parliament Hill and paid silent tribute, while wreaths of flowers were laid at the foot of the cenotaph which has been erected in front of the Victory Tower of the Houses of Parliament.

Laying of the wreaths at the Cenotaph was led by Governor-General Byng. He laid a beautiful wreath of poppies, representing the Dominion of Canada, and saluted. The Speaker of the Senate was next, followed by Sir James Lougheed, on behalf of the Prime Minister.

> Sick soldiers from the hospitals attended in automobiles, and once again they sang as in the old days on a Sunday morning before moving 'up the line,' 'O God, Our Help in Ages Past,' thrilled to the sadness of the 'Pipers' Lament,' played by the United Empire Pipe Band.

Pipers played and marched up and down whilst the wreaths were laid. Royal Canadian Mounted Police guarded the entrances to the grounds.

It was reported no speeches were made, 'only the atmosphere created to evoke for each man and woman in the vast crowd the sadness and the triumph of those four years of war'. Uniform-wearing men had been allowed to wear a poppy, pinned over their hearts.

Canadians knew who had put the Remembrance Poppy on their lapels. Anna, 'the Poppy Lady of France, the founder and promoter of the Inter-Allied movement of the Memorial Poppy Days', marched in the parade with the men of the GWVA, and placed her 'wreath of Poppies adorned with French colors' at the foot of the commemorative pylon, which had been temporarily erected in front of the Victory Tower.

For a couple of days afterwards, the familiar photograph of the younger Anna appeared in newspapers: '"Poppy Lady" Brings Flowers From the Fields of Flanders'. Text underneath Anna's image read:

> 'THE POPPY LADY' who has come to Canada with her inspiring message, 'We Shall Not Forget.'
>
> She has brought with her more than two million reproductions of the scarlet flowers which grow over the graves of the men who fell in action in France and Flanders fields during the Great War, and on Thursday these tokens will be worn in memory of Canada's heroes. She is helping Canada unite with France on Armistice Day, to honor the dead who sleep in French soil.

Anna returned to Toronto for Armistice Day. The Toronto GWVA asked her to present a wreath for them to the mayor on Armistice Day, for placing at the Cenotaph in front of the City Hall. It was reported she was accompanied by some widows and orphans.

On the eve of Armistice Day, Toronto's *Daily Star* printed an article headed 'MADAME E. GUÉRIN EXPRESSES HAPPINESS OVER PROSPECTS'. Anna explained that 'she was feeling very happy over the success of her venture and felt that the G.W.V.A. would make far more for their relief work than she had ever dreamed they would.' But the newspaper brought up the 'Guérin' saga yet again.

The article quoted Mademoiselle Mary Guerin:

'My objection to the work of Madame Guérin,' explained Mlle.
Guerin this morning 'is that she came to Canada representing the American-Franco Children's Legion which was organised in 1919 and has its headquarters in the United States and is represented in France by a committee. It was organized to strengthen and develop affection between America and France.'

Mlle Guerin argued that she had refused to go to the USA many times, even though she could have raised far more money. She kept her organisation entirely Canadian. The confusion of names had lost her money.

Anna was given the last word. She was able to defend the merit of her poppies. They had been sold to the GWVA at 6 cents each and, of those 6 cents, she was able to pay 3 cents for the work to make them. Ottawa's Poppy Drive raised over $7,000 and results showed that the poppies averaged 25 cents, instead of ten cents, which meant much more profit for the GWVA.

From the October, while Anna carried out her itinerary and Yette was busy in Toronto HQ, their friend Blanche began touring Saskatchewan, Alberta, and British Columbia. Representing Anna, she explained the League's work. She advised the GWVA and its Auxiliary, War Widows, and IODE, and so on, on how to plan 'energetic' Poppy Drives.

Newspapers referred to Blanche as 'the Poppy Lady' of France, although she was not 'the Poppy Lady of France' per se. She began in Saskatchewan. Saskatoon's *Star Phoenix* called her 'Madame Berberon'. The Kiwanis Club pledged support, as it often had in the USA. GWVA Ladies' Auxiliary invited Blanche to tea and presented her with a bouquet of flowers. The article expressed regret this charming French woman could not stay longer.

In the city, every house would be visited on 10 November, so no one would be embarrassed at not wearing 'an emblematic blossom' the next day, Armistice Day.

Blanche explained her mission and something new is learned here:

> So keen was Mme. Berberon's determination to suggest every
> possible means for the quick distribution of the poppies that as
> she talked her long, slim fingers fashioned a remarkably useful
> 'basket' from a manilla bag that had been used to bring cakes
> to the tea. As she pinned a poppy to the side she said: 'You can
> carry your flowers like this.'

So many articles, throughout America, mention 'baskets' or 'bags' for
carrying poppies, with photographs to match, but little is known about them.
The bags were handmade, always looked white, had a similar design, have
been found described as 'cloth', and usually had a poppy pinned to the front.

I wonder if women were always shown how to make the bags or were
given a paper pattern, then left to make them. Certainly, they must have
been easy to make if Blanche made one while she talked.

In Saskatchewan, Regina's Poppy Day alone raised $1,804.39. It was
announced $929.28 was sent to the French Consul-General for women and
children in the devastated areas of France. The balance of $875.11 was
retained by Regina's GWVA for 'application to the Last Post fund and for
local relief'. It demonstrates the GWVA policy of making decisions at the
local level. There had been a rumour beforehand that profits would be going
to America, to swell that country's contribution to Anna's League, but it was
quickly squashed.

As promoted in the run-up to the campaign, Anna was donating a silk
French flag to the school that sold the greatest number of poppies, relevant
to pupil numbers. The Cornwall school, Regina, would be the school to win
it, with 3.03 poppies per pupil.

Blanche went on to cities in Alberta. In Edmonton, its *Journal* called
her 'Madame Vernerun' when she spoke at the Memorial Hall. Archbishop
O'Leary, of the Roman Catholic diocese, gave 'his hearty endorsation to the
project' and many other associations expressed a willingness to participate
in the local arrangements.

In Calgary, on one visit, Blanche spoke to children of Mount Royal
school, the Crescent Heights High School, the Normal School, the
Commercial High School, and South Calgary High School.

In November, Blanche addressed the Ladies' Auxiliary, in GWVA club
rooms, Calgary. In Alberta, ninety GWVA branches took part in the Poppy
campaign. Nearly all of them reported they did not have enough poppies
and they would need more than twice as many for Armistice Day 1922.

There was not a small or large poppy to be had, nor a wreath. Alberta raised about $20,000 ($305,000 in 2021).

Blanche then went on to British Columbia. There were many 'character-revealing incidents' recalled by those counting the money at the end of Poppy Day, on 10 November: a small gold nugget had been donated to one box; a penny, wrapped in tin-foil to look like a quarter, was found in another. Blanche happened to be on Vancouver Island on the morning of Armistice Day, and in Victoria that afternoon.

Vancouver Island alone would raise $4,595.61. France received $2,020.62 and the GWVA $2,574.99. There was a suggestion that poppies be made by the GWVA in 1922 but it was pointed out that one of the chief reasons for distributing French-made poppies was to keep alive the bond of friendship which existed between France and Canada.

And so Armistice Day, 1921, was dawning all over Canada. In her *Synopsis*, Anna wrote: 'When I arrived in New-York I was in time to be on Armistice day in Toronto where I had a tremendous reception as the ORIGINATOR OF THE FLANDERS FIELDS POPPY DAY.'

French-made 'Decoration Day' poppies distributed in Canada were similar to those distributed in the USA and Australia in 1921, as similar as any can be with them all handmade by different pairs of hands. These three countries held Decoration Days and their poppy paper or cloth tags read: 'DECORATION DAY', 'POPPY LADY FROM FRANCE'.

The *Toronto Star* reported: 'While the City Hall was yet dim with early morning darkness the first silent tribute was placed on the cenotaph before it to-day. A nurse who had seen much service overseas paid homage to the dead. From then until noon there was a solemn procession of those who brought remembrances.'

The 1921 'Armistice Message' from the Governor-General of Canada, Lord Byng of Vimy, was widely publicised across the dominion, to reach all the people: 'Government House, Ottawa, Nov. 10. My message to the people of Canada: "Honor the dead by helping the living." (Signed.) BYNG OF VIMY. Governor-General of Canada.'

On Armistice Day, Lord Byng unveiled Montreal's Cenotaph. Byng did this numerous times in both Canada and Great Britain.

At 11.00 am, immediately after the unveiling, two minutes' silence was observed. One mother was chosen, from all the mothers in the city who had lost sons, to lay a wreath at the base of the Cenotaph after the silence. It is a tradition still being carried out in Canada.

In Toronto, the day finished with a ball at the King Edward Hotel. Huge Union Jacks draped the new ballroom. It was given by the IODE

Dreadnought Chapter and its Regent, Mrs Denison Taylor, greeted 500 guests. Anna and her sister Yette arrived with Mrs Albert Edw. Gooderham (Marietta/Mary). During the First World War, Mary and her husband Albert equipped the Daughters of the Empire Hospital in London and, later, they founded the IODE Hospital for Convalescent Children in Toronto.

Mary founded the Protestant Women's Federation and had a longstanding link to the Red Cross, dating back to the South African War. Both Mary and Albert were known for their philanthropic good needs. Albert was knighted in 1935, and thus Mary became Lady Gooderham.

The *Toronto Daily Star* described the clothes Anna and Yette wore. Believe it or not, it appears Anna wore her campaign uniform 'of French blue with narrow belt and tam o'shanter hat to match'. She wore her 'beautiful jewelled medals, one as officer of the French Academy, another as an officer of the Public Education, and one as an officer of "Nicham".' Yette wore a 'becoming dark blue uniform with cap to match'. Certainly, the two women would have been instantly recognisable.

Reportedly, Toronto took 200,000 poppies and raised more than $20,000 during its Poppy Day on 10 November. Organiser Mr George Moore stated the response 'was most generous'. At an early hour, 'Toronto blossomed forth into a poppy garden', as 1,500 women, girls, and boys tagged people with scarlet blossoms. The *Toronto Daily Star* noted how the city distributed nearly all the small poppies and 'nearly 13,000 of the larger numbers of wreaths, crosses and sprays'. There were taggers at the Metropolitan Street Railway termini, to catch the workers. The Boy Scouts were on duty too, doing a 'valiant service'.

We know Anna was asked to present the GWVA wreath to the Toronto mayor. This could be the *Daily Star* describing it: 'On behalf of the children of France who are grateful to Canada for her help, a spray combining the flowers of the field of France and Canada, poppy, cornflower, daisy, field together with Canadian and French flags, was presented to the mayor this morning to be placed on the cenotaph.' It supposedly came from 'Mlle Guerin' but perhaps it was 'Mme'?

St John, in New Brunswick, was just one city reporting that few in the city were without a 'poppy of Flanders field' on Armistice Day. Scores of willing women, from all organisations, assisted the GWVA. Traffic and all business ceased during the two minutes silence. Nelson, in British Columbia, was another where supplies of poppies were exhausted early. Three times the number of poppies could have been sold in Nelson.

A week after Armistice Day, Anna attended an emotional meeting of the National Poppy Day Committee, in Montreal's Windsor Hotel.

Lady Williams-Taylor chaired it. Montreal's *Gazette* printed a long article about that campaign committee meeting.

Lady Williams-Taylor exclaimed, 'I can hardly trust myself to speak of Poppy Day. How little we foresaw five weeks ago what that day would be, what an ecstasy of remembrance, what an indescribably spiritual welding together of the finest and highest emotions of all classes it would prove.' The honorary treasurer's statement showed $31,381.67 was raised as follows:

> Tag-day proceeds, $24,974.82; Thanksgiving Day collections at three theatres, $1,303.65; sale of wreaths, etc, $1,830.40; donations, $1,557.50; province (incomplete), $1,113.30; accounts due, $600. The expenditure totalled $3,456.17, leaving a net total of $28,925.50, which will be divided between the Disabled Soldiers' Employment Association of Montreal and the Children's League of Paris.

It was said to be probably the largest sum raised in Montreal during a one-day tag collection.

Anna, representing her French Children's League, 'returned thanks on behalf of her organization for the effort put forth by Montreal, and told how the inspiration for the Inter-Allied Poppy Day movement came to her from Col. John McCrae's poem'.

For Winnipeg, it was reported that gross receipts were $8,689.52. After the campaign expenses had been subtracted, there was a net profit of $8,255.66. Of this, $4,000 would go to Anna's Children's League, and the balance of $4,255.66 was equally divided between the Provincial Chapter IODE and the Ladies' Auxiliary of the GWVA.

On 6 December, Anna's sister Yette and friend Blanche sailed on the Canadian Pacific ship *Sicilian* from St John, New Brunswick, to take poppies to Cuba. The *Gazette*, of Montreal, announced their departure, adding, 'Mlle. Boulle's sister was the originator of the idea which attained such unusual success among all the former Allied nations.'

In Anna's aforementioned February 1922 letter, written from Montreal, she recalled the 1921 poppy campaign in Canada. She had arrived from New York City, from the VFW campaign:

> here in Canada, the Great war Veterans have had with 1,000,000 small poppies and 200,000 large ones $90,000 clear profit for their relief work in their different branches, and the French side will have about 80,000 dollars. I am just arrived here to settle

this part. On the $80,000 the French Poppies will be paid, the expenses of the Campaign also and the balances, clear profit will go to the poor children of the battle fields; I am proud to say that my delegates, two of them, left here to do the work with the Veterans while I was in England, have done splendidly, having run this campaign for the Veterans with their help.

When the final figures were announced, in March, they were scaled down somewhat. The *Ottawa Citizen* quoted the amount of sold small poppies as 735,066 and, for the large poppies, 69,049.

Consequently, final monetary figures were reduced. The Legion's Treasurer Sir Arthur W. Currie handed the Consul-General for France, at Montreal, a cheque for $60,780.03 for 'the orphan children in the devastated areas of France'. GWVA branches gained $70,000.

The next chapter within Canada's Remembrance Poppy history involves one Brigadier Captain James Learmonth Melville MC. As Anna Guérin was recognised, at the time, as the 'Originator of the Poppy Day', so was James well-known for his work with Canadian disabled veterans, occupational workshops for veterans, and the poppy.

I learned of James Melville's involvement with the Canadian poppy from conversations in 1978 and 1979, which were recalled in the *Times Colonist* of Victoria, BC, ten years later. The article was titled 'How a modest flower became a potent symbol' by Rev. Jock (John Arthur) Davidson.

As his parishioner at Dominion-Chalmers United Church in Ottawa, the Rev. Davidson visited 'Jimmy', as he was known to many old soldiers (especially those of the Royal Canadian Engineers), at the city's National Defence Medical Centre. It took place a few days before Remembrance Day in 1979. Jimmy was in his ninety-first year.

Jimmy was a Glaswegian by birth. He had arrived in Canada just over a year before the First World War began. Jimmy had served with the Royal Canadian Engineers in the war, winning the Military Cross in France, at Vimy, and a Bar at the Canal du Nord. He lost a brother in that war. At the end of the war, Jimmy became Principal of the Vocational School for Disabled Soldiers. He married Clare Gladys King on 31 May 1920, at the Dominion Methodist Church, Ottawa.

In 1921, Jimmy was appointed Unit Director of Administration in the Department of Soldiers' Re-Establishment. He was 'put in charge of what were called "sheltered workshops," which had been set up to provide employment for disabled veterans.' The post of Director of Vetcraft and Orthopaedic Services followed.

Jimmy served as a Chief Engineer of the Canadian Army overseas for part of the Second World War. One of his and Clare's sons, Robert, was killed whilst serving in the Second World War. Jimmy returned to Canada to become the Chairman of Canada's Pension Commission, in 1943. The Reverend Davison had served during the Second World War also, with distinction, and had gained a Mention in Despatches with the Royal Canadian Corps of Signals.

From the 1979 conversation, together with the interview which he knew Jimmy had given a year before, the Reverend Davison discovered Jimmy's role in developing the remembrance poppy ethos in Canada.

Jimmy told of meeting Anna, 'who had the idea of making money for assistance to French war orphans. She had come to Canada because she was aware of Canadian interest in the poppy as a symbol.' Apparently, 'the authorities sent her to see Jimmy Melville'.

Jimmy described Anna as a very kind lady and told how he persuaded her to let him have the Canadian manufacturing rights for making poppies. He had hoped 'the symbolic poppies could be made in the workshops he had helped establish for disabled veterans, with the object of selling them on behalf of them and their dependents. I promised her that we would operate on a non-profit basis, and I kept that promise.'

Jimmy added: 'I found a Madame de Witt in Toronto who made the [machine cutting] dies for us, and after that all the rest of the work was done in the veterans' workshops. We sold the finished flowers to the Great War Veterans Association, and they took care of all the marketing and distribution, with profits going into a special fund.'

Rev. Davison described Jimmy as 'a gracious and gentle man', who claimed no credit for the remembrance poppy's development in Canada. Jimmy said, 'It was Madame Guérin who started it all, I just picked up on a good idea.' When Jimmy died in 1980, Rev. Davison officiated at his funeral, and read McCrae's poem 'In Flanders Fields'.

And so Canada had said 'au revoir' to Madame Guérin. In 1922, most poppies were made by Canadian returned veterans. In Toronto, men in the Christie Street Hospital made them. However, as reported, a small number of poppies were supplied by Mlle Mary Guerin's Franco-Canadian Orphanages Society's orphanages in France. Mary Guerin was actually in charge of Toronto's Poppy Drive.

In Montreal, the central depot was at the Bank of Hochelaga at 363 St Catherine Street West. The city was divided into at least forty districts and, from that depot, 100,000 small and 75,000 large poppies were allocated. Each District's Captain reported to the central depot on the afternoon of

9 November, signed a receipt, and took their allotted boxes of poppies. Motor car owners generously provided their vehicles to facilitate this.

In Alberta, Edmonton's Poppy Day was held on Armistice Day. The *Journal* headlined with: 'Millions Wear Poppies "In Remembrance" for Those Who Saved Empire. FRANCE OBSERVING SPIRIT OF THE DAY.' Flags flew at half-mast; snow showers threatened; there was a nip in the air; but the ladies braved the weather with their baskets of poppies and distributed them.

The *Journal*'s long, emotional article described the day. Everybody felt bound to wear a poppy, there was no need to beg for a sale. Small 10-cent poppies were popular, as they had been with Anna, but people also loved the large poppies. One old lady buyer was mentioned. The article stated she got off the streetcar; she was not in 'the fur coat and limousine class, by any means', and her old purse looked lean and 'weather-beaten, with no bulge of money.' The sides of the purse were shrunken and wrinkled, just like its owner.

The old lady asked for a poppy and the 'eager-eyed girl with the basket' handed her one of the small ones. But the old lady said, 'No – I must have a big one – a big one.' She placed the poppy into the folds of her old, faded grey scarf and it shone like a ruby.

The siren sounded from the Hudson's Bay Company walls, traffic stopped, and walking paused. An old man murmured 'In Flanders' fields the poppies blow,' and someone sobbed. It was the old lady with her large poppy. 'Her old eyes are strained and wet with unshed tears – she, too sees that far-off field where the poppies blow – perhaps.'

Vet Craft Work Shops, for the disabled veterans, slowly became established, offering occupational therapy. In 1923, Work Shops made what were called 'Artcraft' poppies, under Jimmy Melville's DSCR. The *Winnipeg Tribune* described how to identify the official poppies: every poppy had 'a sticker attached bearing the vetcraft trade mark'.

In Vancouver, there had been a Red Cross Drive in September 1921, and it was proposed that the money raised would fund a badly needed workshop for local disabled men. The Disabled Veterans' Association refused the offer. The DVA was determined the government would not renege on its responsibilities to returned service men.

The DVA did not want others to bear the brunt. However, by November, Vancouver's Work Shop was operational. Basket-making, hammered brasswork, woodwork, and so on were carried out. Obviously, it was better for men to have a donated Work Shop than not.

Interestingly, on 11 May 1923, the Hon. H. S. Beland, Minister of the Department of Soldiers' Civil Re-establishment, received a deputation from veterans working at the Vetcraft Shops in Toronto and Hamilton. They had been on strike, for the basic rate of pay of $75 per month for all single men and $100 per month for all married men. Their request was granted and backdated to 1 May 1923. Additionally, men were given an extra 5 cents per hour for each dependent child.

Reportedly, in 1923, Lillian Freiman became a member of the National Poppy Day Advisory Committee. She chaired Ottawa's annual poppy campaign nearly every year until her death.

In 1924, Winnipeg's *Tribune* reported that some cities' poppies, in 'former years', had been commercially made. It reminded readers that all the poppies that year were made in Vetcraft workshops throughout the Dominion of Canada. They would be sold on Armistice Day, under the auspices of joint veterans' organisations.

In June 1925, Ottawa hosted the 'British Empire Services League' conference, where the poppy was adopted as the Empire's emblem of remembrance. It is now known as the 'Royal Commonwealth Ex-Services League'. In 1925, Canadian veteran organisations merged to form the Canadian Legion.

In 1931, after pressure from the Canadian Legion, the Canadian parliament amended the Armistice Act; 11 November would be set as the day to pay tribute to those 'who gave their lives that freedom might prevail'. The Legion would become 'Royal' in 1960.

On 30 November 1933, Ontario-born General Sir Arthur William Currie GCMG, KCB, National Poppy Day Campaign Treasurer, died. As a tribute, poppies with a 'Currie Button' were made.

Between 1928 and 1929, Currie had been Dominion President of the Canadian Legion of the British Empire Service League, to give it its full title at the time. Poppies with a 'Currie Button' were manufactured by disabled returned men, in 1934 and 1935. The paper 'Currie Button' replaced the CLBES crest paper centre.

The 'Currie Poppy', or 'Currie Button' poppy, had been suggested by Lieut.-Col. Léo R. La-Flèche, DSO, ADC, Chairman of the Canadian Legion's National Poppy Advisory Committee. Mrs A. J. Freiman was one of his associates. It was one of a number of changes La-Flèche suggested, in order to make poppies and wreaths more attractive. All members of the Legion were urged to have 'as their yearly objective the sale of 5,000.000 poppies'. It was hoped the 'Currie' poppies would prevent Remembrance Day 'bootleg' poppies, from Japan and Germany.

It was reported that poppies were coming into the country at $4.50 a thousand and that could be stopped with the introduction of the 'Currie' poppy. People should be encouraged to only purchase poppies from Vetcraft. To date, I have seen four versions of 'Currie' poppies:

1. A one-layer four-petal poppy; stamens; black painted metal button, with 'CURRIE' in a relief scroll design; with a pin.
2. A large double-layer poppy; more stamens; no centre button; very long stem, with leaf; the poppy was approximately four inches dia. to the widest point of the opposing petals; one petal had the black painted metal button, with a 'CURRIE' relief scroll; one petal's reverse had the printed words 'MANUFACTURED BY VETCRAFT'; and another petal's reverse had printed words 'DISTRIBUTED BY CANADIAN LEGION'; total length approx. ten and a half inches.
3. A two-layer circular poppy; no defined petals; with stamens; metal 'CURRIE' button; with leaf similar to a maple leaf.
4. A one-piece four-petal poppy (same as 1); without stamens; with a central paper 'button', rather than a metal relief one. The paper centre depicted a head and shoulders sketched profile-image of General Currie, along with the words 'CURRIE' above 'REMEMBRANCE DAY'.

'Vetcraft Industries Ltd' ceased manufacturing the remembrance poppies in 1996, when 'Veteran Affairs Canada' ceased supporting the company. The Royal Canadian Legion took responsibility and contracted out the manufacture of poppies to a Toronto company.

In 2021, the Royal Canadian Legion marked the centenary of the Poppy Day with a 'Tribute Poppy'. It was a paper replica of Anna's 1921 French-made poppy, and its accompanying card featured her. Canada also marked the centenary with a commemorative stamp and a coin.

I have a very tenuous link to Julian Hedworth George Byng, Governor-General of Canada. In 1913, he purchased Thorpe Hall in Thorpe le Soken, Essex, fifteen miles from my home. This is where two of my research projects overlap each other. Byng was born at Wrotham Park, Hertfordshire, on 11 September 1862, which was designed for his ancestor Admiral John Byng, by Isaac Ware in 1754.

In Canada, it was said, 'Everywhere Julian Byng has served there has been a bit of fighting; and everywhere there was a bit of fighting Byng was in it; and every time Byng was in it he came out a bigger Byng than when he went in.' He was already a highly decorated soldier after serving in Sudan and South Africa when, in April 1902, he married.

In 1910, Major-General Byng took charge of the East Anglian Division, with its 'important military centre' being in Colchester, Essex. When the First World War broke out, Major-General Byng was serving in Egypt. He quickly embarked for Europe.

After serving in Flanders and Gallipoli, Julian Byng was appointed Commander of the Canadian Corps in 1916, leading his Canadian 'Byng Boys' to a victory at Vimy Ridge in April 1917. Arthur Currie was serving with Byng during this time, as senior Canadian commander. As Baron Byng of Vimy, KCB, Julian was Governor-General of Canada from 1921 to 1926. He had the unenviable task of unveiling numerous First World War memorials in both Canada and Britain.

They say that behind every great man is a great woman and, for Julian Byng, this was (Marie) Evelyn, née Moreton. While he served overseas during the First World War, Evelyn served 'at home'. Like so many of her social position, she kitted out her home and turned Thorpe Hall into a British Red Cross hospital, known as Thorpe Hall Voluntary Auxiliary Detachment Hospital and/or 'Lady Byng's VA Hospital'.

Evelyn was recorded as 'Donor. Commandant. Matron' on her British Red Cross volunteer card. It was natural for a donor to become a commandant, the person taking charge of their own hospital, except for nursing and medical responsibilities.

Evelyn began equipping Thorpe Hall in August 1914. It had 33–40 beds and received its first batch of soldiers in October. It was operational up until 16 August 1915, when the last two patients were discharged. It had treated about 200 men, many of them Belgian sick or wounded. The majority of voluntary nurses had been local women.

Lord and Lady Byng returned from Canada in 1926 to live at Thorpe Hall again. In memory of the time the couple spent in Canada, Evelyn set about creating a beautiful rock garden at the front of the Hall and a 'Dominion Border'.

In 1928, Byng became 1st Viscount Byng of Vimy and was appointed as Chief Commissioner of the London Metropolitan Police. In 1932, he was promoted to the rank of Field Marshal.

The Byngs were friends with King George V and Queen Mary and, after the King died in 1936, Queen Mary visited Thorpe Hall. For the Queen's visit, a 'Queen Mary Suite' was designed and furnished, new gates to the estate were erected, and Evelyn Byng designed a 'Queen Mary's Walk' for the grounds.

Lord Byng of Vimy died at Thorpe Hall on 6 June 1935. He is buried at the eleventh-century parish church of St Leonard, in the nearby hamlet of Beaumont-cum-Moze.

Newfoundland was a British Empire self-governing dominion and not part of Canada when the First World War broke out. Newfoundland and Canada were intrinsically linked by their topographic positions, of course, but Newfoundland did not become part of Canada until 1949, after resisting for more than eighty years. Background facts about the province and the war appeared in an article on 15 August 1922.

Toronto's *Daily Star* wrote of Newfoundlander Sir Patrick McGrath, the owner and editor of the *Herald* newspaper. He held many other positions, including Financial Secretary of the 'Newfoundland Patriotic Association', voluntarily set up for the war. The article is interesting to anyone not an expert on Newfoundland's war history, which I am not.

It told of Newfoundland sending 6,500 soldiers and 2,000 sailors 'into Armageddon'. About 25–30 per cent of those who saw action 'over there' were killed.

Sixteen million dollars were spent on the war by Newfoundland and that did not include what its government had to outsource; for example, $100,000 went on hospital services because it did not have its own hospital.

Initially, there was no War Department. Instead, the aforementioned Association carried out all the 'raising, equipping and replenishing the Newfoundland regiment'. The government passed any legislation asked of it. It was not until 1917 that a Department of Militia was created. At the end of the war, it brought everyone back to civilian life.

In reality, Patrick McGrath carried out the duties of 'a minister of finance, an auditor-general, a purchasing agent, and other duties too numerous to catalogue'. Patrick, and his associates, worked in an unpaid capacity. The article said that 'If knighthoods were rightfully in flower while Flanders poppies bloomed, one of them was coming to the editor of the Herald, who was also, the president of the legislative council.'

At the time of Anna's poppy campaigns, Newfoundland had the GWVA, as Canada did. Originally, this Newfoundland GWVA had been the 'Soldiers and Rejected Volunteers Association', which was formed in St John's, Newfoundland, on 11 April 1918. The SRVA reorganised itself along the same lines as the GWVA in Canada.

I have been made aware that Newfoundland's strongest ties were not with Canada but with New England 'Boston States' because of fishing. There was also a migration of Newfoundlanders to these American states, mainly to Massachusetts and New York.

With such close connections to these American states and thus American influence, perhaps, the American Legion collaborated with the GWVA in the poppy adoption in Newfoundland. Perhaps Frederick W. Galbraith Jr. had written to Newfoundland veterans before his death, given he had written a letter for Anna to give to Canadian veterans.

Alternatively, Newfoundlanders may have independently initiated the adoption of the poppy in 1921, after learning that other Allied nations had adopted it. The Newfoundland GWVA's Secretary Treasurer, Royal Newfoundland Regiment Captain Gerald J. Whitty, OBE, MC, is one person linked to running the first poppy campaign there.

Whitty was GWVA Dominion Secretary and editor of *The Veteran* magazine. In 1924, Whitty and a Lieut. W. King were killed when a car struck them as they waited for a bus after attending a Newfoundland Regiment reunion. The four passengers in the car were also killed when it plunged over an embankment, although the driver survived.

One of Whitty's closest friends was Lt. Col. (Padre) Thomas Nangle, who had been in charge of Newfoundland burials in France during the war and up until 1925. Nangle was a close friend of Field Marshal Haig and it is felt the Padre contributed much to the commemoration of Newfoundlanders. Many consider Thomas Nangle was the main advocate for Newfoundland adopting the poppy.

Newfoundland's 'National Poppy Day', held on Armistice Day, was organised by the Ladies' Auxiliary of the GWVA, together with the National War Memorial Committee. Mrs W. B. Fraser, Vice-Chairman of the GWVA Ladies' Auxiliary, was in charge of the organisation. She and 'willing assistants', including friends, conducted the poppy sales, which were sold in aid of the GWVA and war memorial funds. As always, women were the backbone of the poppy campaign.

By 21 October 1921, some 12,000 poppies had already been ordered by Newfoundland Great War Veterans' Association. On 25 October, the St John's *Evening Telegram* reported some poppies were now 'in transit from London'. That, no doubt, meant en route via rail from London to Liverpool, to be put on a ship bound for St John's. At a guess, poppies had come into the Port of London from Le Havre.

On 27 October, the *Evening Telegram* reported on the origin of the idea of a Remembrance Poppy but not Anna Guérin's role in it:

> The children of the devastated areas of France gave the nucleus of this idea, which is rapidly gaining recognition, when they gathered the red poppies which grow with profusion in Flanders and Northern France, and decorated the graves of the fallen heroes near their homes. The suggestion from the childish hands was seized upon by the French Children's

League, which has been endeavouring to formulate plans in order to provide for the thousands of orphan children of the war area at work making silk replicas of the poppy, with the idea in mind that they could be sold and the proceeds devoted to this pressing need.

The article noted the United States had 'advanced' the idea the previous year but did not mention Canada, although it did quote the same three 'worthy objects' as the Canadian GWVA:

The inauguration of the custom of wearing a poppy as a memorial flower on Armistice Day, and thus cherish in perpetuity the memory of the Sacred Dead.

As a means of assisting the National War Memorial Committee and the G.W.V.A. The receipts to be equally divided.

Extending much needed assistance to the orphan children of France by purchasing at a reasonable price the product of their handiwork.

It was hoped as many people as possible would help in carrying out 'this most worthy campaign'. In order that enough poppy supplies would be available, outport settlement committees were asked to cooperate with the War Memorial Committee in order to calculate to what extent the poppy would be worn on Armistice Day.

These coastal fishing settlements were smaller than St John's but they were just as significant. A newspaper suggested the 1921 outport response was low. In 1922, it was noted that, because the outports were 'entering wholeheartedly into the scheme' that year, more poppies would be sold.

There was a worry about the poppies arriving on time, though. The *Evening Telegram*, on 10 November, noted they had still not arrived and printed an article about the next day:

Provided that the s.s. Sachem, which is bringing the poppies to be sold on Armistice Day, arrives in time, the streets to-morrow will be invaded by a detachment of young ladies, who will sell the emblems 'of Flanders Fields' in aid of G.W.V.A. funds. It will indeed be a flinty-hearted person who will refuse to purchase a poppy … The object is a worthy one and the poor man's mite is just as welcome as the rich man's cheque. No one should be seen on the streets to-morrow without a poppy.

And so 11 November 1921, dawned in Newfoundland. Its Poppy Day was a 'close call' because the French-made silk poppies only arrived in St John's on the ship SS *Sachem* that same day. The ship had left Liverpool on 3 November, carrying fifteen passengers, one infant and 700 tons of cargo, which included the poppies.

On 12 November, the *Evening Telegram* noted the SS *Sachem* had 'arrived in port yesterday afternoon' but it must have arrived during the morning for the cargo to be unloaded early enough for the poppy sale.

So, because of the late arrival, it was only the people of St John's who could pay tribute to their 'heroic dead by wearing the Flower of Remembrance – the Flanders poppy'. Even if the outports had ordered poppies, there was no time to deliver them.

On Armistice Day, St John's *Evening Telegram* printed a short piece describing the day. It was extremely cold but a large number of 'young ladies were stationed throughout the city'. 'No one who did not have one of the red emblems of "Flanders Fields" was allowed to pass these keen eyed girls, and quite a large sum must have been collected towards the deserving object.'

In the same edition, frustration was vented by an irate reporter: 'Shameful Apathy. NON-OBSERVANCE OF SILENCE BY MANY.' The reporter wrote that apathy was shown in the city by many during the two minutes silence. They had hoped that every single person would show respect and a few did, but

> on the street traffic rolled along as before, motor cars kept on going, long carts did likewise, people went on as if nothing untoward were happening; everywhere apathy or ignorance of what was being commemorated was apparent ...
>
> There was no excuse for not having heard the signal as the chimes in various city churches gave warning of its approach. There should be very little excuse for a profession of ignorance of the ceremony. What then was the reason for the indecent neglect of the commemoration? Surely, after all the talk we have heard of slack times, people are not going to say that they were too busy to stop for two minutes!

The rebukes continued in a similar manner. Of course, Newfoundland would certainly not be alone in incidences of indifference.

At 8.00 pm on Armistice Day, the GWVA celebrated with a dance at the Civilian Conservation Corps Hall, at Kings Beach, St John's. Prizes won during the summer, for GWVA sports, were presented by His Excellency the Governor.

Mrs W. B. Fraser and her coworkers were thanked for their 'indefatigable' effort and it was announced that the money raised by selling the poppies was $1,016, which was divided between a 'War Memorial Unlimited' fund for St John's war memorial and the GWVA. Through the latter, 'bona fide' distressed ex-service men would be helped through winter.

In 1922, the Empire's Dominions were also calling Armistice Day 'Remembrance Day', just like the 'Mother Country' of Great Britain.

The 1922 Poppy Day was held along the same lines as the year before. Although, as already mentioned, outport settlements participated.

About 40,000 poppies were imported from England. Principal outports, with GWVA branches, received about 25,000. Mrs Fraser took charge of St John's distribution again, with an 'energetic band of young ladies'.

The *Evening Telegram*, on 19 October, gave notice of 'Remembrance Day. NOVEMBER 11TH'. The GWVA prepared to have Armistice Day as a Poppy Day again. Magistrates, Post Office officials, school teachers, and others were all 'canvassed' about their willingness to assist.

Responses from the 'outport' settlements were described as 'very encouraging' in 1922. Funds raised were used for relief of ex-servicemen and their dependents in Newfoundland. The main ethos was remembrance and 'proud mourning' for their dead, that covered 'the plains of France and Flanders and elsewhere'.

The article stated it was only right that thoughts were, for at least one day, 'turned to those, who, in the fullness of their youth and in the prime of life, laid down their lives for civilization'. It continued that their task came to an end on 11 November (in 1918) but it was the day the task began for others and poppies would remind them to build up 'a nation worthy of the ideals for which they fought and died'.

Come Armistice Day in 1923, people of Newfoundland were still remembering the Armistice and living with the effects of the First World War. On the eve of Armistice Day, the Evening Telegram described the next day as an 'ANNIVERSARY OF A GREAT DELIVERANCE'.

At home, in 1918, the Armistice news was

> received with mixed feelings of surprise and unutterable relief; in the field, with consternation and dismay. No longer unsurmountable was that barrier that for four years had held our troops at bay, embedded in the mud of France and Flanders. The dogged, indomitable line of khaki had won out in that gruelling

test of endurance, and broken and disorganized, the front of the enemy had given way. The series of successes which our troops of late had won were on the point of materializing into an overwhelming victory, when the word was passed along to cease fire.

The article reminded readers that poppies were being distributed that day and all should wear the poppy the next day, Remembrance Day. During the two minutes' silence, they would think of the 'great army of warriors' who did not return and the 'broken down heroes' who did.

Newfoundland holds another flower dear – the forget-me-not. It was first worn as a remembrance flower on 1 July 1924. On that day, Earl Haig unveiled Newfoundland's National War Memorial. In 1916, it was the first day of the Battle of the Somme and a terrible day for Newfoundland losses at Beaumont-Hamel. The date became the province's Memorial Day.

The forget-me-not is now worn in the province, and wherever its people find themselves, on each 1 July. All those lost serving, in times of conflict or peace, are remembered – as they are on 11 November.

A Newfoundland veteran explained that the forget-me-not 'fell out of fashion' for a time. During the 1969 Provincial Command Convention, it was decided to wind down the forget-me-not fundraising campaign because interest and fundraising was to solely focus on the poppy campaigns and a cheap local source of the flowers was not available.

But the forget-me-not's significance did not diminish and it continued to be worn. In 2015, the wearing of the forget-me-not was given official authorisation by the Rituals and Awards Committee of the Newfoundland and Labrador Provincial Command of the Royal Canadian Legion. A year later, in 2016, Centenary events to commemorate the Royal Newfoundland Regiment's losses at Beaumont-Hamel spurred on another revival. Like the poppy, the forget-me-not is worn on the left lapel.

There is a poignant and astonishing story behind the making of thousands of forget-me-not lapel pins today. In essence, it is a personal First World War story, together with a passion for remembrance that lies behind their handmade manufacture in Port de Grave, Newfoundland.

This story began when a Newfoundlander, 17-year-old Eric Francis Taylor, went off to serve in the First World War and never came home. Whilst serving with the Royal Naval Reserves, he contracted meningitis. He died on 14 March 1915, and is buried in Glasgow, Scotland.

Eric's niece Florence Morgan-Thom, and her husband Barry, travelled across the Atlantic and visited his grave. It was emotional for Florence to visit the grave of the uncle she had never known and to honour a young lad from a family that had been in Newfoundland for 300 years.

Having an aptitude for flower arranging, Florence began her remembrance handicraft by making wreaths for her local Bay Roberts Royal Canadian Legion branch. Whilst enjoying her retirement, Florence was asked to create a few forget-me-not pins in 2011 and has not looked back since.

When I first heard of Florence, in 2016, she was making 200 pins a day. It is a non-profitable venture for her and a full-time labour of love. Florence and Barry were making approximately 102,000 remembrance forget-me-not pins a year, back then. What an amazing achievement by two retirees – and they are still going strong today!

Florence is now 80 years old, but she and Barry are proud to still play their part in resurrecting the forget-me-not tradition. Orders come in from the Newfoundland and Labrador government, many Legion posts, and other groups, sometimes for as many as 2,000 at a time.

Today, the forget-me-not sits equally, side by side, with the poppy in Newfoundland.

On 6 July 2021, in a Royal Canadian Legion press release, the Dominion President Thomas D. Irvine, CD, referring to Anna, stated: 'We are proud to be the safekeepers of this special symbol, brought to us by a visionary woman. Every time I see a Poppy I think of our fallen, and I thank them for their sacrifices.'

Chapter 8

Great Britain and the Poppy

Placing Great Britain here is deviating from the order in which the nations adopted Anna Guérin's 'Inter-Allied Poppy Day' idea. In reality, it should be Australia now but, because Anna took time out to visit Great Britain from Canada, it is logical to go away from that succession.

After succeeding in securing support in Canada for her 'Poppy Day' scheme, and after sending Colonel Moffat off to Australia, New Zealand, and South Africa too, Anna next looked towards the mother country of the British Empire. When Anna was in Port Arthur, in the first week of July, it was noted she would proceed to England 'to ask the Prince of Wales to become head of the Poppy Day movement in England'.

The mention of the Prince of Wales is not as far-fetched as it might sound because it was reported that Anna performed for members of the British Royal Family during her British tours, between 1911 and 1914. Given her powers of persuasion and charm, she was more than capable of achieving a personal audience with HRH the Prince of Wales. However, I have no proof that she did.

The Prince of Wales had become the British Legion's first Patron, and Earl Haig its first President. The British Legion had been formed from four British veterans' organisations on 14 May 1921: the National Association of Discharged Sailors and Soldiers; the Officers' Association; the Scottish Federation of Ex-servicemen; and the Comrades of the Great War. 'Royal' did not become part of its title until 1971.

Having left her sister Yette and friend Blanche in Canada, in charge of arrangements there, Anna left for England on the new Cunard liner SS *Albania*. The Ship Passenger List named 'Guérin, Anna. Lecturer. 40 [she was really 43 years old]; French' within the 'NAMES AND DESCRIPTIONS OF ALIEN PASSENGERS' list. The 'Date of Arrival' in Liverpool was given as 29 August 1921 (a Monday), and the *Scotsman*'s 'Shipping Intelligence' report, on 30 August, states: 'CUNARD LINE … *Albania* lands passengers Liverpool, 7.30 A.M., 30th.'

It is evident Anna never wasted her time. After disembarking, I am sure she would have boarded the first available train south to London. Her proposed destination, shown on the ship's Passenger List, was the Piccadilly Hotel. It was conveniently placed, as it was only just over a mile's walk to the British Legion headquarters at 26 Eccleston Square.

One guess is that Anna sent a cablegram to the British Legion from Canada. I doubt she would have set off without an appointment booked. Anna always used her time efficiently and, regardless of when she made contact, I wager her appointment with Legion men was 31 August.

In her 1941 *Synopsis*, Anna described going from Canada to London, 'where the English Veterans' Organisation was in great need'.

In advance of Anna's appointment at Eccleston Square, the British Legion's Vice-Chairman, Lieutenant-Colonel George Rawlinson Crosfield, DSO, asked the Legion's General Secretary, Colonel Edward Charles Heath, DSO, if he would meet with Madame E. Guérin.

Colonel Crosfield was a strong advocate of the First World War comrades' association Fédération Interalliée des Anciens Combattants (FIDAC), as Anna's American Legion ally, the late Col. Frederick Galbraith, had been before his death. George became FIDAC President in 1925, leading approximately 8,000,000 service men in nine countries.

George Crosfield was known to the American Legion and attended its third convention in Kansas, Missouri, as Anna had. He addressed the Legionnaires and a long article in an *AL Weekly* issue described him as 'a gallant and courageous military commander' and stated he followed Lord Byng's noble motto: 'Honour the dead by serving the living.'

After the Kansas convention, George went into Canada. He was representing the British Legion in both countries. George met GWVA men, visited Vetcraft Workshops, and visited an artificial limb factory. Having lost a leg in the Great War, he had a personal interest in disabled ex-servicemen finding employment. In Britain, George was on the Lord Roberts Memorial Workshops for Disabled Soldiers committee.

Anna wrote in her *Synopsis*:

> Field Marshall Haig, the President, called a meeting where I explain the Idea which was adopted immediately, but they had no money in the Treasury to order their Poppies. It was September and the Armistice day in November. I offered them to order their Poppies in France for them, so my own responsibility, that they would paid them after [sic]. Gladly they accepted my offer.
>
> Sir Francis went to Paris with me and we made the arrangement, we ordered for 1 million flowers of silk poppies.

The Legion's Francis William Crewe Godley could be Anna's 'Sir'. Anna's 1941 reminiscing was after he was knighted, as Francis William Crewe Fetherston-Godley. It is almost unknown to find Anna making an error but, evidently, she should have written 'Sir Herbert'.

A description of Anna's visit to the British Legion in 1921 is found in a press release taken from an issue of the *Legion Journal* in 1942. Colonel Edward Charles Heath remembered it was Sir Herbert Brown going to France with Anna in 1921, as well as recalling other events. He recalled that the poppy idea came to the British Legion 'somewhat mysteriously. There were grave doubts at first as to whether it would "take on."'

> In the late summer of 1921, Colonel Crosfield asked me if I would meet a Madame Guérin. This little French lady came to Headquarters to show us some small artificial poppies of a type then being made by certain French women and sold for the benefit of the children in the devastated areas of France.
>
> Would the British Legion care to adopt this emblem as a means of raising money for its own purposes?
>
> There were two firms in France ready to supply the material. She would want a certain percentage for her own organisation in France. The Finance Committee of the National Executive Council was concerned with the raising of funds, which were sorely needed if benevolent work on any reasonable scale was to be undertaken.
>
> The project was put to them.
>
> Poppies! Who wants poppies? Madame Guérin – who is she? What are her credentials? Do the two French firms exist?
>
> It was August – the sale and collection, if it were to be made, was due for November 11. There was no time to make suitable arrangements on this side of the Channel. If we were to do anything with the idea we must use the French organisation.

Colonel Heath is quoted as saying, 'We shall always be grateful to that good lady, Madame Guérin, for her part in the scheme.'

As the Legion's Honorary Appeal Secretary, Sir Herbert Brown was sent for and consulted. He was asked to go over to Paris with Anna. 'He reported to the next meeting of the Finance Committee that all appeared to be in order. The firms did exist; they were ready to supply the material to the organisation for making the poppies; the women in the devastated areas of France would make them.'

Colonel Heath recalled Sir Herbert was asked to go back to Paris and order 1½ million poppies. Before Sir Herbert left, Colonel Heath said to him, 'For goodness' sake order three million, whatever else you do.'

Colonel Heath's recollections show the British Legion to be as cautious as Canada's GWVA, but perhaps that caution was based on the Legion having 'no money'. The British needed to be sure about who they were dealing with. Neither of those two countries knew Anna like the USA. Anna's offer to supply poppies, before payment, would be very welcome. She had used her own money before, of course, in the USA.

The significant contribution Sir Herbert Brown made, in getting Anna's 'Poppy Day' idea off the ground, may never be fully known.

Sir Herbert Brown KBE (1869–1946) was a son of Charles Brown, of the flour milling business Charles Brown & Co. Ltd., in Croydon and Bermondsey. Having joined the family business in 1910, Herbert became its first Chairman when it became a limited company.

Sir Herbert forged strong links with hospitals in the area, becoming Chairman and subsequently President of the Croydon General Hospital. Over time, he gave over £20,000 to the hospital. He was a Governor of St Thomas' Hospital and Richmond's Star and Garter Hospital. Herbert was a very successful philanthropist and was knighted in 1920.

Sir Herbert Brown's family was no different to any other. During the First World War, his sister drove a Voluntary Aid Detachment ambulance and three sons enlisted; his son John Gordon, who was awarded the Military Cross in 1916, was killed five weeks before the Armistice.

By 16 September 1921, the British Legion was making known its decision to adopt the poppy as the remembrance flower. On that day, the *Evening Post* in Wellington, New Zealand, reported that the Returned Soldiers' Association was considering a proposal to 'adopt the red poppy of Flanders as the national memorial flower', which the American, Canadian, and British ex-servicemen's organisations had done.

On his return trip to France, to order more poppies, perhaps Sir Herbert accompanied Lieut.-Col. Crosfield, DSO, for part of the way at least. Crosfield went to begin a venture in the devastated areas of France. He was taking a party of nearly 200 unemployed ex-servicemen. They left from Folkestone on 20 September.

The next day, the *Taunton Courier & Western Advertiser* wrote of how 'war memories were revived' at seeing the men. The party was cheerful, showing 'joy at the prospect of at last securing employment, even though this might entail a lengthy sojourn abroad'.

Lieut.-Col. Crosfield explained the work would be mostly unskilled; the men would live in huts and would 'receive the trade union rate of pay in France of two francs (nominally is 1s 8d) per hour for unskilled work and 2.50 francs for skilled labour'. This was a trial-run and, if it was a success, other parties would be sent out to France.

On 27 September, we know Canada's GWVA received a cable from Anna. She stated the British had adopted her scheme and added 'already complete success is assured by the manner in which the campaign is being receiving [sic] by the people generally.'

I cannot say where Anna was when she sent the cablegram. It may be logical to assume she had returned from France by then because she had to get up to Liverpool ahead of leaving the port on 1 October, or she may have been sent it before crossing the Channel. She had been in Europe for just over four weeks, proving her credentials to Sir Herbert and, during this period, she may have visited Belgium and Italy too.

Many British promotional articles contained lines from Canadian John McCrae's 'In Flanders Fields'. However, the Guérin name is hardly discovered in online contemporary newspapers. I wonder if there was a conscious effort not to promote Anna's involvement.

Compared to most other countries, mention of Anna in Great Britain was negligible. With no evidence to the contrary, people could not help but think Poppy Day was Earl Haig's idea. What was reported as Haig's idea was for 11 November to be known as 'Remembrance Day'. It would coincide with a 'Poppy Day', like no other flag day.

Once the orders for Anna's French-made poppies were placed, the British Legion said 'farewell' to Anna Guérin. Had there been enough time to manufacture all the poppies in Great Britain, I think a British 'cheerio' would have been uttered earlier.

Before returning to Canada, Anna may have shared some advice. That said, Great Britain had held Flag and Flower Days for years.

However, I have seen photographs of British poppy sellers with some familiar Guérin-trademark sashes but gone were the handmade cloth bags, replaced with large trays suspended by a cord, around the neck, like the sellers of refreshments in cinemas.

Once the decision was made, British Legion communiqués were sent out en masse to newspapers, County Lord Lieutenants, and heads of municipalities (mayors, mayoresses, and so on). Mainly, they were sent from Earl Haig's Appeal's Organising Secretary, Captain W. G. Willcox; Hon. Appeal Secretary, Sir Herbert Brown; or Earl Haig himself.

Nottingham's *Evening Post*'s headline on 5 October was 'THE FLANDERS POPPY. EARL HAIG AND REMEMBRANCE DAY – NOV. 11ᵀᴴ'. The article passed on the desire of Field Marshal Earl Haig, President of the British Legion, that 11 November, Armistice Day, should be a 'real remembrance day'. It was noted that another scheme being launched was 'the wearing of the Flanders Poppy to the memory of the men who rest beneath the flower on the fields of Flanders'.

Readers were told the poppy had been accepted in Australia, Canada, and the USA, as the national memorial flower to be worn on 'Remembrance Day' and that 'There is an added value to these poppies in the fact that they are made by the women and children in the devastated areas of France.' Profits were for the British Legion 'Haig's Fund'.

Lord and Lady Haig were raising funds as early as mid-1917, when Lady Haig's Fund for the Relief of Disabled Officers became active, especially in Scotland. By mid-1918, events like an international football match at Celtic Park, in Glasgow, between Scotland and England, were taking place for the Sir Douglas Haig Fund for Disabled Soldiers.

By mid-1919, the Fund was referred to as the Sir Douglas Haig Fund for Disabled Officers. By 1920, it was known as Lord/Earl Haig's Fund for Disabled Soldiers and Sailors. On 31 March 1921, the entertainment profession held a national Warriors' Day. Cinemas, music halls, and theatres all raised money for the benefit of Earl Haig's Fund. One huge event was a Fancy Dress Ball at Covent Garden's Royal Opera House.

By the time a cheque for £115,140, raised on Warriors' Day, was handed over at the end of May, the British Legion had been formed and the money went into its Unity Relief Fund instead. For a few years, the entertainment industry made donations intermittently to its Warriors' Day Fund. These decreased as Poppy Day became more profitable.

Four British ex-servicemen's organisations merged to create the British Legion, at a Unity Conference on 14–15 May 1921, at Queen's Hall, Langham Place, London. More than 800 delegates attended from the British National Federation of Discharged and Demobilised Sailors and Soldiers; the Comrades of the Great War; the National Association of Discharged Sailors and Soldiers; and the Officers' Association. Thomas Frederick Lister, a wounded ex-serviceman, presided over the meeting.

Earl Haig was not present at the meeting because he had been touring South Africa. Haig and Thomas Lister were the two prime movers in bringing all the British ex-servicemen together into one organisation. Mr Lister, who would receive a CBE in 1927 and a knighthood in 1961, became the British Legion's first Chairman.

Sir Herbert Brown, who went to France with Anna, had been Hon. Chairman of the Officers' Association. Through the merger, the British Legion inherited his Appeal Department and its £10,000.

Anna was not found identified as 'Originator of Poppy Day' per se. Rare press mentions enlightened: 'The poppy plan, though now greatly developed, originated with Mme. Guérin, wife of a French judge'; 'it will be financially helpful to the women and children in the devastated areas who are engaged in making the poppies'; 'poppies from France'; and 'The idea is of French origin.' I have not found any publicised interviews with Anna, as had occurred in North America.

Anna recalled the 1921 British poppy campaign in 1922: 'the success was even greater' than Canada, and 'the British People have taken that in the right spirit, it will go on now, every year, nationally in Memoriam, "Lest we forget" ... The Prince of Wales, Field Marshall Haig, are at the head in England ... The motto is: "Honor the dead in helping the living; buy and wear a Flanders Field Poppy on Memorial Day."'

She reminisced in 1941: 'Their first National Flanders Poppy day was an enormous success and it has developed so well, so big that for the past 15 years the ENGLISH EMPIRE was selling 25,000,000 Flanders Poppies on Armistice day, poppies made by the disabled soldiers.'

Not every council felt they could fulfil Earl Haig's request to be responsible for a Poppy Day 'on Armistice Day for the benefit of the funds of the British Legion'. Budleigh Salterton, in Devon, was one. The council passed on its letter from Earl Haig to the local British Legion Branch. Commandant of the Branch, Captain Bone, replied to the Council 'deprecating' its action: 'it was regrettable that the impression should get about that the Council were not sympathetic with the appeal.'

Budleigh Salterton Council Chairman explained 'that a letter had been sent in reply pointing out that the Council could not carry out the effort, but were anxious for the success of Poppy Day, and would be quite prepared to see the matter through in their private capacities.'

It was said that 'Capt. Bone had sent a telephone message expressing thanks for the Council's action, and regretting the tone of his original letter.' A decision was made to form a committee of council members and so on, 'for the purpose of carrying out Earl Haig's suggestion.'

Unlike in North America, Anna was not hands-on with the first British Poppy Day. No doubt, she described how her successful Poppy Days and Drives were carried out, with efficiency and enthusiasm, by mothers, wives, daughters, and sisters, and British women did not disappoint.

Women, including those from war service organisations and the British Legion's Women's Section, were called upon by Earl Haig 'to give him just a few hours of their time'.

Earl Haig asked 'earnestly' for women 'to help by selling poppies' on 11 November and papers printed 'Local Helpers Wanted' advertisements ahead of Armistice Day.

The *Grantham Journal* noted:

> The work of organising the sale of Poppies in each district is distinctly the work of ladies, and those who served during the war, in Women's Units, or worked in a voluntary capacity at home, are specially invited to pull together once again. It is suggested that those ladies entitled to wear uniform on occasions, and decorations and medals, should do so on 'Remembrance Day,' and volunteer to sell Poppies.

The *Western Daily Press* declared:

> POPPY DAY. Field-Marshal Earl Haig is appealing for the loan of motor-cars for 'Poppy Day' in Bristol. They will be useful to-day, to-morrow, Friday, and Saturday. Will those willing to lend communicate with Capt. Willcox, Poppy Day Offices ... Lady helpers are still required to sell Flanders poppies on Armistice Day. The Army Council has given permission to soldiers to wear the poppy in their uniform head-dress when not on duty.

After Poppy Day, the key role played by women in the distribution of the poppies was appreciated. Only formed 1–3 August, the British Legion Women's Section was able to justify its existence. From 1 October 2016, after a certain amount of publicly aired resistance, the Women's Section was integrated into the organisation as a whole.

As the King had proclaimed on 9 November 1919, and repeated in 1920, there was another two minutes' silence in 1921: 'That at the hour when the Armistice came into force, the 11th hour of the 11th day of the 11th month, there may be for the brief space of two minutes a complete suspension of all normal activities – so that in perfect silence the thoughts of everyone may be concentrated in reverent remembrance of the glorious dead.' There are South African and Australian links to this 'Silence' initiative, which will be mentioned again further on.

Because some city and town groups were too slow in placing their poppy orders, some could not receive poppies from France. Extra poppies had to be sourced elsewhere.

The *Folkestone, Hythe, Sandgate & Cheriton Herald*, two years later, reminded readers about the 1921 Poppy Day, although some facts would be new. Headed up as 'THE FLANDERS POPPY. BEING MADE BY DISABLED EX-SERVICE MEN', it was very informative. The article began by stating that all the small poppies, the 'dainty emblems', would now be made by Major George Arthur Howson's factory at St James Road, Old Kent Road, by sixty disabled ex-servicemen.

The *Herald*'s article continued:

> When the idea of Poppy Day was first suggested to the British Legion in 1921 by Mme Guérin of Paris, there were only six weeks in which to organise the scheme throughout the country. The Legion purchased the small 'poppies' for 3d. in France, where they were manufactured by the women and children in the devastated areas. These poppies cost £15,510.
>
> The first orders for the 1s. poppies were given to London manufacturers, but the demand was so great that it was impossible to get enough to London, and they had to send to France, Coventry and many parts of the country, and were even then unable to meet all demands.

Sir Herbert Brown and Captain W. G. Willcox sent a message out in 1921. They told of poppies made of silk and cotton, at

> a fixed price of 3d. as the lowest price at which Flanders poppies can be sold; whilst the larger silk poppies can be sold at not less than one shilling each. In one case we hope the usual sum given will be 6d., the other 2s. 6d.: unless we average 4½p. and 1s. 9d., the Poppy sale will not be a success: every penny will go to the help of the ex-service man through the medium of the British Legion. Many people tell us that in these hard times people cannot afford more than 1d. In reply we can only say we want a sacrifice.
>
> We want the Nation to know that they are honouring the dead and the living, and that the Poppy is worn as a symbol of 'Remembrance'. 'Remembrance Day' it is not 'Poppy Day'. May all bear that in mind.

And so Armistice Day dawned: 11 November, Britain's first 'Poppy Day'. One quote read: 'No one could have foreseen how the idea was going to grip the public imagination as it did.'

Newspapers described aspects of the day. All London turned red, apparently; it was rare to see anyone not wearing 'Haig's buttonhole'; Princess Alice sold poppies outside Windsor Castle; Sotheby's interrupted a regular sale to auction off a basket of poppies. It made £10 but it kept being auctioned and made a total of £100; chorus girls, from the 'A to Z' stage show at the Prince of Wales theatre, sold poppies outside it; at St Paul's Cathedral, British actresses sold kisses for 10 shillings each; and Earl Haig's car drove around London, decorated with many poppies. Later in the day, some Poppy Girls stepped out and stopped it, stripping it of its poppies, because they had sold out of their own stock.

The *Hartlepool Northern Daily Mail* described the scene: 'The true measure of the public gratitude to our fallen heroes seemed intensified a thousand fold'; poppy sellers were besieged and 'every business of every nature bowed its head in reverent homage'. It wrote that in London all moving things 'came to a stop'; 'Many women wept'; and 'men stood silently and bareheaded during the two minutes.'

It was not all plain sailing, though. Aberdeen did not receive its French-made poppies, due to unsettled weather and 'a mistake on the other side of the Channel'. However, the people of the city improvised.

Instead, women, ex-servicemen, and others distributed flags. Theatres, cinemas, etc. gave permission for collections to be made on their premises. 'A bevy of fair young ladies in Highland costume' visited the Fish Market and collected a large sum of money.

The stock of these flags was very low but everyone gave generously. Additionally, to show support, many people wore different red flowers in their buttonholes to symbolise the poppy.

Other places improvised too, making their own poppies when their French-made supplies sold out. Having asked for a supply of 10,000 poppies, Tunbridge Wells only received 6,000. These were all gone early in the day, so, from 10.00 am to 4.00 pm, helpers at the Committee Room worked hard making poppies of scarlet paper to satisfy the demand. It was reported that Tunbridge Wells raised £236 17s. 8d.

In Dorchester, although the weather was cold, many sellers had run out of poppies before noon. Through the initiative of the Mayoress, poppies were made from red ribbon. Dorchester raised £35, which was considered an excellent amount, bearing in mind there were so few poppies.

Northampton did not hold a Poppy Day in 1921, but forwarded a donation of £25 to help Earl Haig. It promised to set up an organisation to see to it that the town and county were supplied with poppies in 1922.

Human stories of Armistice Day in London were shared to parts of the Empire. One Special Correspondent, from New Zealand, reported several incidents from London. One was of tense moments during the two-minute silence at the Cenotaph, when the silence was broken by 'one agonising cry' from a woman who could not stop crying.

Other scenes at 'a railway station' were also described, and this must have been Paddington. The Cheltenham Flyer train should have left at eleven, but it did not move at the eleventh hour, on the eleventh day of the eleventh month. A 'sudden startling hush fell'.

Men in a train compartment took off their hats, bar one. That man 'grumbled fiercely and noisily at "all this blank nonsense of holding up an important train"'. For the two minutes, no one spoke and, when the guard's whistle was heard, the grumbler found himself quickly manhandled off the train onto the platform, by two 'hefty countrymen'. When the train moved off, the grumbler was not on it.

The *Northampton Mercury* looked back to that 1921 Poppy Day, ahead of the 1937 Armistice Day: 'How many Northampton people who will be wearing a Flanders Poppy on Armistice Day are aware how the movement originated? It was a French woman, Madame Guérin, who first thought that the poppy would make an appropriate emblem to sell in aid of ex-Servicemen in distress.'

Having a choice of poppy caused a little dissent, with one poppy seller in Hull feeling strongly enough to write to her local newspaper. She thought it was a 'very wrong idea' to have a silk and cotton poppy:

> The poor man's penny, given with a free heart (in many cases it is a struggle to spare) is belittled by the ones who wish their gifts to be advertised ... many a working girl and man gave their silver, but asked for no distinction, whilst one with a haughty demeanour asked for a silk poppy. On being told that our stand had no silk poppy, he replied, 'Very well, I will go to another stand where they have the silk flowers.'

It was an example of how some people felt – to have the choice was divisive. The inference could be made: coppers for cotton poppies, silver for silk poppies. But this was how it would be for decades.

199

On Armistice Day in 1921, the author of the 'A Woman's Point of View' column in the *Yorkshire Post and Leeds Intelligencer* shared her observations. She had read appeals for poppy sellers, in London and the North, and noticed the response 'was not what it might have been'. Women could not be blamed, she said. She commented about 'early days of the war emblem' and flags, when sellers were called to volunteer. They 'came forward in large numbers, but later on all flag-selling became discredited.' I wonder if the author was thinking of the Poppy Day in Whitby, Yorkshire, when writing of 'early days of the war emblem'.

She continued:

> Women were said to sell flags to avoid doing anything else, indeed worse, to pick up acquaintances. A good many busy women will recall the last time they sold emblems for the Y.M.C.A. in the London streets, when the majority of the people they approached replied with something like this: 'Can't you really find something better to do than this sort of thing?' If poppies are to be sold each year on Armistice Day women will come forward fast enough to sell them, if it is understood that it is for the men, and not to pass the time, that they are doing it.

Reportedly the poppies sold in 1921 raised £105,842. This is usually rounded up and referred to as £106,000.

At some point, after Anna's poppies were sold on 11 November, one Major George Arthur Howson, MC suggested his Disabled Society's factory could make the poppies although, it is noted, even he doubted whether making poppies would be a great success.

Thus, making poppies in Great Britain began in this factory. Major Howson, MC and Major Jack Brunel Cohen, MP founded the Society in 1920, with twenty disabled ex-servicemen. Both were ex-servicemen and Major Cohen had lost both legs. Howson became Chairman of the Society, and Cohen sat on the committee. Both were involved with the founding of the British Legion in May 1921.

The veterans made poppies for Great Britain and other parts of the Empire, on behalf of the British Legion. Not every dominion made poppies so they were sent out to places like Gibraltar, Hong Kong, India, Malta, South Africa, as well as to the British Army and expatriates abroad.

It was a hostile employment environment for returning ex-servicemen, regardless whether they were disabled or not. Men did not have the right to have their old jobs back and, as a result, it was stated that 350,000 men were out of work. All Allied nations were facing a similar problem.

It was reported by Manager Captain Bishop on 5 October 1922 that the Factory had made 4,000,000 poppies in three months. There were sixty men employed at what was now being called the Poppy Factory. They had started making poppies for next year and it was predicted that 'by 11 November, 1923, they would make 27,000,000'.

In 1923, most Poppy Factory employees were those who had lost a leg. The Factory was working full-time and more than 14,000,000 small poppies, 250,000 large size, and 300 wreaths had been made by September. The Factory had a canteen, a piano, and was a 'very happy company'.

The Society was always trying to keep prices low because it paid the Trade Union wage of 1s. 2d. an hour and such artificial flowers could be obtained more cheaply, made by female and child labour. The poppies cost 'barely ½p. each' to make, in 1923. That year, the Factory filled many other orders including 180,000 cornflowers for the Ypres League, for Ypres Day. It was felt that if the Factory was more well-known, it could accommodate more orders. In 1925, it became affiliated to the British Legion and moved its factory to a larger site in Richmond, Surrey. Accommodation was built to house some of the men on site.

That same year, a 'Festival Commemoration Performance' took place on Armistice Day at London's Royal Albert Hall, in aid of the British Legion. It became a permanent annual event and, since 1927, it has been known as the British Legion Festival of Remembrance.

In March 1926, Lady Haig opened a Poppy Factory in Edinburgh. When she visited Dundee that November, the *Dundee Evening Telegraph* noted that 'Great difficulty was experienced in getting collectors'. Lady Haig 'appealed for more workers'. There were thirty men employed initially, with a waiting list 'of many hundreds. People should be careful that they were buying the genuine Haig poppy.' There were always fake poppies around to worry about, some even from Germany.

Major Howson formulated the idea of the Field of Remembrance in the summer of 1928. It was said that many doubted the idea, just as 'Poppy Day' success was doubted. However, at the next Remembrance time, Major Howson and his wife took a group of his men to outside St Margaret's church, near Westminster Abbey, with some poppies and a collecting tin. Some of the men stuck poppies in the ground. Thus, in 1928, the tradition of the 'Field of Remembrance' had begun. At first, single lapel poppies were used, with people encouraged to buy two: one for a lapel and one for a 'Field'. Then, in 1932, small wooden crosses were introduced which bore an artificial poppy in their centres.

Several British newspapers in 1936 stated it was yellow British Haig Fund poppies that were sold in France. It was a politically led decision. The change came about from the fear that people could be mistaken as Communists, who had taken to wearing a red poppy badge.

Legion branches in the South of France had instigated the change because political feeling was stronger there. As a result, it was decided to change the colour, to be tactful and to avoid a 'political clash'. A poppy wreath for Notre-Dame Cathedral was kept red, however. It was placed below the British Legion tablet there, which commemorates the British Empire's First World War dead. The tablet survived unscathed the devastating 2019 fire at the Cathedral.

An article in the *Sunderland Daily Echo* stated that the dominions and colonies shared, with Great Britain, in thinking of those who had 'laid down their lives in the Great War'. It also described the ceremony in Delhi, India, where 1,200 British and Indian ex-servicemen marched past the Viceroy, Lord Linlithgow, at the Memorial Arch.

By the time the Poppy Factory's Major Howson died, on 28 November 1936, his men had increased to 368. The newspapers stated they were making more than 30,000,000 poppies each year now. On his final Armistice Night, although seriously ill, an ambulance drove him to watch the 'Field of Remembrance' pilgrimage at Westminster. After the King planted his cross, he went and specifically spoke to the Major.

After the first Guérin French-made cotton and silk poppies, British-made poppies were made in many designs, sizes, and materials, in the following decades. Right from the start, 'Haig Fund' poppies needed to be authenticated, in an attempt to foil forgeries – many from Germany.

Initially, poppies were identified by metal centres, bearing 'Haig/s Fund', in an attempt to foil the forgeries. The poppy materials ranged from cotton lawn to sateen, silk, crêpe paper, and printed card.

In the 1930s, centres also bore 'HF' initials. A large waxed poppy was introduced for motor vehicles. Between 1942 and 1944, 'Austerity' poppies emerged because of Second World War shortages. The poppies produced were smaller and made only in sateen or cotton, had centres of paper, printed with the words 'Haig's Fund', and cardboard stems, replacing the usual metal stems.

Bitumen centres arrived post-Second World War, with leaves going and returning. By the time the Poppy Day's centennial year of 2021 arrived, the

British Remembrance Poppy design had been a standardised since 1967: a one-layer paper design, with green leaf, black plastic 'Poppy Appeal' centre, and green plastic stalk. In 1994, authenticity was no longer identified by 'Haig/s Fund' but by 'Poppy Appeal'.

In Scotland, Remembrance poppies are distributed by Poppy Scotland, one of the Royal British Legion's charities. They are made in the Lady Haig's Poppy Factory in Edinburgh, which Lord Haig's wife founded in 1926. Her poppy design is considered the most botanically accurate, with four petals and no leaf.

Onwards from 1921, the odd mention of Anna Guérin would emerge to prove she had not been totally forgotten. One such mention was in February 1944, within the *Home Front* magazine. With the front cover depicting a First World War serviceman working beside a Second World War ex-RAF serviceman making 'Austerity' poppies, it was mentioned that it was a 'French woman, Madame Guérin, who suggested the Poppy as a symbol to the Legion.'

In 2018, to commemorate the centenary of the First World War Armistice, '1918–2018' was printed in gold on the Scottish poppy petals and on the leaf of the other British poppy.

In 2021, after a century of near obscurity for her in Great Britain, the Royal British Legion acknowledged Anna in its book, *We Are the Legion: The Royal British Legion At 100*, by Julia Summers. PoppyScotland marked the Poppy Day centenary by printing images of '100' on its poppies.

At the Royal British Legion's 2021 Festival of Remembrance, held at the Royal Albert Hall on 13 November, BBC presenter and broadcaster Huw Edwards acknowledged Anna in his opening introduction.

All the British publicity during the Poppy Day centenary year proved Anna Guérin was, at long last, being fully recognised in Great Britain as the 'Originator of the Poppy Day'.

Chapter 9

Australia and the Poppy

Anna Guérin sent Colonel Samuel Alexander Moffat off to New Zealand, Australia, and South Africa, in that order. She was not in a position to visit personally to promote her 'Inter-Allied Poppy Day' scheme, leading up to Armistice Day 1921. After weeks in Canada, plus making a visit to England and Europe, she had time constraints.

Before Colonel Moffat arrived in New Zealand, Australian veterans had adopted Anna's 'big idea'. Even before he had left Canada, Australians had become the second nation of the Empire to adopt it.

On 5 August, at the close of its sixth annual congress, in Brisbane, the Returned Sailors' and Soldiers' Imperial League of Australia announced the red poppy, so 'conspicuous on the fields of France, should be adopted as an international emblem on armistice day' and, I feel, Canada has to be credited with this early decision.

We know Secretary Turley of the Canadian GWVA had cabled the Australian RSSIL, suggesting that they adopt the poppy as their memorial flower, as the Canadians had. The cable also stated that Madame Guérin '"the poppy lady from France," was in Canada with millions of silk poppies made by the women and children of devastated France, and begged the Australian soldiers to promise her their moral support, and to take up a poppy campaign for Armistice Day in Australia.' By return, the RSSIL asked for Madame's credentials.

Some of the finer details are discovered within a statement from Mr B. F. McDonald, President of the New South Wales branch of the Returned Sailors' and Soldiers' Imperial League. His statement, in support of the Poppy Day movement, appeared in several newspapers.

The GWVA replied that Monsieur Jean Adrien Antoine Jules Jusserand, who was French Ambassador to the USA (1902–1924) had stated that 'the committee was entirely dependable'.

Jusserand declared he was personally acquainted with Madame Lebon, who was the managing president of the Paris Committee; he 'gave his assurance that any funds sent to her would be most usefully and economically applied'; and he 'confirmed personnel and enterprise of the Guérin Committee'.

Had it not been for Australian veterans releasing that significant fact, Canada's contribution to the expansion of Anna's 'Inter-Allied Poppy Day' scheme would have probably remained hidden.

Colonel Moffat landed in Australia on 13 September 1921 – he arrived in Melbourne, from New Zealand. He did not need to persuade veterans to adopt Anna's idea, but he would tour, promote, and help make arrangements for the poppy distribution on 11 November.

The headquarters of the RSSILA was in Melbourne at that time and Colonel Moffat was entertained there on the 14th by representatives of the RSSILA. The veterans' organisation is now known as the RSL, the Returned and Services League.

On 14 September, the *Melbourne Argus* announced that he would visit various counties, to organise the wearing of a replica Flanders Poppy on Armistice Day each year. Poppies were made by French orphaned children. They would be worn in recognition of 'gallant deeds performed on Flanders fields by the Allies' and in memory of the fallen.

Both Australian and New Zealand papers reported that Colonel Moffat was a Chevalier de la Légion d'Honneur and a former Red Cross Commissioner for the United States. He was linked to Madame Anna Guérin of the French Children's League, Australian relief work in France and Flanders, Austria, Hungary, Balkan States, the 'Duchess of Sutherland's Hospital Fund', and the Serbian Child Welfare organisation.

How Anna came to engage the Colonel has not been discovered but his reputation would have preceded him and his connection with Australian relief work in France (whatever that was) meant he was an ideal person to promote Anna's memorial poppy scheme 'down under'.

Writing in her 1941 *Synopsis*, Anna described the time spent visiting the British Legion men in London in September 1921 when she added 'Colonel Moffat, meanwhile was doing a very good work in Australia and New-Zealand.'

Australia seems to have been the same as the USA with regard to veteran group structure. The Returned Sailors' and Soldiers' Imperial League of Australia had State branches and each branch had a President. Each State branch had to officially adopt the poppy idea.

Newspapers confirmed the replicas would be worn as badges on Armistice Day, 11 November, 'for the purpose of raising funds for the relief of the children in the war zones of France'.

'There is a wealth of sentiment in the idea,' Colonel Moffat said. He added, amongst other comments, that the blood-red poppy 'will assist to maintain the bond of friendship between France and Australia'.

After a quick return to New Zealand, Colonel Moffat arrived back in Australia. Sailing from Auckland on 5 October, he arrived in Sydney. Then it was on to Brisbane, arriving on the mail train during the night of 7 October. On 12 October, he called on the Consul for France, Major H. R. Carter. Two days later, Colonel Moffat addressed a meeting at the Town Hall where Harry John Charles Diddams, the Mayor of Brisbane, presided. It was declared that the city's 'Poppy Week' would commence on 4 November. Proceeds would be divided between the French orphans and Australian ex-servicemen.

Colonel Moffat told of the losses France sustained and explained the country's future depended on these orphans. German occupation of places such as Lille meant children's health had suffered severely. Such children needed restoring to 'normal health and strength'.

Brisbane followed along the same organisational theme as Anna's Poppy Days in other countries. As usual, women were the linchpins. Brisbane's Executive Committee comprised 'the Mayoresses and wives of shire council Chairmen in the metropolitan area'. From that Brisbane hub, the word was carried further via more meetings in places like South Brisbane Town Hall and Odd Fellows Hall, Toowong.

Colonel Moffat must have made a great impression on Australian veterans because he was made an honorary member of the RSSIL, a compliment rarely conferred by the League. He left Brisbane for Sydney on Saturday, 15 October, on the SS *Canberra*.

The Morning Herald wrote 'POPPY DAY' was 'INTERNATIONAL' and 'FOR REMEMBRANCE'. It told of all the Allied governments cooperating with the movement. As Anna had arranged, in the past, there would be no Customs duties paid on the poppies and there would be free transportation of them, on railways and steamships.

Colonel Moffat was received by the Governor of New South Wales, Sir Walter E. Davidson, on 20 October. Both he and his wife Dame Margaret 'willingly extended their patronage to the movement' and agreed to serve on the honorary committee, which was promoting it.

Ironically, there were no street sales in Sydney on Armistice Day in 1921. There was a regulation limiting street sales to two days a year but 'the Idea' was still carried out by selling before 11 November, in hotels, shops, theatres, and the like. It was, the *Morning Herald* wrote, because 'it is believed that the people of New South Wales are as truly patriotic today as they were during the war, and will be only too willing to join in celebrating Armistice Day in this manner.'

The *Herald* of 29 October, and other newspapers across the country, would continue to remind readers of what was already known: that the poppies would be coming 'through Madame Guérin'; Colonel Moffat, with his own 'original credentials' was her representative; and 'the moneys destined for France were to be sent by the Returned Soldiers' League direct to the French Children's League Headquarters in Paris, or to any organisation for relief of French war orphans.'

The aforementioned Mr B. F. McDonald was stating, by that date, that 400,000 poppies had arrived in Sydney. 'The public,' added Mr McDonald, 'may rest assured of the bona-fides of this movement, and the league will see that the moneys derived from the sale of the poppies go to the object already made public. An earnest appeal is made to the women to assist this worthy movement.'

And assist the 'worthy movement' the women and girls of Australia did. Groups such as the Red Cross Society, Catholic Girls' Guild, Girls' Friendly Society, Housewives' Association, Girls Guides, Mothers' and Wives' Association, Nurses' Association, Overseas Australian Services Society (OAS Society), Sailors and Soldiers' Mothers' Association, Victoria League, Voluntary Auxiliary Detachments, Wattle League, and state schools were amongst those recruited to distribute poppies.

Poppies were sold at one shilling each. Newspapers gave differing alternatives for how the proceeds would be shared: after reimbursing French children, the balance of the money would go to the RSSIL (no percentages given); half the money would go to the orphan children who make the poppies and the other half, minus expenses, would go to the RSSIL for service men and their dependents; 45 per cent would go to France, 45 per cent to the RSSIL, and 10 per cent to the Warriors' Day Fund.

Local newspaper columns carried advertisements for public meetings, where the best ways of conducting a sale would be discussed and people could commit to volunteer. For instance, in Mackay, Queensland, a long article explained all the details and called for 'a large attendance of the public' on 25 October. The initial idea was a Poppy Sale on 11 November, and another some days prior to it.

In Melbourne, Colonel Moffat attended a dinner given by the Federal executive of the Returned Sailors' and Soldiers' League of Australia at the Francatelli Café on 4 November. He was introduced by the president as the 'first ambassador of the French committee which was trying to make Armistice Day a universal celebration'. The Colonel asked for sympathy for the children of the devastated areas and said that, at the end of 1918, '290,000 French homes were completely wrecked and 230,000 were partially wrecked. France was already coming back. Of her devastated areas one third was yielding a two thirds crop.' While distributing relief in Lille, after the Armistice, he 'found children aged 10 years wore the same size clothes as Melbourne children of six years'.

On the eve of the 1921 Armistice Day, in New South Wales, the *Gosford Times & Wyong District Advocate* wrote about its ladies and the poppies they would sell that day and the next day. Red Cross Society members, together with the members of the Gosford Sub-Branch of the RSSIL, would be selling 2,750 poppies that day and the next. They must have had two sizes to sell because the prices were quoted as being one shilling and one shilling and sixpence. Some Red Cross women were also going to sell poppies from a stall that day, Thursday, which was Market Day.

'Madame Guérin, the "Poppy Lady"' was mentioned, along with duplicating all the facts about Canada encouraging Australia to adopt her idea, her credentials, Colonel Moffat being her representative, and so on.

And so Armistice Day dawned in Australia and Poppy Day went hand in hand with Warriors' Day, on that commemoration day.

In her *Synopsis*, Anna wrote of the success in 'England' being greater than that in Canada but she followed that with: 'the success has been also very good in Australia.'

Distributed poppies were described in Australia's newspaper the *Northern Miner* (Charters Towers, Queensland) on 11 November 1921: 'The stalks of the poppies bore little strips on which were printed the words: "Decoration Day 1921. The poppy lady from France."' This distinguished Anna Guérin's French-made poppies from any forgeries.

His Majesty the King wished for a two-minute silence throughout the Empire on Armistice Day, at 11.00 am. He requested 'a suspension of all normal business, works and locomotion throughout the British Empire'.

This was carried out with reverence, generally, although there was criticism in Newcastle, NSW. The *Sun* printed its public condemnation that the city did not observe the silence: 'When eleven o'clock struck there was nothing to distinguish the day from any other, except that a fairly large crowd of people gathered at the post office.'

The Rev. Joseph Lundie, of Hamilton Presbyterian Church, spoke of 'the relief it was when the armistice was signed'; that it was 'fitting that they should turn aside for a few minutes to pay a tribute of gratitude to the men who fought'; and 'that it was also owing to the courage and endurance of our men that the crowd was there that day'.

'It is a strange thing in a city like this, that we cannot give up our business for a few minutes,' he continued. 'It only shows that we have short memories. We sent them away with flags waving and bands playing and our promises that we would look after them and their dear ones. We welcomed them when they came back, but eaten bread is soon forgotten, and I am afraid that that is the case with many.' The article went on in a similar vein.

In contrast, a more positive story came out of Broken Hill, NSW. At the Returned Soldiers' Hostel, returned soldiers all stood to attention for the two minutes as one of their own, Bugler Nankivell, sounded the 'Last Post'. Business employees stopped, and all work in the Government and public offices was suspended for the silence.

Flags flew from Broken Hill's Court House, Town Hall, Returned Soldiers' Hostel, and so on. All the trams stopped running. After the silence and onwards, into the night, many women and a number of schoolgirls sold the French-made poppies.

Emotive newspaper articles abounded on Armistice Day. One came out of Tasmania: 'BUY A RED POPPY. A DIGGERS' APPEAL.' Major Burford Sampson, DSO, MID, a respected Launceston man and soldier, wrote of the 'mighty debt' owed to France and that, by buying a red poppy that day, it would 'liquidate a trifle of that same debt'.

Major Sampson had been wounded twice in Gallipoli and, in France, he was wounded a third time. He knew of no more deserving cause than to help the French children in the devastated war zones.

'Though three years have come and gone since "cease fire" sounded, and the mighty armies of men ceased to kill and destroy, the need for help and succour is great, particularly amongst the little ones.' He recounted how a lady friend who was working with returning refugees had written to him recently, from the Somme.

With still an urgent need for warm winter clothes for boys and girls, the friend had asked for old woollens. She was substantiating everything that Anna had said, and was saying elsewhere still, and what Colonel Moffat was saying on her behalf now.

Sampson implored:

> Just picture these children, living amongst grass-grown ruins in hastily constructed wooden dwellings or iron huts. Winter is coming on, and those of us who wallowed in the Somme mud and morasses of the salient in winter time know how cruel and bitterly cold it is. Imagine little girls and boys, too, often ill-clad and not on a plentiful army ration, cheerfully carrying

on amid the depressed gloom of a village lying from year to year in ruins, overgrown with weeds. The French children have scarcely any toys. Some have never seen one.

Major Sampson felt that, between the Australian returned soldiers and the 'noble band of womanhood who did such wonders for them, during the long years of the later bitter struggle', the day would raise a considerable sum for the children of the devastated areas of France.

He concluded: 'So buy a poppy, fashioned by the hands of some little Annette or Jeanne, and help those who help themselves. Kind deeds speak louder and last longer than brave words.'

The Bass Strait had been no obstacle in the Australian poppy campaign. The Tasmanian State secretary of the RSSIL had written to all councils on the Island, explaining the reason for the appeal for funds on Armistice Day: half of proceeds would be devoted to the veterans and the balance would be handed to the French Committee to restore the devastated regions of France. It was requested that no other appeals be made on that day.

Large places, such as Hobart and Launceston, promoted well. In addition to the women's groups already mentioned, helpers in Hobart and Launceston came from Chalmers Church Women's Guild, the Free Kindergarten, St Andrew's Guild, and Invermay Girls' Friendly Society. Launceston was conscientious enough to name the many women who had helped in its sale, and the organisations they represented.

Smaller places in Tasmania, like Zeehan, did not need an army of women. Zeehan only needed a brigade, a Girls' Brigade. Miss Campbell organised the distribution of only 200 poppies.

Australia was falling into line with every one of the allied nations, or so it was written in the *Eastern Districts Chronicle* of York, Western Australia:

> when in every town in America, Britain, France, Belgium, and Portugal, replicas of these flowers will be sold and worn as emblems to the memory of those who fell in the Great War ...
>
> Only those who saw what France and what the kiddies of France suffered, have any idea of the extent of their need, of their bravery, and above all of their love for 'the Aussie, the Digger.'

Sometimes, newspapers felt it was more important to name-drop the French President's wife Madame Millerand rather than mention Madame Guérin, the 'originator' of the idea: 'FIRST LADY OF FRANCE AIDING IN "WEAR

A POPPY" MOVEMENT ... The "Wear a Poppy" movement is sponsored by The Children's League in France of which Madame A. Millerand, wife of M. Millerand, President of France, is the leader.'

Readers of Launceston's *Daily Telegraph* were informed that this French League was a 'clearing house for the relief work among the children of the war-torn areas, and the funds raised through the sale of poppies will go toward the amelioration of the condition among these children and the wounded veterans.'

The article stated Madame Millerand had been the 'heart and soul in relief work ever since the declaration of war' and she had 'given many hours daily to it and still continues to do'. Those sentences could have easily described Anna Guérin.

After Armistice Day, Colonel Moffat sailed from Sydney on board the ship *Makura* on 15 November, heading for Auckland, New Zealand. The New Zealand veterans had decided to wear their poppies for the next Anzac Day – 25 April 1922. By 13 December, he was back in Sydney, from Wellington, New Zealand.

Anna wrote of sending Colonel Moffat to South Africa, but the only proof is an application he made whilst in Melbourne. On 23 December, he applied at the American Consular Service to have South Africa added to his passport. It was from Melbourne that Colonel Moffat sailed for South Africa on 31 December, on the ship *Aeneas*.

Anna would eventually write to Mr G. J. C. Dyett, Federal President of the RSSIL. It would be announced that he had heard from 'Madame E. Guérin, known as the "Poppy Lady" of France, who initiated the Inter-Allied Poppy Day scheme'. Anna wrote that the statement of expenditure and receipts that she had received in connection with the Australian Poppy Day, held on Armistice Day, 1921, 'was the clearest she had received in connection with any campaign.'

Anna added that France was grateful 'for the genuine interest of the great country of Australia towards France and her poor women and children for whose relief the money was raised.'

Only New Zealand kept the faith with Anna Guérin for longer than Australia. The country continued to be loyal to French-made poppies up to and including 1926. Anna not being able to visit Australia did not mean the Australian veterans' passion for her French-made poppies waned. Anna showed her appreciation by writing and sending flags.

From 1 November 1922, newspapers like Tasmania's *Launceston Examiner* informed their readers that the President of the Returned Soldiers' and Sailors' Imperial League of Australia had heard from Madame Guérin, 'organiser of the French Children's League'. Conveyed were her thanks for the sale of poppies in 1921.

'Until recently,' Anna wrote to the President,

> I thought it would be possible for me to come to Australia this year and to assist you in the success of your second Poppy Day. It is with many regrets that I have been compelled to postpone this pleasure. I know that your people and your organisation would have welcomed the news that I should have brought from those flanders fields which your gallant soldiers so nobly saved.

Anna continued it would have been a 'great joy' and a 'privilege' to her to speak in Australian schools and to Australian veterans. However, it was necessary for her to visit other Allied nations instead, 'lest they should forget that they must have in memoriam their Poppy Day on the anniversary of armistice'.

She was able to advise the veterans that the Children's League was offering a service where poppy wreaths could be laid on graves of brave relatives. It had evolved after requests had been received from many mothers and dependants in Canada, England, and the USA.

It was suggested that all nations' returned soldiers' organisations could make this known to parents of deceased soldiers, buried in France. Some might wish to subscribe to a wreath. Wreath-laying would be carried out by local committees, according to instructions.

The mayor of the nearest town or village to any given cemetery would send a certificate to each relative or business that subscribed, in order to prove that a wreath had been placed on the grave. To enable a mayor to send the certificate of wreath-laying, the name and address of the subscriber must be given, along with the name, rank, number, unit of the dead soldier, and the name of the burial place.

Anna wrote: 'Our idea is that all such wreaths should be placed on the graves during the week of Easter. The poppies are made of waterproof material so that the wreaths shall last a long while.' Traditionally, Easter was a time when the French visited their relatives' graves in cemeteries, so it was a logical period to choose.

Anna had obviously been communicating with the RSSIL beforehand because she was able to state that it had given this idea its 'wholehearted support'.

In her letter, Anna described the wreaths on offer as being made of eleven large poppies and two palm leaves, 10 inches in diameter, and noted that the cost of a wreath would be £1 each. Relatives and businesses wishing to have a wreath laid were asked to send their payment to the RSSIL State Secretary or to their local Branch Secretary.

Poppies were little silk replicas again, in 1922 – 'the exact replicas in size and colour of the poppy that blooms in Flanders fields, and were made by the war widows and orphans of the devastated area in France' – although there were a few poppies left over from 1921. The *Register*, of Adelaide, South Australia, wrote on 9 November 1922: 'To buy them will be greater than a duty – a service of honour.'

Between 3 and 6 October 1923, the seventh RSSIL annual conference took place. President H. S. Humphrey drew attention to a bannerette and flag Madame Guérin had sent them. They were her 'token of gratitude for the money raised for the widows and orphans of French soldiers on Poppy (Armistice) Day'. The conference resolved to write a letter of appreciation to her. It was also decided that, if Armistice Day fell on a Sunday, Poppy Day would be held on the Saturday.

Anna was still publicly recognised as the '"Poppy Lady" of France, who initiated the Inter-Allied Poppy Day scheme'. In 1924, Anna was still selling poppies to Australia. She was the 'French lady, Madame Guérin' who 'conceived the happy idea of despatching to Australia thousands of poppies for sale, the proceeds to be devoted to giving attention to the graves of Australian soldiers in France'. An article in the *Warwick Daily News*, of Queensland, informed readers that not every Australian town had been participating in Poppy Appeals.

On 8, 11, and 20 November 1924, Warwick held its first Poppy Days, organised by the Warwick branch of the RSSIL ladies' committee, with assistance from the Women's Club and the Country Women's Association. The call went out to Warwick residents: 'Remember those lonely graves among the poppies in Flanders. Buy a Poppy.'

In 1925, Australia was still as one with New Zealand, because it was remaining loyal to Anna Guérin and France.

When Lord Stonehaven, Governor-General, and Lord Stradbroke, State Governor of Victoria, placed a wreath of poppies at the memorial tablet of Melbourne's Anzac House, it was one made by the children of France. Although there was a feeling emerging and increasing that it was necessary to put Australia and Australians first, it was not only about poppies.

Protestations had begun to be openly aired. On 13 February, that year's RSSIL annual state conference began in Brisbane. Local members attended, as well as from other states.

Brisbane's *Telegraph* reported on the considerable amount of business being discussed, all with the welfare of Australian returned servicemen in mind. One of the matters was the 'influx of aliens'.

For instance, the Prime Minister had stated that preference should be given to returned servicemen being employed on the Brisbane-Kyogle railway line but the conference shared its 'extreme disappointment' that he had failed to keep his 'definite promise'.

As far as the Poppy Appeal was concerned, all those present at the conference, bar one dissenting voice, resolved to 'emphatically' protest against funds being sent to France after each poppy appeal.

The funds were probably only the wholesale cost that Anna charged, rather than anything more, but it was still a case of money going out of Australia. It was noted that 'Madame Guérin had sent out ten thousand poppies which arrived on an already overloaded market'.

As in other First World War Allied countries, Australia had a lot of destitution amongst its returned servicemen. There had to be frequent appeals in newspapers for funds, second-hand clothing, and goods. It was quoted that some Brisbane sub-branches of the League were refusing to take part in the Poppy Appeal, in its present form.

In contrast, Melbourne's *Herald* positively described the appeal as one 'for the children of the devastated areas in France' and it extolled the virtues of the 'memorial emblem of the Allied Nations in the Great War'. They 'bloomed freely' on its streets on Armistice Day.

The paper told of 150 poppy sellers, each one a 'relative of a soldier'. More than 20,000 1/- poppies and 2,000 2/- poppies were issued. It was written that 200 2/- poppies only took an hour to sell at the Tattersall's Club. But not all Melbourne's money was going to France because a portion of it went to the Memorial Building Fund of Anzac House and the public 'responded whole-heartedly'.

In 1926, ahead of Armistice Day, national newspapers tried to allay any fears by stating that, although the country was still using French poppies obtained from Madame Guérin, only a proportion of sales would go to benefit the orphans in France. Enthusiasm was still there, though, for Poppy Days. Ladies from metropolitan sub-branches were ready to do their bit and many in the country had ordered supplies.

It was still expected that all in the dominion would 'show their appreciation of the sacrifices made by Australian soldiers in the great war and wear a poppy in remembrance'.

It was not until 1927 that disabled Australian veterans, together with their dependents, were reportedly making remembrance poppies to be distributed on the streets of Australia. Shepparton's *Advertiser* reported poppies as 'silken' and 'beautifully got up'.

Finally, Australia had politely said, 'So long/au revoir, Madame Guérin.'

Anna's representative Colonel Samuel Alexander Moffat needs more written about him. He was an enigma initially, just as Anna Guérin had been. American newspapers referred to him as only 'Colonel Moffat', because his reputation needed no further introduction, and some of the Australian newspapers referred to him as 'Alfred'.

As is often the case, good things come to those who wait and to those who dig deeper. Eventually, Colonel Moffat was identified. Samuel Alexander Moffat was Scottish, born at Comely Park Place, Gallowgate, Glasgow, Lanarkshire, on 24 January 1878. His parents were blacksmith Samuel Moffat and his wife Margaret, née Robertson.

On 20 September 1888, Samuel arrived in the USA with his mother and sisters Agnes, Jeanne, and baby Mary. They arrived on the SS *Waldensian*, which had sailed out of Glasgow. Their father Samuel had obviously gone ahead, to find work and somewhere to settle down. They were like many families who went seeking a new life in the New World, including members of my own Scottish family.

On 12 September 1906, Samuel married Ethel Busiel Morse, on Rhode Island, New England. Samuel's occupation at the time was the YMCA General/Financial Secretary in Saratoga Springs, NY State. When the 1910 Census took place on 15 April, Samuel was with Ethel in Brooklyn. His occupation was a Social Worker for the 'Boy Scouts of America'. He became a nationalised citizen later in the year, on 5 August.

By 1911, Samuel was Business Secretary for the organisation and, a year later, he was 'National Field Scout Commissioner'. Samuel would tour different states, visiting scout councils.

After the USA entered the war, Samuel Moffat publicised the fact that Boy Scouts were selling $300,000 worth of War Savings Stamps every day across the country, in addition to selling millions of dollars' worth of Liberty Bonds.

At some point, Samuel Moffat became an American Red Cross Commissioner. When the Armistice was signed, he was the Red Cross Director General of Belgium Staff. Later that month, he went to France, where he 'had the privilege of helping to entertain and clothe 10,000 stunted children at Lille'. Between August 1919 and April 1920, he was American Red Cross Commissioner to Hungary, with the rank of Major.

A year after the Armistice, conditions were still dire in Hungary and Samuel was in charge of feeding 33,000 children, over half of them in Budapest alone. He expected that number to increase to 100,000.

He announced in the Budapest newspapers, near the end of 1919, that he would give gifts of babies' clothing, milk, soap, handkerchiefs, and in addition a sum of 100 crowns in cash to each mother having a baby born on New Year's Day in Budapest. These were all scarce. That day, 180 babies were born, so Samuel was poorer by 18,000 crowns, and all the commodities promised, but he wrote home saying it was worth it.

From March 1920, Samuel Moffat's passport shows he began to visit many other countries in Europe. From the American Red Cross headquarters in Paris, he reported that 97,000 children were dying of starvation in Vienna, Austria. Of 187,000 children, from 6–14 years of age, only 7,000 were sufficiently nourished. Samuel now held the rank of Lieut.-Colonel.

Between April and July 1920, Samuel was the American Red Cross Commissioner to Serbia. By June 1920, he was referred to as 'Colonel' when he, other Red Cross personnel, and British observers had to be rescued from the Ukrainian region, where the Bolsheviks were advancing against the Poles. It was far too dangerous to stay and be shot at.

Samuel had become a well-travelled and high-profile individual within the American Red Cross. On 24 November 1920, he arrived in San Franscisco, via Germany, Suez, and the Orient. Within four months, he was working for Anna Guérin's Children's League.

In her 1941 *Synopsis*, Anna Guérin wrote about her Children's League headquarters moving to New York in 1921, adding 'Colonel Moffat, the right hand of Mr. Hoover (while he was feeding Europe) arrived at that time from Austria and joined us in our work.'

Ahead of the US Memorial Day, he took part in promoting the wearing of the poppy. He described the conditions he had seen during his Red Cross service. He considered France had suffered more than any other place in Europe, with the exception of Poland and Vienna.

Then, as we know, Samuel sailed from Canada in August, taking Anna's 'big idea' to Australia, New Zealand, and South Africa. After all those duties, he finally travelled to Europe in February 1922, 'in transit [to] France'. But Samuel had found love in New Zealand and returned.

Obviously divorced, he married fellow divorcée Louis Gordon Hawkins (née Kettle) in 1923, in New Zealand. Louis had three children by her first husband and all took the Moffat name. Before the end of the year, Louis and her children had arrived in Seattle, Washington State to make a home with Samuel.

Samuel was an Organizer for Churches and Colleges in 1930. In 1940, he was Field Director of the National Conference of Christians and Jews. He was known as 'a forceful speaker with an enlightened attitude on inter-religious matters'. Two years on, Samuel was found employed by the New York fundraising firm of Ward-Wells Dreshman.

Colonel Samuel Alexander Moffat died at home, in Bergen, New Jersey, on Saturday, 16 October 1948. A private funeral service and commitment was held at the Snell Funeral Home, Ridgefield Park, New Jersey on Monday, 18 October at 10.00 am. The death notice, appearing in the newspaper, stated 'Kindly omit flowers'.

An obituary for Samuel Moffat appeared two days later, in The Record, of Hackensack, New Jersey. The headline read: 'Moffat, Scouting Organizer, 70, Dies In Ridgefield Park. Aided Red Cross In World War I, Introduced Poppy, and Helped Y.M.C.A. Over The Top.'

Samuel's obituary documented a little of his life. 'Madame A. Guerin, The Lady of The Poppy' was mentioned, not as 'the Originator of the Poppy Day', but more as a partner to Samuel. One paragraph inaccurately read:

> The poppy was adopted by the Veterans of Foreign Wars and the American Legion mainly through the efforts of Moffat, and they organized their first campaign for relief funds through the sale of poppies.

However, this was 1948. By now, Anna's true part in history was forgotten.

Chapter 10

New Zealand and the Poppy

Colonel Samuel Alexander Moffat arrived in Auckland, New Zealand at 7.00 am on 27 August 1921, from Vancouver, Canada. He sailed into port on the ship SS *Makura*.

New Zealand newspapers reported, as Australian ones had, on Colonel Moffat's reputation. It may have just been ten days before he was off again, going across to Australia. Before he left, he attended a meeting of the Standing Sub-Committee of the Dominion Executive of the Returned Soldiers' Association in Wellington.

At that meeting, Colonel Moffat submitted a proposal that, along with the American, Canadian, and British servicemen, New Zealand's Returned Soldiers' Association adopt the red poppy of Flanders as its national memorial flower. The matter was discussed and it was agreed that Colonel Moffat would compose a 'a detailed memorandum on the subject for submission to the Dominion Executive'.

What Colonel Moffat wrote to the Association was published. He began at the beginning: 'Shortly after the armistice was declared, the French Children's League was started in France for the amelioration of conditions among the children of the devastated regions.'

He wrote of the League's adoption of the poppy as its memorial flower and of the invitation, being extended to all veterans of the First World War Allied nations, to adopt the 'poppy of Flanders field' too.

Colonel Moffat mentioned the 'great war poem':

> No emblem typifies the fields whereon was fought the greatest war in history nor signifies so truly as the last resting place of those who died for the liberty of mankind. The poppy of Flanders' fields was known throughout the world in connection with the war, and was immortalised in Colonel McCrae's great war poem, in which appear the lines: 'In Flanders' fields the poppies grow Beneath the crosses row on row.'

Colonel Moffat said his mission to New Zealand and Australia was 'to extend a cordial invitation to the Returned Soldiers' Association to join in wearing the poppy'.

He told of a large quantity of the replica poppies being made by the war widows and orphans of devastated France; that the poppies were shipped from Paris to the participating countries; that every Government had rescinded the duty on the poppies; and steamship companies and railroads, regardless of ownership, had granted free transportation.

It was planned, he said, to sell the poppies 'at a nominal price' in all local associations throughout New Zealand and, after campaign expenses had been deducted, the monies would be 'divided in part' between the work of Madame Guérin's Children's League and relief of New Zealand's wounded soldiers or any other relief the association choose.

It was also agreed at the meeting that if Colonel Moffat could return to New Zealand before 26 September, he would be invited to attend the Dominion Executive meeting on that day and discuss the proposal.

Colonel Moffat did make the meeting, the Dominion Executive of the NZRSA officially passed a motion and adopted 'the red poppy as the memorial flower of the fallen of the Allies'.

It was agreed a sub-committee would be set up to work out the details and choose a suitable day. Significantly, at this early stage in the proceedings, the option of either Armistice Day or Anzac Day for wearing the poppy replicas was considered.

Anzac Day had been commemorated annually on 25 April since 1916. It was just as significant a date as Armistice Day, for remembering when Australian and New Zealand Army Corps landed at dawn on the Gallipoli peninsula on 25 April 1915.

On 1 October, Colonel Moffat was off again to Australia, leaving Auckland on the *Riverina*. Arriving on the 5th, he remained in Australia for just over a month. On the evening of 10 November, Colonel Moffat boarded the *Makura* and headed back to Auckland.

An event that occurred on board the ship was written about in several New Zealand newspapers. A small sale of the 'red poppy of Flanders' raised £40 among the passengers. Half the proceeds were donated to the Australian Returned Sailors' and Soldiers' Imperial League and half to the New Zealand Returned Soldiers' Association. With Colonel Moffat on board, surely it must have been instigated by him,

And so Armistice Day 1921 dawned in New Zealand. There had been no national Poppy Drive in the country. By now, it was obviously common

219

knowledge that French-made poppies had not arrived for the Armistice commemoration. It could be assumed there were no poppies on lapels, but the newspapers suggest otherwise.

The *Western Star*, of Riverton, in its Armistice Day issue, reminded readers of the Armistice being signed, just three years past, and told how the NZRSA had adopted the poppy as a memorial flower, 'in memory of the fallen'. It added: 'Replicas of flowers were sent to New Zealand and in the large centres were worn as a proud adornment.' That suggests that some poppies had arrived, only enough for limited distribution.

From 23 November, over a few days, articles appeared in newspapers, in both the North and South Islands. Being identical, the source had to be official, which gives them credibility.

Articles stated the NZRSA had received 'about 200,000 artificial poppies'. Was the *Western Star* correct and the 'proud adornments' were French-made poppies on some New Zealanders' lapels on Armistice Day, but not in a 'National Poppy Day' sense?

Napier, on the North Island, had expected a shipment of poppies before Armistice Day but its Poverty Bay Herald reported 'the flowers had not arrived' so 'willing workers, realising the worthiness of the object, set to and made 2000 little poppies'.

Public response was so great that more had to be made: 'The sight of so many little red poppies in Napier on Friday was evidence of the feeling of the British people towards the widows and little orphans of France, who sacrificed and suffered so much during the great war.'

Regardless of availability of any poppies, the New South Wales State Government had refused to allow the sale of the League's red silk poppies on Armistice Day. That initial decision 'raised the ire' of the Sydney Returned Soldiers' Association, and it passed a resolution expressing disapproval of the State Government's attitude. The Mayor of Sydney was asked to convene a public meeting of protest.

That said, on Armistice Day (also known Warriors' Day), there were some poppies sold in Sydney. This sale raised £1,125 but that was only part of the £6,000 raised by the characteristic street stalls. Proceeds went to the Warriors' Fund, to help unemployed returned servicemen.

On 11 November, Ashburton's *Guardian* newspaper, on the South Island, wrote of 'how liberty was saved and tyranny overthrown'; 'the qualities of courage and self-sacrifice, exemplified: by New Zealand's soldier sons, those who gave their lives and of their physical manhood that freedom, liberty and justice might not vanish from off the earth'; and 'remembered the sacrifice of our manhood and how the burden was lifted at the signing of the armistice'.

In Ashburton,

> all movement ceased for two minutes, and a quiet hush fell
> over the town. The thoughts of most were somewhere away
> overseas, straying amid the French fields of scarlet poppies, or
> lingering on a sandy beach lapped by the blue Mediterranean.
> Beautiful is the sentiment of remembrance; grand is the
> thoughtful moment wherein we recall those who went hence
> for the honour of their country.

The observance of Armistice Day was 'simple, but wonderfully expressive.'

Greymouth, South Island, had no official service but it observed two minutes' silence, flags flew at half-mast, and muffled church bells rang.

At Parliament House, Wellington, the Members rose at 11.00 for the two minutes' silence. Afterwards, the hymn 'O God, Our Help in Ages Past' was sung by Members and the members of the public who were in the galleries. To conclude, a verse of the National Anthem was sung.

In Christchurch, it was reported that Viscount Jellicoe was a VIP at its Cathedral service; the two minutes' silence was observed and all movement stopped. When Colonel Moffat visited Christchurch, he said the Flanders Poppy was an appropriate emblem of the fraternity which existed between the Allied armies. Perhaps the city saw a homemade poppy on the lapel, perhaps it would have to wait until Anzac Day for a French one.

Now, before the end of November 1921, it was being reported that 'Poppy Day' would be held before Anzac Day, in order that 'the flower may be worn as a memorial on that solemn and historic anniversary' and part of the proceeds would go to children of devastated northern France, and part to the RSA 'to form the nucleus of a fund for the immediate relief of soldiers and their dependants'.

Anna wrote in her *Synopsis*: 'The New-Zealand Veterans have chosen as Memorial Day, Anzac Day, beginning of April. But every thing shows that it will be also a success.'

In December, an article in *Quick March*, the national paper of the NZRSA, challenged Lieut.-Gen. Sir G. M. Macdonogh (KCB, KCMG, Adj.-Gen. to the Forces). As he unveiled Beaumont College's War Memorial, in Windsor, England, he 'expressed a regret that the poppy had been chosen to commemorate the fallen, as it was a pagan flower representing oblivion'. The article's retort was: 'the important thing about the poppy is not what the ancients thought about it but what the moderns think about it. The poppy may have been an emblem of forgetfulness of long ago; today it is an emblem of remembrance.'

Colonel Moffat left Wellington, New Zealand and arrived in Sydney on 13 December. On 31 December, he sailed out of Melbourne on the *Aeneas*, with England being his final destination.

En route, he would rendezvous with South African veterans. He had been a very successful ambassador for Anna and La Ligue. But he would return to New Zealand for love, as we have seen.

And so 1922 arrived and the New Zealand Returned Soldiers' Association began looking forward to their poppy campaign ahead of Anzac Day in April that year.

A Press Association telegram, out of Wellington on 31 January, enlightened New Zealanders through many local newspapers to the fact that the New Zealand RSA had 'received 396,000 artificial poppies from France for distribution throughout the dominion prior to Anzac Day, on which anniversary they will be sold and worn in sacred memory of those who fell in the late war.' Part of the proceeds would go to women and children of devastated France and part would be kept by the RSA, to benefit returned service men in need of assistance.

New Zealand's shipment route of poppies would have been no different to any other Allied country: a sea voyage from France to a British south coast port, then a train journey to the port of Liverpool, ahead of loading on an assigned ship, for its final destination.

Of course, by not adopting Anna's 'Inter-Allied Poppy Day' idea until 26 September, the NZRSA was late ordering poppies. Put that together with the fact that New Zealand was quite isolated, with a lengthy sea voyage, and it was probably inevitable that the poppies could be late arriving. It would have all impacted on when they were delivered.

On 13 February, Melbourne's *Evening Post* printed a 'Customs Duty Refunds' list of goods entering the country and the French-made poppies featured in this list: 'Flanders poppies to be sold for the benefit of wounded soldiers in New Zealand, £376.'

Anna always secured free entry into a country for her poppies, with free movement within it. Custom Refund entries for the French poppies coming into New Zealand are found in 'Appropriations Chargeable on the Consolidated Fund and Other Accounts' files.

New Zealand's official line is that the ship carrying Anna's poppies to New Zealand 'arrived too late for the scheme to be properly publicised' before Armistice Day on 11 November 1921. The Remembrance Poppy event was postponed until close to the New Zealand Anzac Day commemoration, which would be on 25 April 1922.

So, when did the aforementioned 396,000 poppies arrive? Do the telegram of 31 January and the Customs Refund for the poppy cargo, thirteen days later, suggest the poppies arrived in January 1922? My hunch is that the 1922 poppy order was shipped to New Zealand on the SS *Westmoreland*.

During research, the *Westmoreland* ship loomed out at me. The poppy-ship had to sail out of Liverpool and the *Westmoreland* did, on 3 December 1921, laden with a cargo of 6,000 tons for New Zealand – for Auckland, Wellington, Lyttelton, and Dunedin, in that order. The ship arrived at Auckland on 10 January. On 21 January, it arrived in Wellington, from Auckland. That port's consignment was 1,800 tons. It left Wellington on 26 January, to discharge the rest of its 'Liverpool cargo' at Lyttelton and Dunedin. On 31 January, the NZRSA sent out a telegram – 396,000 artificial poppies had been received.

During research, I communicated with commemoration organiser and author Gavin Marriott. He recalled once seeing, a long time ago, the name of the ship that brought the cargo of poppies to New Zealand. When I asked him if the name *Westmoreland* jogged his memory, he replied: 'The name of the ship I saw mentioned resembled a place name around here. We have a suburb in Christchurch called Westmorland. It had several syllables, I do remember.' Time will tell if the hunch is correct.

After Colonel Moffat's promotion of Anna's 'Inter-Allied Poppy Day' idea and its adoption by the New Zealand Returned Soldiers' Association, the country's women began doing all in their power to get people in the mood ahead of Anzac Day.

In Wellington, the Returned Soldiers' Club women decided to hold a street day on 3 March. It was called the 'Diggers' Poppy Day' because the Flanders Poppy was 'so well known and associated with soldiers' efforts all over the Empire'. As well as street stalls, a 'plain and fancy-dress masked ball' and a light supper were organised. All manner of 'handsome articles' were raffled. A sum of £505 16s 9d was raised and it all went towards benefiting the country's returned men.

It was reported in February that every branch of the NZRSA and every member of every branch was 'expected to work hard for a successful Poppy Day, just before Anzac Day this year'.

The RSA had 396,000 lapel red poppies at 1/- each to dispose of. There were also 4,000 large poppies, at 2/- each, suitable for wreaths. The latter, it was suggested, could be placed on war memorials by children. It was reported, of every 1/- raised, 3d would go to the French children and the remainder would be used by the NZRSA.

From this point, the NZRSA set about promoting its Poppy Day which, generally speaking, would be held on 24 April, in order that the poppies could be worn the next day – on Anzac Day.

In Christchurch, Mrs W. Wood of the Womens' National Reserve Committee was to be in charge of the city's Poppy Day, as she was meant to be on Armistice Day. She described the split of proceeds in fractions: one-quarter would go to the poppy makers in France and the remainder to the NZRSA. New Zealand women were getting organised.

The NZRSA Standing Sub-committee recommended, after expenses, the remainder should go soldier unemployment relief during the winter. If all poppies were sold, a lot of money would be raised.

It was noted there were indications that many 'comrades will have a struggle to exist during the winter'. It made it known it 'would work in conjunction with the Public Works Department and local bodies in all cases', regarding the allocation of funds in a district. Ultimately, though, headquarters had the final say.

There was a priority to receiving relief, and the descending order was: married men with children and no pension; married men with children and a small pension; married men and single men with dependents; and single men without dependents.

Some places had had the opportunity of seeing examples of poppies early. District secretaries had to allocate the poppies to various towns. To give you two examples, 122,100 poppies were allotted to Wellington City and 65,600 poppies were allotted to Otago and Southland. The large poppies were sold to the 300 largest schools in the dominion for school wreaths. Twelve poppies were required to make a wreath and, at 2/- each, that amounted to 24 shillings (or £1 4s) for a wreath.

On 10 March, the NZRSA printed a rallying article in its *Quick March* paper: 'Wear a Poppy. Every man, every woman, every boy, every girl, who will wear a R.S.A. poppy on Anzac Day will be showing a badge of remembrance.' It described how buying a poppy would help 'children in the war-ravaged parts of France' but would also assist unemployed returned service men by providing helpful and good work. These men and their dependents were suffering much hardship, as they were in the other Allied nations.

Six weeks previously, sixty-three Returned Soldiers' Association branches had been sent a circular letter by the general secretary. They were each encouraged to be 'the most energetic'; to 'show the best results'; and 'take the most pains to get the help of all willing works'. Basically, branches were set a challenge to be the most successful, to show the best results.

The NZRSA had also been in contact with 240 townships that had no branch, to the same end.

Because of physical environs, not every community could take part in a Poppy Drive. For instance, the County Council of Akaroa and Banks Peninsula announced in late March that it was difficult to make such a collection because of the scattered nature of its district.

In mid-April 1922, the *Auckland Star* and other newspapers printed a short paragraph, mentioning 'Madame Guérin, "poppy lady of France" and director of the French Children's League'. Anna had cabled the General Secretary of the NZRSA, notifying him that she was forwarding six French flags. These should be awarded to the six towns selling the most poppies during the poppy campaign.

For the NZRSA, Poppy Day was 'the biggest philanthropic social' campaign it had ever undertaken. By 19 April, there were between 1,000 and 1,200 unemployed ex-servicemen throughout the country and the veterans' organisation was attempting to obtain work for them.

This would relieve general unemployment. The NZRSA made a point of explaining that, apart from deducting expenses, it was not retaining one penny of the money raised. The funds raised in a district were to be spent on relief work in that district.

A couple of days before the Poppy Day, the public cry went out to all: 'Do not step aside from a collector on Poppy Day, and thus side-step your responsibilities to the men who offered their lives upon the altars of duty, home and country.'

And so 24 April 1922 dawned. It was New Zealand's first National Poppy Day, on the eve of Anzac Day. Preparations had been made in nearly every city, town, and village in the country, where it was feasible to do so, and success was generally expected.

The NZRSA publication *Quick March* furnished readers with many facts about the first New Zealand Poppy Days, once they had all been gathered together: 'New Zealand held out a collective hand for the bright red Poppies of Remembrance.'

The allotted 14,000 large poppies were not enough to meet the demands from the schools and other institutions desiring them for wreaths. Likewise, even though there were nearly 300,000 smaller buttonhole poppies, there were not enough. Telegrams poured into the NZRSA requesting more poppies, but none remained.

In Wellington, the poppy sellers were so busy that people had to queue and wait their turn. By the middle of the afternoon, the city's quota was sold out. Many searched the streets but the answer was the same everywhere – 'sold out'. Many were too late and disappointed. It was reported that takings for Wellington City were £1,427, and the amount for the city and its environs totalled £1,723.

Aucklanders had never responded so generously to such a sale and the 'Poppy Lady from France was the city's favourite'. There were poppy-decorated stalls and, by midday, it was rare to see anyone who was not wearing the 'red emblem of the battlefield'. Not taking the district into consideration, Auckland City raised over £2,000.

Christchurch held two Poppy Days – 21 and 24 April. The grand sum of £1,081 9s 3d was raised. At the end of April, there were over sixty unemployed returned service men registered with the Repatriation Department of Christchurch.

New Zealand's ladies' committees 'rallied enthusiastically' and, as a result, sales elsewhere were comparable. As a result, the NZRSA concluded it was a sale which would 'live long in the people's memory'. So many people helped that it was not possible for the NZRSA to thank everyone for their 'kindly remembrance of comrades to whom unemployment has brought anxiety and suffering.' It was believed New Zealand's total would reach that which the NZRSA had striven for.

It was in the run-up to the next year's Poppy Day, in *Quick March* again, that a veteran recalled the first real Flanders Poppies he had seen. Under the pseudonym of 'Sniper', he recalled this poppy campaign.

He described a scene that could illustrate the 'In Flanders Fields' poem at Houplines, a suburb of Armentieres. He described the Communication Trench 'threading its way through the beautiful orchard en route to the front line. This orchard was dotted all over with beautiful red poppies, and so were some "Tommy" graves in the orchard.' Seeing the poppies, he had thought they were typical of a soldier's life: 'to-day red and full of life, to-morrow a thing of the past, destroyed by War's deadly blast.'

He added it was a 'happy choice that Madame Guérin ... chose the little red poppy as the emblematic flower for sale through the Allied countries on Armistice Day. The "Poppy Lady of France" had hundreds of thousands of miniature silken poppies made in Northern France ... a vast amount of organisation had to be carried out ...'

'Sniper' considered that opinion was unanimous afterwards: the campaign was the most successful and best organised ever witnessed in New Zealand. He noted that 245,059 small poppies were sold at 1s each, with 15,157 large ones sold at 2s each. The NZRSA had striven for between £10,000 and £12,000 but had collected £13,166 overall.

'Sniper' stated that '£3694 15s 7d was cabled to France to relieve distress in the battle-areas ... Madame Guérin disclosed the pleasing fact that New Zealand was highest in her contributions to the widows and orphan children who had helped to make the poppies.'

He noted that '£9471 went to the New Zealand Returned Soldiers' Association – never in its history had "so much practical good been done" during the winter of 1922.' It was noted payment was not given as dole money but paid as wages for useful work carried out in towns and cities. Married ex-servicemen were assisted first and, he added, 'many a wife must have blessed the successful "Poppy Day"'.

'Sniper' stated that 'in every hamlet, town, and city' there was insufficient supply of the beautiful large poppies in 1922.

Before Armistice Day, 11 November 1922, the *Northern Advocate* (of Whangarei) highlighted the fact that Anna had written to the NZRSA. She was introduced as 'The Poppy Lady of France, for such is the official title of the organiser of the Poppy Day movement'.

The 'organiser of the Poppy Day movement' had written offering her thanks to the NZRSA and the New Zealand people for the success achieved on April's Poppy Day.

'Allow me to thank you,' she wrote, 'for all your amiability to Colonel Moffatt, my representative, who had the great chance to come first in your beautiful country.' It reads that her charity had received a letter from the NZRSA, giving details of the 'wonderful ways the campaign was handled, so that so many flowers were disposed of in such a small country'. She asked to be excused for the delay of her letter and that they accept her expression of deep gratitude. She had been travelling in 'European allies' in relation to their Poppy Days on Armistice Day.

She personally acknowledged receipt of the money raised in New Zealand. By using so many of the Flanders Poppies, 'so many poor widows and orphans of those battlefields' had been helped. She was proud to state that, proportionately, New Zealand had obtained the 'best result for the first year of Poppy Day'.

Anna referred to this second year, when Poppy Days would take place again elsewhere, on Armistice Day. England and Scotland, she said, were hoping to sell 15 million poppies. France and 'little Belgium' would also use 'this simple and magnificent way to honour the dead'.

She wrote of hoping to sail to Australia and New Zealand at the end of November but she had been forced to 'postpone this pleasure'. Instead, she was sending six military fanions, or flags. She asked that they be given to NZRSA posts, to schools or clubs, which helped the most during the Poppy Day – a small token of remembrance and gratitude.

It appears, in another letter, that Anna had drawn attention to another option for a family's or an institution's act of remembrance. Anna wrote that many mothers had asked how much it would cost to have a wreath of poppies placed on a loved one's grave.

In order to economically meet this demand, Anna was proposing to each Allied veteran organisation, as part of their publicity for their campaign, the following idea: a beautiful wreath would be placed on every New Zealand soldier's grave, on Anzac Day. The cost would be 10 shillings; 2s and 3d should be kept by the veteran organisation, the remainder would be sent to Anna's League.

Anna suggested that banks and other large establishments would surely send the price of one or several of these wreaths, if they had lost employees. She was going to ask Colonel Moffat to write to the RSA.

Like Australia, New Zealand continued to be loyal to Anna Guérin, to the 'Poppy Lady of France'. In actual fact, New Zealand was the most loyal of all the First World War Allied nations.

It is just a question of including snapshots for the next few years. In 1923, a Customs Refund entry for the poppies, for the year ending 31 March 1923, has not been discovered.

From an article by 'Sniper' again, in April 1923, we learn that 250,000 small poppies and 30,000 large ones were ordered for that year and each district had received these several months prior. 'Sniper' told of the noble work 'this humble scarlet little flower' was doing for all the Allied nations' returned soldiers.

The article mentioned the work of 'noble lady-sellers for without them last "Poppy Day" would not have been the success it was'. It told of the movement being born in France, which had spread. Information 'from Madame Guérin (the founder)' disclosed how New Zealand's contributions were the highest made to the widows and orphan children who had helped to make the poppies.

In Ashburton, some of the poppies were made by the local Returned Soldiers' Association because there had been a limited supply coming from France. The foreign silk ones were disposed of at 2s 6d each and the locally manufactured ones were sold at 1s.

In a *Quick March* issue of 10 May, an article extolled the virtues of the New Zealand women, noting that no history of the Great War could be complete without mentioning their service. It acknowledged the 'noble service performed by' New Zealand women, which was continuing during the Poppy Days: Auckland's total collection was around £1,600; Wellington made about £1,000; and Christchurch raised £853. The day had been another success. It was stated that 'it is difficult to see how it could be otherwise.'

'Sniper' stated that no other country could claim to have had the same contributions, per head, that the New Zealand collectors had achieved since 1915 – the date of the country's first 'Street Days'.

Ever since then, 'Sniper' stated, come snow, rain, or shine, New Zealand ladies had 'never deserted the cause of our soldier boys'. The same women could be found standing on the same street corners collecting, many times a year: 'Zealandia's ex-soldiers will never forget the practical patriotism and kindness meted out by our women-folk.'

In Christchurch, demand for poppies was so great that the supply was exhausted shortly after midday. In November, the Canterbury District Executive reported it had received a beautiful French flag from 'Madame Guérin, the "Poppy Lady of France"', for presentation to the branch of the Returned Soldiers' Association selling the most poppies prior to Anzac Day. It was decided this flag should be presented to Christchurch.

The Customs Refund entry for 'Flanders poppies to be sold for relief of unemployment in New Zealand', for the year ending 31 March 1924, was £919. That year, 'Lest We Forget' became the poppy tag trademark.

Christchurch held its Poppy Day on 23 April 1924. Determined to win the flag again, the cry went out: 'no effort will be spared to this end'. An offer was received by the Christchurch organising committee from members of the Woman's Christian Temperance Union to assist and it was decided to 'solicit the aid of the large schools and colleges, several of which had been very helpful last year'. Sadly, though, the French flag was not retained by Christchurch – I have no idea who did win it.

On the day, Ashburton raised £80 but that was down on the 1923 result. Apart from the fact that the supply of poppies was lower than usual, there was a reduction in the price – 1 shilling each. Auckland raised approximately £994. Wellington sold 15,000 poppies.

In June 1924, a Mr R. B. Jacobs was a critical voice at the RSA Conference. He did not see a connection between Anzac and poppies: 'It seemed wrong to benefit financially by appealing to people's sentiment.'

He suggested Poppy Day be held on or near Armistice Day and Messrs R. B. Bell and E. F. Andrews spoke against. The Rev. J. McCrae argued Anzac Day and poppies went together. 'People like to buy poppies and wear them on Anzac Day, and if Poppy Day was altered to Armistice Day the sale of poppies would go down by 50 per cent.'

Mr W. E. Leadley moved not to have the custom interfered with and it was his motion that was carried. As for the Poppy Day proceeds, it was agreed local branches should control the distribution, with special attention being given to the relief of unemployment and the New Zealand Veterans' Home, at Auckland.

Some places, like Dunedin and the Otago province, held a Poppy Day on 1 August, to commemorate the tenth anniversary of the start of the First World War. Dunedin raised a gross £492 10s.

The Customs Refund entry for 'Flanders poppies to be sold for relief of French war orphans and the children of the devastated regions in France, and for the benefit of returned New Zealand soldiers', for the year ending 31 March 1925, was £1,748.

Poppy Day, in 1925, was on 22 April. In Christchurch, the ladies were anxious to regain the French flag, presented by 'Madame Guérin, the "poppy lady of France"', that had once been theirs.

A poppy seller, at Napier, met one man who received a poppy but refused to give more than 3d. The seller 'argued and urged in vain' and handed back the man's 3d. Her example of generosity then stirred him: he pocketed it and offered 6d instead.

Again, no Customs Refund entry for poppies has been discovered for the year ending 31 March 1926. Poppy Day was held on 23 April. In Auckland, it was reported that Poppy Day proceeds would be 50 per cent to the Veterans' Home; 30 per cent to disabled soldiers; and 20 per cent to the relief of needy cases among fit men.

In Christchurch, it was noticed that few people in the city were not wearing a poppy on their lapel. Energetic collectors raised at least £650. Dunedin also had a successful Poppy Day, raising at least £630 – that was nearly £100 more than in 1925.

The Customs Refund entry for 'Flanders poppies to be sold for relief of French war orphans and the children of the devasted regions in France and for the benefit of returned New Zealand soldiers', for the year ending 31 March 1927, was £353.

Poppy Day was held on 22 April. In Auckland, apparently, there was 'an abundance of red poppies to sell' and it had not been necessary to order a supply of poppies made in France that year.

The Customs Refund entry for the year ending 31 March 1928 was £143: 'An amount of £143 paid as duty on artificial poppies imported from England by the R.S.A. for sale to the public is to be refunded.'

In 1928, French-made poppies were still sent to New Zealand. However, some were bought from the workers of the British Legion, namely the Poppy Factory. They were a small variety, and well finished. The local executive also had some large poppies made in Auckland.

The Customs Refund entry for the year ending 31 March 1929 reads 'A refund of £215 is to be made by the Customs Department in respect of the duty on artificial poppies imported by the R.S.A. for Poppy Day sales.' The year 1929 was the first that New Zealand's poppies were not made in France. All the poppies were purchased through the British Legion. Again, an order would be fulfilled by the Poppy Factory. New Zealand had said 'kia ora/goodbye, Madame Guérin'.

The Customs Refund entry for poppies, for the year ending 31 March 1930, reads: 'Artificial poppies to be sold for the benefit of returned New Zealand soldiers – £310.'

Poppy Day was held on 24 April and 30,000 poppies were delivered from the Poppy Factory, in Richmond, Surrey. 'Buy a poppy for remembrance and wear it on Anzac Day.'

The year 1931 was the first in which disabled veterans in New Zealand made the poppies that were distributed on the streets of New Zealand.

In 2022, the *New Zealand Post* worked together with the veteran organisation Royal New Zealand Returned and Services' Association New Zealand and commemorated Anna Guérin's role in history. On 2 March, *New Zealand Post* Collectables released First Day Covers to celebrate 100 years of the New Zealand Poppy Appeal.

One First Day cover envelope held Anna Guérin's image and the five commemorative stamps each held a different poppy, including one of the Guérin French-made ones.

Chapter 11

Other Allied Nations and the Poppy

I know nothing about Anna's work in Belgium and Italy, although in her 1941 *Synopsis*, Anna Guérin wrote that she went 'to England, Belgium, Italy' herself. I make no apology for believing she did visit Belgium and Italy.

I accept all Anna wrote because, by the time I came to read her words, I had already proved approximately 99 per cent of its contents. I knew she had accurately recalled her work, as I had evidence to prove it. If I had to guess, I would say Anna probably visited Belgium and Italy after going to France in September 1921, to prove her credentials to the British Legion.

Cuba adopted the poppy prior to the 1921 Memorial Day. Anna's sister Yette and friend Blanche left Canada for Cuba on 6 December 1921 from Canada's east coast Port of Saint John, New Brunswick. They sailed on the steamship SS *Sicilian*, taking with them large cases of poppies. It was hoped the poppy campaign in Cuba, a country 'where such a tag day was practically unknown', would prove successful.

A National Poppy Day Committee was established to organise the arrangements. It is assumed Yette and Blanche stayed with a 'Madam La Bouse, Prado 36, Bajos, Havana'. They named her as the friend in the country 'whence alien came', for the ship's manifest. Surely this Madame La Bouse was on the Cuban Poppy Committee.

Yette and Blanche were in Cuba during December 1921 and January 1922 – 'during the Christmas season'. Returning to the USA, Yette's final destination was Indianapolis and Blanche's was New York City. In early February 1922, Anna wrote: 'My two delegates arrived yesterday from Cuba where they have sown the Idea splendidly.'

Both Yette and Blanche would have felt at ease visiting Cuba because it was intrinsically linked to France. French immigration into Cuba had begun in the eighteenth century and increased in the nineteenth century, when there was an influx of French people into Cuba from Haiti. Haiti was a French colony and indigenous people were fighting for their independence.

Santiago de Cuba was a popular place for French people to make their home and some settled so well that they married Cubans. Anna Guérin's first husband's Rabanit family is a good example of this.

In 1898, Cuba became a United States protectorate. Although it gained its independence in 1902, a bond with the USA remained. Like the USA, Cuba had initially been neutral but, when the USA declared war in 1917, Cuba followed. Cuba seized the German ships which it had been allowing to dock there and it became a base to protect the area from U-Boat attacks. Many Cubans enlisted, but were never needed.

There was an American Legion Post in Cuba so it must have helped promote the 'Poppy Day', but I know nothing more of it.

I can write a little more for South Africa, although a lot of it may be considered tenuous. Anna wrote that she sent Colonel Moffat, her representative, to Natal and the proof is with his passport. He applied for an amendment on 23 December 1921, whilst staying at the Menzies Hotel in Melbourne, to have South Africa added to it.

Colonel Samuel Moffat sailed for England, and France thereafter, from Melbourne, Australia, on the ship *Aeneas*, after his campaign down under. It could have been around 23 January 1922, when the ship docked at Port Natal (Durban), where he must have met South African veterans. Research has not brought forth any details.

There is a South African connection to the origin of Armistice Day's two-minute silence. This is South African Sir Percy Fitzpatrick, who lost two brothers in the First World War.

The late Ken Gillings, of Pinetown, South Africa (South African Military History Society) personally drew my attention to Sir Percy Fitzpatrick. On 27 October 1919, Sir Percy suggested a minute's silence be observed every year on Armistice Day. Sir Percy's suggestion was put through to King George V.

However, there is one other gentleman who should be mentioned. In the same way I have credited Anna Guérin with her place in the 'Remembrance Poppy Day' history, there is this little-known Australian who made a contribution to the history of this remembrance custom of silence. This is Edward George Honey (1885–1922).

Honey was working at London's *Evening News* in 1919. Under the name of 'Warren Foster', he wrote suggesting something of the same: 'five minutes of bitter-sweet silence' for 'national remembrance'.

Edward Honey found the 1919 Armistice Day to be more like a celebration than a commemoration. His idea was considered, though, because he attended a private rehearsal at Buckingham Palace. The final decision was a compromise because it was felt five minutes was too long but, to be fair to Edward Honey, Sir Percy's one minute was too short.

Sir Percy received a letter from Lord Stamfordham, stating the King 'ever gratefully remembers that the idea of the two minute Pause on

Armistice Day was due to your initiation – a suggestion readily adopted and carried out with heartfelt sympathy throughout the Empire.' I do not know if Edward Honey received a comparable letter.

The final proclamation made by the King was: 'That at the hour when the Armistice came into force, the 11th hour of the 11th day of the 11th month, there may be for the brief space of two minutes a complete suspension of all our normal activities... so that in perfect stillness, the thoughts of everyone may be concentrated on reverent remembrance...'

Two minutes of silence continues to be observed at the eleventh hour on Armistice Day, but it now features at other acts of remembrance.

Anna Alix Boulle may have been French, but France only took the poppy to its heart for a short time. Although France showed solidarity with the USA in 1920, and with other First World War Allies in 1921, by wearing the Flanders Poppy, it was the cornflower (le bleuet) that was adopted as the country's memorial flower, for Armistice Day lapels.

The young French Army recruits who arrived at the Front in 1915 were given the nickname of 'les bleuets' because of their new 'blue horizon' coloured jackets. Thus, there was a personal connection with the dainty blue flower that grew profusely on the battlefield, alongside the poppy.

As with the Flanders Poppy emblem, it was the fairer sex that was responsible for les bleuets/cornflowers being worn on lapels in France. Two French women are credited with this idea – widow Suzanne Lenhard and Madame Charlotte Malleterre.

Suzanne Lenhard was the Matron of l'Hôtel des Invalides hospital, in Paris. Her husband had been killed on the Massiges battlefield, in the Marne département. Charlotte Malleterre was the wife of General Gabriel Malleterre and her father was General Niox, the Commander-in-Chief of l'Hôtel des Invalides.

The two women set up workshops for maimed, facially disfigured French veterans ('les gueules cassées') of l'Hôtel des Invalides. These men made les bleuets/cornflowers as an aid to their rehabilitation and as a means of earning money of their own. Such an occupation was the only thing many would have been able to cope with.

Anna, and her French lecturing companion Monsieur Oliveau, of course, knew the plight of all of their ex-servicemen and it spurred them on to fundraise in the USA for some of them.

It is recorded that those first 1918 cornflowers had petals of cloth and stamens of newspaper strips. To begin with, these cornflowers were sold mainly within the capital city of Paris, and not on a national scale.

'La Fédération Interalliée des Anciens Combattants' (FIDAC) was formed in 1920, in France. Here, we remember that Anna's American ally, the American Legion's National Commandant Col. Frederick Galbraith, and the British Legion's George Crosfield, were strong advocates of it.

We get an indication of the empathy, perhaps even the conflict of interests, surrounding the cornflower and the poppy, from a Bulletin of l'Association générale des mutilés de la guerre (the General Association of the Mutilated of the War) in early 1935.

A French delegate at the fifteenth annual congress of FIDAC, held in Westminster, London, in September 1934, wrote about what he or she had learned. Written in French, the piece was entitled 'Le bleuet de France' ('The cornflower of France') and was 'described with great emotion'.

I cannot say if this particular delegate was male or female. Women were in attendance, certainly, as members of the FIDAC Auxiliary.

The delegate described how the British chose the poppy as its 'emblem of recognition and remembrance' to honour its dead and, on 11 November, 'there is not a Briton who does not have the honour to pin on his chest this poppy of memory. In addition bouquets, wreaths of poppies are deposited at the foot of all the memorials and on grassy slopes.'

Small wooden crosses were described, which were placed in front of London's Westminster Cathedral, each decorated with a poppy – 'these crosses evoke distant cemeteries'. It was added that all towns and colonies 'imitate this symbolic homage'.

This fundamental question was asked:

> Given such a touching example of fidelity and gratitude, how would the French remain insensitive? And why should we not imitate our English friends?
>
> By putting all of us on the same emblem, veterans and young people, we would gather all our hearts in a common sense of pride for our past and faith in the future
>
> This is the thinking of the Auxiliary members of FIDAC advocating the adoption of a national flower of remembrance.

I interpret those three quotes to be what some Auxiliary members of FIDAC thought and felt, when they were considering a national flower of remembrance – they were advocating the poppy.

But cornflowers were chosen, which were also wild flowers of the battlefields – 'A modest flower, a perennial flower, which already symbolised the heroism of our young classes on the eve of victory.'

The Women's Auxiliary of the FIDAC approached the National Institution of Invalids and asked them to make the flowers. FIDAC suggested creating the cornflowers from tissue paper.

Thus, the cornflowers were made by these victims of war, 'with materials provided by the city and its colonies'. The cornflower had not yet been officially adopted as the memorial flower of France.

In 1928, the French Republic's President, Gaston Doumergue, had granted his patronage to the creation of le bleuet. In 1934, 'le Bleuet de France' charity was officially formed. It was appreciated that the success of 'le Bleuet de France' rested solely with the generosity of the people.

Mr Rivollet, the French Minister of Pensions, between 1934 and 1935, granted his patronage to the charity too. He set the example by laying a wreath of 'le Bleuet de France' cornflowers, on 1 November 1934, at the tomb of the Unknown Soldier, under the Arc de Triomphe.

Another fact recorded is that for the 1935 anniversary of the Armistice, a grass field was created under the Arc de Triomphe. It was 'available to the public' to receive crosses and it was called 'Champ d'honneur et du souvenir' (Field of Honour and Remembrance). To copy Great Britain, with a field, is a compliment.

The delegate concluded: 'Success and long life to "Bleuet de France" which will take root in our soil and its colour in our sky.'

The 1935 bulletin concluded by mentioning badges and wreaths could be ordered at 'le Bleuet de France' workshop, at 6 Boulevard des Invalides, Paris VIIme, via Mrs S. Lenhardt, President and Director.

The 1935 bulletin stated les bleuets were sold with 'an official tri-color stamp' which was copyrighted, perhaps including the paper tag. After the Second World War, authorisation was given to sell them on 8 May, the anniversary of the 1945 'Victory in Europe' date, too.

A 1960 'le Bleuet de France' pamphlet refers to the year before. Collections of 8 May and 11 November 1959 were quoted as being 'only a total of 190 million old francs'. The word 'only' is significant because of the following paragraph (read '1921' for '1924'):

> The aim sought is to give Bleuet collections the importance acquired by our British friends with the 'Flanders Poppy'. Indeed, the 'British Legion' created in 1924 puts the 'Poppy of Flanders' on sale in all the British Empire on the day of the 11 November and the benefits are returned to the social works of this organisation. To Great Britain and the various territories

of the Empire, this sale annually records about 950,000 pounds sterling, i.e. more than 1,200 million old francs.

The success of the Flanders Field Poppy was obviously something the 'Office National des Anciens Combattants et Victimes de Guerre' was, and still is today, trying to aspire to with the cornflower.

Among the numerous tasks assigned to the ONACVG, from 1917, is the one relating to assisting les Pupilles de la Nation. These are orphans adopted as wards of the French nation, as their fathers were 'morts pour la patrie' – they had died for the fatherland.

Gustave Alfred Léon Baussart was one of these Pupilles de la Nation. He was born on 18 September 1907, at La Gorgue, Nord. He was a son of Alfred Léon Baussart and wife Marie Louise Roussel. After marrying, they lived in Hulluch, Pas-de-Calais. Alfred was a mine worker at Lens, 6.4 km south. Alfred and Marie had another son but he died.

Alfred was a Reserve Infantryman and, at the outbreak of the First World War, he was immediately recalled to duty but 'died for France' on 6 October 1915. Like most civilians, Gustave and his mother became refugees, after surviving the German invasion of October 1914, on the Nord-Pas-de-Calais Front, between La Bassée and Lens.

They found sanctuary 420 km away in Tours, which lies between the rivers Cher and Loire. It was in Tours, on 26 December 1919, that Gustave became a Pupille de la Nation. He had suffered a lot during the war years, including receiving shrapnel wounds.

Marie and Gustave did not return to Hulluch, because it was totally destroyed. Instead, they made their home in La Gorgue, 21 km away. Gustave had a family of his own but his life was very unsettled. He had many jobs: gardener, wooden shoemaker, and so on. He spent a lot of time in hospital. Gustave died on 5 December 1973, aged 66.

In 1959, the ONACVG provided assistance to 130,563 pupils. There were 66,519 boys and 64,044 girls, with many nearing the age when a choice of a career or trade had to be decided. The 'Ministere de l'Education Nationale' awarded scholarships and the ONACVG provided additional assistance.

The ONACVG and 'le Bleuet de France' organisations merged in 1991. Today, together, the same ethos as the Royal British Legion and other ex-Allied nations' comparable veterans' associations exists.

Where the ONACVG differs from other veteran associations is that it is run by the French government. The ONACVG is not a charity as the Royal British Legion and the Australian RSL are, for instance.

In the same way the artificial poppies have provided funds, and still do, for several veteran organisations, les bleuets raise funds for the ONACVG (National Office of Veterans and War Victims) to support the 'most unfortunate' veterans, veterans' widows and orphans, and victims of war. Today, children of victims of terrorism are also supported.

Apart from offering an artificial flower for a donation, be it a poppy or a cornflower, all offer additional items relating to their own particular memorial emblem. This marketing strategy produces additional funds, which continue to be necessary to continue their good work.

Anna Guérin may or may not sympathise with the commercialism of the emblems, as we experience it today. In her *Synopsis*, she referred to taking poppies to the USA in March 1923, and observed that in America: 'already the Flanders Poppies had been commercialised and it is why the NATIONAL POPPIES DAYS have never had the tremendous success that they have had in the ENGLISH EMPIRE'.

But, in that era, 'commercialism' relating to the poppy was simple – it meant that poppies were not being made by disabled ex-servicemen, they were being made by professional artificial flower manufacturers.

Anna's fears of commercialisation with the Flanders Poppy were generally unfounded. With les bleuets, though, the manufacture was outsourced to China for many years. However, in 2014, the First World War Centenary year and eightieth anniversary of the foundation of 'le Bleuet de France' charity, it was announced that its artificial cornflowers would be made in France once again, by French veterans.

When needs must, Anna did what she felt was required of her, in order to assist and relieve the plight of women and children of the devastated areas of France. Her 'big idea' was a progression of that, to help Allied veterans at the same time. Veteran organisations today have to do what is required of them and the demand remains ongoing.

Chapter 12

Life After the Poppy Campaigns

In the USA, the American Legion's reneging and readopting of the poppy had begun a slow decline in its relationship with Anna, but the Legion still purchased her poppies in 1923, 1924 and 1925 and she attended the sixth American Legion National Convention at Saint Paul, Minnesota, held between 15 and 19 September 1924.

A newspaper described Anna as 'Mme. E. Guérin, Vallon, France, founder of the Interallied Poppy days'. During the Convention, Anna presented Iowa's State Commander, Bennett A. Webster, with a French military flag. It is deduced it was for selling a significant number of her poppies. Certainly, Iowa City smashed all local records in its 1924 sale.

Additionally, it is recorded Anna sent the Secretary of the Commercial Club in Lincoln, Nebraska, Walter Whitten, a box of about '200 silk poppies of exquisite French workmanship' which she wished to be given to the American Legion with her compliments. Walter had been Anna's friend since she first visited Lincoln in June 1918.

Anna had taken her 'Inter-Allied Poppy Day' idea to complete fruition. As one 'pro-Anna' American newspaper stated in October 1924, 'Now each country claims the right to make its own poppies.' New Zealand and Australia would be the exceptions to that rule.

Anna could begin to think of herself as something more than the selfless humanitarian she had been for much of her adult life. On average, she travelled to the USA once or twice a year and stayed for six months or three months respectively. Leaving from Vallon, her visas were issued in Marseille and she sailed from there; from Paris, visas were issued in that city and she sailed from Cherbourg or, very occasionally, Le Havre.

On 2 December 1924, Anna returned to New York for six months. Apparently, she was there to lecture before American Legion Posts. I have no idea what that involved.

In 1925, Anna made various visits to the USA. One reason for a visit, or visits, must have surely been connected to the aforementioned order of poppies for the Massachusetts American Legion.

Another reason was that New York's Mrs Mercedes McAllister Smith had re-emerged again that year. On 10 June 1925, Mrs Smith began another lawsuit in the Supreme Court for $200,000 damages for slander. She claimed that, on 9 May 1921, the five defendants 'conspired to injure her good name'.

She stated she had been an official of the 'American and French Children's League' in 1921, tasked with raising funds for the charity. After refusing to join the new 'American-Franco Children's League', a malicious French government report was circulated about her. As a consequence, President Harding had 'neatly severed' his link to her.

Mercedes Smith said it gave her much physical and mental distress. After two days, defendants were reduced to: George W. Burleigh, attorney; Barry N. Smith, head of the National Information Bureau; and Anna. It was reported these three offered no defence and this 1925 court jury awarded her six cents in damages, but Judge Delehanty called it 'obviously inadequate' and set another trial for October 1925.

Anna was back in Vallon for 29 July 1925, when her daughter Renée married Paul Marcel Rolland Guibal at Vallon Town Hall. Aunty Yette (Juliette Boulle) was able to be present at the celebration too.

Groom Paul Guibal had been awarded the Croix de guerre medal and, at the time, was the 'Inspecteur des finances' in Madagascar. Renée and Paul's official family home was 5 Square Charles Dickens, Paris. It was commonplace that on marriage, a woman gave up any occupation she had – for Renée, this meant ceasing medical studies.

Paul's work continued to be in Madagascar and, in January 1930, he was appointed Madagascar's Central Financial Administration Deputy Director but, within two months, Paul died on the Island.

To digress, one of two 'major witnesses' was a very interesting family friend – American William Henry Hunt. At the time, William was the United States of America's Consul in Saint-Étienne, Loire, and had been since 1906. Prior to that, William had served in Madagascar.

William had arrived there in 1898, as Clerk/Assistant/Vice-Consul to Mifflin Wistar Gibbs, US Consul in Tamatave, succeeding Gibbs when he retired in 1901. William married Gibbs's daughter in 1904.

Anna and William remained friends after they had left the Island. For instance, in 1912, Anna gave a 'Conférence' on Madagascar in Vallon and William chaired it. Described as an 'eminent compatriot' by the mayor, Anna gave her lecture to an audience of 300.

William had said he knew of Anna's role as 'founder and director of schools when few Europeans still dared to live' in Madagascar. He went on to give 'a dazzling testimony to endurance, self-sacrifice, and courage not expected there, our countryman claiming that she [Anna] was a matter of admiration for all the settlers'.

William was born into slavery, in Tennessee. He was of mixed race and his father was a white slave owner. William's slave mother also had white heritage. In reality, he was quarteronne, as Renée and Raymonde were.

By 1925, the American Legion's 'Poppy Lady of France' had been superseded by Auxiliary member Moïna Michael. The Legion nominated its 'Poppy Lady of America' for the 'Pictorial Review Prize': 'for the woman who made the greatest contribution to civilization that year'.

The $5,000 prize went to Mrs Cora Wilson Stewart, pioneer leader of pro-literacy 'Moonlight Schools'. Anna's total management of US Poppy Days, her originating the 'Inter-Allied Poppy Day', and the Legion's previous commitment to her no longer meant anything to the Legion.

Anna may have routinely returned to New York after Renée's marriage but there is no record of an outward or inward voyage.

One problem I have encountered in my research is that not every ship's manifest is online. However, I know Anna was in Vallon for the 1926 Census, taken on 7 March, but back in New York again on 14 April, 'staying for Decoration Day', at least.

Possibly, Anna arrived for a particular court judgement, relating to Mrs Mercedes McAllister Smith. It would seem that Judge Delehanty's trial had not materialised. Instead, on 30 April 1926, the Appellate Division of the Supreme Court of New York, which deals with appeals to reverse decisions, reinstated the June 1925 jury decision of six cents' damages to Mrs Smith. This was an end to the whole issue. Who knows if all this had an impact on Anna's social reputation?

Back in France, Anna's daughter Raymonde was married on 28 November 1927 to André Julien in Paris. André Julien taught at the city's prestigious l'Ecole Polytechnique. By all accounts, he was a 'charming gentleman and a very good amateur painter'. According to the social structure or class prestige of the time, Raymonde and Renée had both made 'beaux mariages'. After the wedding, Anna went straight to Cherbourg and sailed for New York on 30 November.

On 15 February 1928, and on 22 January 1929, Anna sailed from Cherbourg to spend six months in the USA as a lecturer. Only one piece of evidence has been found to show she was doing some lectures – an article noted she had cancelled a lecture in St Louis, Missouri.

By 1930, Anna was a grandmother of two – one each from daughters Renée and Raymonde. Both families lived in Paris and Anna continued to have a foothold in both the United States and France.

By now, Anna's sister Yette was settled in New York. Yette loved America. When she became an officially naturalised American citizen in 1931, her occupation was vice-president of Anna's antique business. Yette was unmarried and, for a long time, she shared an apartment with friend Blanche Berneron, who had also helped Anna with Poppy Days. Blanche would become naturalised in 1935.

In 1930, the American Legion awarded Georgia's Moïna Michael its Distinguished Service Medal, 'for her part in originating the Memorial Day poppy program'. When, once, Moïna had only appeared briefly in American newspapers, the Legion was recognising and promoting her, for the work she was doing in its name now.

This was also the year Moïna Michael's name began to seep into the newspapers of First World War British Empire nations. Moïna's name began replacing Anna's when, in reality, Moïna had played no part in the Empire's adoption of Anna's 'Inter-Allied Poppy Day' idea.

In New Zealand, 'Madame Guérin'/the 'Poppy Lady of France' was known whilst she supplied poppies from 1922 to 1928. But, two years later, in 1930, although Anna is mentioned in articles, it is second to Moïna.

The first mention found of Moïna in British newspapers was in November 1933, when Princess Elizabeth, the British heir apparent, was sent a 'Poppy Lady' doll, which had been modelled on Moïna.

The doll was sent by the children of Georgia, USA, to commemorate British General J. E. Oglethorpe's landing on Georgia soil in 1733.

Moïna was described as the 'Poppy Lady of Georgia', the person who gave Americans the idea of wearing a poppy in their buttonholes, and who had been honoured by the American Legion. Announcing Moïna's death, in 1944, the British public were being told she was the person who originated 'Poppy Day'. She was the 'Poppy Lady of the World'. It is wagered that few Britons knew any different.

In Australia, there was no word of Moïna found until the very end of 1938, when a Queensland article told how she was responsible for the American Legion adopting the poppy, that her 'poppy plan' had spread around the world, and that Anna was 'the agent'. No more mention was found until the announcement of Moïna's death, when all of Australia was being told she was the originator of Poppy Day.

It seems the Canadian press had not printed anything on Moïna until the worldwide press release announced her death. Additionally, one British Columbia newspaper duplicated a New York article. It told of Moïna originating Poppy Day, carrying it to the American Legion in 1920, and, because of all the money raised across the world during Poppy Days, the article's New York author believed Moïna had done more for disabled veterans than anyone else. Honours included ones from Georgia: a marble statue and a Distinguished Citizen of Georgia citation.

The article stated Moïna had finished her annual poppy anchor only two weeks previously, to honour the servicemen lost at sea. It was 7ft long and held the 300 paper poppies she had made. It is acknowledged that Moïna's advocates are proud of her dedication to the poppy, Georgia, the USA, and American Legion veterans.

During the 1930s, Anna ran an antique shop – her French Antiques Company, at 160 East, 56th Street, New York City. In the States, she was referred to as president of this company. I believe Anna had her antiques shop from 1932 and into the 1950s, at least. The 160 East, 56th Street building was multi-occupancy; for instance, there was the Maragliotti Studios, which was considered 'one of the world's most famous and mural and decorative painting firms'. It carried out artwork in many prestigious ecclesiastical, public, and private properties.

Also in the building was A. Bleiman, an auctioneer, but, when Anna and family members sold antiques, Parke-Bernet Galleries, Inc., at 30 East 57th Street, New York, was instructed. It was approximately a quarter of a mile or three blocks away. It was described as 'America's largest fine art auction house'. Sotheby's bought it in 1964.

Shipping items, large or small, from France into the USA would not have fazed Anna. She would have gained so much experience from negotiating and shipping millions of poppies around the world.

Yette and Blanche supervised the shop. Both were the managers of an antiques business in the 1940 US Census. They lived only six minutes from the shop. This was still the case for Yette in the 1950 US Census.

A week ahead of 1931's Memorial Day in the USA, the Alaskan *Fairbanks Daily News Miner* printed the most extraordinary article mentioning Poppy Lady Madame Guérin and her Poppy Day idea.

It is extraordinary inasmuch as an American Legion Auxiliary member wrote it. She wrote the truth about the origin of the Poppy Day, at a time when the Legion was writing Anna out of history. It had been a while since Anna and the American Legion were mentioned together.

Miss Elizabeth Louisa Spencer took part in an American Legion Auxiliary essay contest, on the 'Origin and Meaning of the Poppy'. She was an exception to the rule because she publicly mentioned Anna.

Elizabeth began by writing about 'one million of the cream of American manhood' going to France. Many did not return but, of those who did, they carry the memories of a 'horrible, screaming hell'. She wrote of the battlefields 'brilliant with acres of red popies [sic], fertilized with the blood and flesh of our boys who are still "over there"'.

> The wearing and making of the red poppy is a beautiful idea, originated by E. Guérin with the assistance of Commander Galbraith. Madame Guérin was impressed by the fact that the French peasants believed that the poppies of Flanders were thick and red because of the blood spilled there; the theory of the peasants is undoubtedly true. She thought that it would be a great honor to the dead for each person to wear a poppy on his breast the Saturday before Memorial day.
>
> At the Annual American Convention of 1921, Madame Guérin assisted by Commander Galbraith persuaded the head of the organization to accept the idea of having our wounded make these poppies. The idea was accepted and each year the output of poppies increased. Accordingly, each year the funds of the American Legion increased. The red poppy has now become almost universal among the nations of the Allies. The output of the British Legion is from twenty to twenty-five million each year, and this legion claims that most of the support comes from the red poppy sales.

She wrote much more about wounded soldiers and logistics surrounding distribution, with no mention of Moïna Michael.

On 9 December 1932, Anna set sail from New York for France. That same day, the *Gazette*, of Montreal, Canada, reported her being a passenger on board the White Star liner *Majestic*, bound for Southampton and Cherbourg: 'Madame Guérin is going over to France to purchase $50,000 worth of the finest vintage of champagne in France, which she intends to bring back to the United States to sell in the event of the 18th Amendment being repealed.'

The 18th Amendment of the US Constitution had been ratified in January 1919, establishing the prohibition of intoxicating liquors in the USA. If Anna did buy champagne, she had to wait for the Amendment to be repealed on 5 December 1933 to ship it over to America.

By December 1938, Anna had begun naming daughter Raymonde as her next of kin on ships' manifests, not her husband. Her granddaughter confirmed that Anna and Eugène Guérin did separate. This would have occurred at some point after the 1936 Census was taken, when both were resident in Vallon.

On 3 September 1939, Great Britain, France, Australia, and New Zealand declared war on Germany. On 19 May 1940, Anna sailed from Saint-Nazaire on the ship *Champlain* for New York. The USA would become her safe haven for the whole of the Second World War.

Her daughters and other family members had to endure the enemy occupation of the country. Family lore tells of Renée being conscripted into working in a German-run hospital somewhere near Arras.

It may have been more luck than judgement, but Anna left before the Germans entered Paris on 14 June. She and her fellow passengers were lucky to sail safely away when they did because, a month later, on 17 June, the British ship RMS *Lancastria* was sunk off the port.

The ship had been diverted to Saint-Nazaire to evacuate British Army, Navy, and Air Force personnel, diplomats, and civilians, ahead of the Germans closing in to capture the port. Accusations suggest the news of the sinking was withheld initially, because of the horrific loss of life.

The exact numbers for the loss of life involved is not known but reports state it was far more than the *Lusitania* and *Titanic* losses put together, which are estimated to be a total of around 2,700. Some estimates are as high as 4,000, with less than 2,077 surviving. It is called 'the forgotten tragedy' of the Second World War.

As a result of the German occupation of France, Anna stayed in New York. She spent the war years in America. During this time, if Anna's name was mentioned within American newspapers, she was referred to as 'Madame A. Guérin, of New York'.

In 1940, Moïna Michael, the 'Poppy Lady of Georgia', was 71 and getting her affairs in order. Her thoughts had turned to writing her autobiography, along with her version of the Flanders Poppy history, and she began seeking permissions ahead of its publication in 1941.

Telling her story, Moïna declared she made a pledge to always wear a poppy in remembrance after reading John McCrae's 'In Flanders Fields' poem on 9 November 1918. It is accepted this was the day she wrote her poem, which Anna complimented her on in 1919. I could describe it as Moïna's epiphany moment.

This occurred while Moïna was working as a war-effort volunteer at the YMCA's 25th Conference of Overseas War Workers/Secretaries at Columbia University, New York. A teacher by profession, Moïna had worked there for two months as an assistant secretary.

At her own expense, Moïna set floral arrangements to create a homely environment for the YMCA men and some gave her a donation as recompense, in gratitude for this gesture. Moïna went out and purchased some artificial poppies with this unsolicited donation and gave the poppies out to some men on her return, in remembrance. This has been written into history as the first sale of a Flanders Field Memorial Poppy.

I cannot look beyond one definition of 'sale', 'the exchange of a commodity for money'. I cannot help but see the event as two separate incidents, rather than one exchange. I know others will disagree.

On 13 December 1918, Moïna signed a contract with Publicity Agent Lee Keedick. Her 'Flanders Fields Memorial Poppy campaign' began. As I see it, Moïna wanted to nationally promote the Flanders Poppy as a memorial emblem but, initially, as a 'Victory Emblem'.

Moïna had two 'Victory Emblem' designs patented on 11 March 1919. One design was discarded: a Torch of Liberty and a Flanders Poppy entwined, with a vintage cavalry sword. The one chosen was the identical torch and poppy but minus the sword. This was the one Moïna offered 'for adoption as a national victory memorial'.

Surviving evidence shows Moïna worked hard promoting this. She and Lee Keedick put their faith in this 'Victory Emblem', which was to be displayed on flags, badges, etc. Initial success was shortlived, though and Moïna herself eventually admitted it was 'disappointing'.

On 31 January 1941, Moïna sent a joint letter to Anna and her sister Juliette, at 686 Lexington Ave., New York City. Apparently, Anna was difficult to find. I believe the last contact between the two women would have been if Moïna replied to Anna's February 1922 letter, about Georgia's VFW Poppy Drive that year. Moïna received Anna's address through American Legion Adjutant Frank Samuel, who had obtained it from former Adjutant Lemuel Bolles. He would be one of the American Legion allies who Anna remained friends with after the Poppy Days.

Moïna addressed Anna and Juliette as dear friends. She stated she had already written her autobiography and was asking permission to quote from their letters and articles, including that of Anna's American and French Children's League Secretary, Isabelle Mack.

The request included quoting from Anna's first letter to Moïna, most probably the 1919 letter Anna wrote to her praising her poem. Moïna also noted it was when Anna announced her own work to Moïna. She also wished to quote from Isabelle Mack's letter, which was probably the one sent to Moïna with a copy of *Le Semeur* in February 1921.

Moïna wrote that the history could not be written without including Anna's part in it. Concluding, Moïna asked to hear from one of them as soon as possible. Anna replied on 9 February.

Anna forwarded her *Synopsis*, her history of the 'National Poppy Days'. Anna's comments at the start and finish of the *Synopsis* timeline demonstrate she was not impressed.

Likewise, in her covering letter, Anna wrote 'I am dumbfounded'. She asked that her poor English be excused and urged Moïna to read her hurriedly typed *Synopsis*. Anna wrote of how surprised she was to receive letters from Lemuel Bolles and others, before she left France. She must have been made suspicious about what Moïna might write.

Anna had been pre-warned of Moïna's intention to claim she was 'Originator of the National Flanders Poppy Days'.

Anna had 'thought it was a joke' and had not paid any attention to the rumour. She wrote it was she who everyone had known as 'Mme E. Guérin the Originator and Founder of the National Flanders Fields Poppy Days in the U.S. and in all Allied Countries of the last War'.

Anna stated she was going to gather all the documents in her possession and hand them all over to a well-known American writer. He could write 'the history of the Poppy Days idea' for her. She would send it to all state and provincial newspapers as well as American Legion and Legion Auxiliary Posts. She believed she was the only person to hold a list of 10,000 Posts, outside of the Legion, which had been given to her when she was working at the Legion's HQ.

So confident was Anna of her status as 'Originator of the National Flanders Poppy Days' that she further wrote that she would obtain the resolution documents from Indianapolis HQ, relating to the Cleveland convention poppy adoption, and gather all necessary affidavits.

Anna wrote she would have her history published before the next Decoration/Memorial Day, 30 May. However, nothing appears to have transpired with Anna's plans to publish her own version.

Anna added: 'I am going to start a great work for England which will, very probably, take me to all the places I have been lecturing from 1914 to 1922.' She would take it to American Legion Posts, Chambers of Commerce, colleges, universities, women's clubs, and so on.

Anna declared, or perhaps it can be construed as begged: 'No, please, do not use my name or the name of one of my organizer, Mrs. Mack, until I know more about what you wish to write.'

Anna headed her *Synopsis*: 'SYNOPSIS OF THE HISTORY OF THE INTERALLIED FLANDERS' FIELDS' POPPY'S DAYS [sic]. By the ORIGINATOR and PROPAGATOR in the U.S. and all Allied Countries: Madame E. Guérin from France and New-York City.'

It preceded Anna's declaration that it was

> absolutely preposterous to think there is 2 originators of the
> NATIONAL POPPY'S DAYS. one for the United States and
> one for the ALLIED as THE FLANDER'S FIELD'S POPPY'S
> [sic] DAYS started in the U.S. at Baltimore, in 1919, after the
> First Convention of the Gold STAR MOTHERS. But here is
> the story…

It was reassuring to realise, when I eventually read Anna's 'story', that I had proved it all bar a couple of facts. My research and Anna's *Synopsis* gave the other equal credibility.

Anna wound up her seven-page *Synopsis* by stating: 'YES THE POPPY'S DAYS were originated by me: Mme E. Guérin from France & New Y. TO HONOR THE DEEDS OF THE GREAT WAR IN HELPING THOSE WHO WHERE [sic] SUFFERING. and In Memoriam.'

On 13 February, Moïna's lawyers Tolnas & Middlebrooks, of Athens, Georgia, replied to Anna on her behalf. They acknowledged receipt of Anna's *Synopsis*, as Anna had asked. The letter demonstrated the two women were now rivals. Once, they were aligned, along with many others, trying to promote the Flanders poppy as a memorial emblem.

The letter to Anna noted she had been doing a lot of lecturing in the United States prior to it entering the First World War, for the children of devastated area of France.

Anna had stated she raised funds as a War Lecturer (meaning for the US Bonds) and for the American Red Cross after the country entered the war, but this was not referred to. Also overlooked were the statements that Anna had been personally invited to the American Legion's 1920 convention; that her 'Poppy Day' idea was thought to be the 'Best MEMORIAM' given to the veterans; and she was known as the 'Founder of the National Flanders Fields Poppy Days'.

Affirming Moïna, the lawyers mentioned the American Legion had awarded her its Distinguished Service Medal on 6 October 1930, its Distinguished Service Citation on 24 September 1940, and credited her with the first claim to the Flanders Memorial Poppy idea.

The lawyers pointed out Anna's Poppy Days began in Baltimore in 1919, to benefit children of the devastated area in France, but it was earlier, on 9 November 1918, when Moïna had thought of the idea 'of using the Poppy from the fields of France as an emblem of the sacrifices made on the Battlefields of France'. It was stated that it was known that Lee Keedick suggested the use of the Flanders Fields Poppy for a 'Poppy Day' long before Anna did.

Ahead of Moïna's book, Lee Keedick verified details. He could only do it from memory, as his records had been destroyed by fire. He wrote that Boy Scouts sold the 'Memorial Poppy' on 14 February 1919. He was the agent for that event. For my part, I am confused by the 'Memorial Poppy' wording because I think that refers to the 'national memorial emblem' with a poppy and torch, otherwise known as a 'Victory Emblem' as per the lecture below.

Keedick recalled a lecture by Canadian Flying 'Ace of Aces' Colonel William A. Bishop, at New York's Carnegie Hall. A Bishop lecture was advertised there for 14 February, but no review can be found for it. Neither I nor a Carnegie Hall archivist can verify that it took place. However, there was a significant Bishop lecture on the 15th.

The *Brooklyn Daily Eagle* reviewed that lecture, which took place at New York's Academy of Music. It wrote of Moïna and her new victory emblem design. A huge 'Emblem' flag, of the Victory Torch and the Flanders Poppy, hung above the stage. Moïna's flag was described as the 'design for a national memorial emblem'. It was described as the first seen in Brooklyn. No single poppy blooms were mentioned.

Moïna's lawyers drew Anna's attention to a letter dated 11 March 1919, written by her to the Federation of Women. It was before Anna was back in the United States. The commercial value of Moïna's idea was mentioned in this letter.

But the 'Idea' expressed in this letter was the 'Victory Emblem'. Moïna wrote the Emblem was to be worn and displayed by every man, woman, and child. It was not a 'Poppy' nor a 'Poppy Day'.

Of her 'Victory Emblem', Moïna suggested in that letter that there was not a more fitting symbol 'to express the sentiment' that the torch had been caught. It was not a single poppy bloom.

It was pointed out that Moïna was extensively featured in February/March 1919 papers, for originating the Flanders Fields Memorial Poppy. I found identical articles about her Poppy and Torch 'War Service Flag' and identical articles depicting Moïna, with her 'Victory Emblem' image – not a single poppy.

Ohio's *Sandusky Register* on 6 April 1919 was also used in an attempt to illustrate a point. The lawyers quoted it as carrying 'an extended summary of the Memorial Poppy and the author of the Memorial Poppy Idea'. The 'Idea' was Moïna's 'Victory Emblem'. This article only promoted Moïna as the designer of her 'Victory Emblem' ('Memorial Poppy Idea'?), offered as a national victory memorial.

Every effort was made to point out all the dates were before Anna had arrived back in the USA on 31 March 1919. This was accurate but the dates refer to the promotion of the 'Victory Emblem', not a single poppy, nor a Poppy Day.

Lawyers stated it was most important for Anna to accede to Miss Michael, 'without controversy' because the facts proved Moïna's claim. However, credit would be given to Anna for using Moïna's 'Poppy Idea' to further her Poppy Days for fundraising for the children of France.

Anna did not accede. Complying with her wish, though, Moïna did not name her as 'Madame Guérin' when the book was published. Anna was only portrayed as the person who utilised Moïna's idea. In a 1939 oral history interview, Moïna described Anna as a 'notable difficulty', and it is presumed that was her true feeling of Anna.

No one can say if it was the wrong decision for Anna to make, to withhold her permission from Moïna. I guess it was a matter of principle for Anna, given the conviction she held for the role she felt she owned – that of being the true 'Originator of the Flanders Poppy Day'.

Anna may have felt she had nothing to lose, as she had already been sidestepped by the powerful American Legion; it is written that 'those in power write the history'.

In mid-1942, Anna was found dabbling in a new war-related venture. She applied for, and was granted, a US patent for four servicemen designs for stoppered bottles. Perhaps this was what Anna meant by 'a great work'. The patent text reads: 'Be it known that I, Anna Guérin, a citizen of France, residing in New York city, in the county and State of New York, have invented a new, original, and ornamental Design for a Bottle or Similar Article.' It would seem that nothing came of them.

Ahead of 1943's Memorial Day, the VFW was irritated by some specific unknown comments. Adjutant Gen. Robert B. Handy Jr. felt compelled to outline poppy history and the Veterans of Foreign Wars' contribution to it. It was done to: 'rout all innuendoes and statements circulated by unscrupulous individuals'; defend the 'pre-eminence of the V.F.W.'; and remind Americans and, perhaps, the American Legion.

Robert Handy Jr. sought to minimise conflict and stated 'the Veterans of Foreign Wars of the United States was the first veteran organization to promote a nationally organized campaign for the annual distribution of poppies made by disabled and needy veterans.'

'Ever since other organizations have taken up the sale of poppies we have urged and worked for co-operation and harmony in spite of opposition, rebuffs, and misstatements that have been used to discredit our rights, our methods and our purposes,' declared Adjutant General Handy, obviously referring to the American Legion.

Robert Handy had been Chairman of the VFW National Buddy Poppy Committee since 1 February 1923 and was 'thoroughly familiar with the activities of other organizations that have sought the exclusive privilege of raising funds for the welfare of disabled and needy veterans and their dependents in this matter'.

Robert recalled the 1922, 1923, and 1924 VFW poppy campaigns and described how the 'Buddy Poppy' came to be and how the VFW was adhering to the policy of veteran-made poppies.

He continued to tell how the American Legion adopted the poppy in September 1920; repudiated it in favour of the daisy in October 1921; but then adopted it again in October 1922, after it realised how financially successful the VFW Poppy Drive had been in May.

Robert emphasised the VFW always sought harmony and its units were encouraged to invite the cooperation of the Legion in joint ventures and, in many places, this happened. He believed the consistent support of its 'Buddy Poppy' dissolved any ignorant prejudice.

He drew attention to the poem 'In Flanders Fields', written by Col. John McCrae, and to Madame Anna Guérin, the 'Poppy Lady of France', who sought and received the cooperation of the VFW early in 1922. He kept one particular VFW rumour alive by stating that the American-Franco Children's League was dissolved in 1922.

He noted that, as it had always done since 1922, the VFW acknowledged Madame Guérin as originator of the idea but the American Legion had 'recognized Miss Moïna Michael of Athens, Georgia'.

Robert Handy said that 'The question of who first sponsored the idea of the poppy as a memorial flower' in the USA would probably never be definitely settled. He was right to state that.

That question was raised again at the end of May 1944. An article appeared in various newspapers released from New York. It may have been prompted by Moïna Michael's death, which occurred on 10 May. The headline was 'The Controversy Continues Over Poppy Originator'.

The article recognised three claimants for the Poppy 'originator' title: Miss Moïna Michael of Athens, Georgia; Madame Anna Guérin of New York; and one Mrs Mary Hanecy, of Milwaukee, Wisconsin.

Although the Legion's Auxiliary stated, for the article, it had 'not entered the controversy' because the dispute had begun before it took over the sale of poppies in 1925, it sang Moïna's praises and not Anna's.

Officially, the Auxiliary stated, the Legion had never 'taken a stand on the matter' but it was acknowledging Moïna and not Anna.

The late Moïna Michael was respectfully defended in her absence; Anna personally justified her claim, citing the facts; and, last but not least, Mrs Mary Hanecy was the third potential 'Poppy Lady'.

In support of Mary, the article quoted American Legion National Adjutant Frank E. Samuel, who in 1940 wrote: 'from our records, you may note that while Miss Michael is generally credited with originating the poppy as a memorial flower, Mrs. Hanecy is likewise credited with originating the idea of the annual poppy day sale.'

Mary's story is that she helped with Milwaukee's official homecoming of the US 32nd Division, which included the 120th Field Artillery. Contemporary articles give the day as 6 June 1919. She was head of the 32nd Division Mothers and, along with the community reception committee, participated in the welcome. One review of the occasion reported that it was a day 'when dreams came true'.

Mary is reported to have been one of the women manning a booth selling doughnuts and coffee. Apparently, she had decorated the booth with poppies but they were twice stripped by patriotic Americans who left contributions behind on the counter, in gratitude.

Contemporary newspapers reported Milwaukee's first Poppy Drive being held between 24 and 31 May 1920, under the auspices of American Legion Sergt. Arthur Kroepfel, Post 1. At that time, Mary was a member of Post 1's Auxiliary and President of 32nd Division Women's Corps, the latter having taken the poppy as its memorial flower.

One Wisconsin article, on 27 May 1920, mentioned Milwaukee's 'Poppy Week' and stated that the American Legion and the Service Star Legion distributed poppies in a number of places at the same time.

Anna's League's Poppy Days may have been those referred to, as they were being supported and assisted by both those organisations then.

In 1932, the Legion awarded a Certificate of Appreciation to Mary for conceiving, in 1919, 'the idea of the manufacture and sale of paper poppies on the streets preceding Memorial Day, and that from this suggestion the first poppy day ever held in the United States was conducted in Milwaukee'. The date quoted was 19 May 1920.

Another certificate was awarded to her, in 1934, stating 'the first poppy day held in America was held at the promotion of Mrs. Hanecy in Milwaukee'. The date quoted was 20 May 1920, this time.

When Mary died in 1948, four years after Moïna Michael, she was identified as 'originator of the idea behind the American Legion's annual

Poppy Day' too. But surely the American Legion had given that honour to Moïna Michael? With tongue in cheek, as Anna declared to Moïna's lawyers, it is 'absolutely preposterous to think there is 2 originators of the NATIONAL POPPY'S DAYS'.

Returning to 1944, Paris was liberated in August. After applying for a Re-Entry Permit, Anna returned to France in July 1945.

Anna arrived back in New York on 29 November 1945, aboard the *Edmund B. Alexander*, from Le Havre. Her daughter Raymonde was next of kin again and still living in Paris.

With the world at peace, Anna began sailing backwards and forwards between France and New York again, staying at her home in Vallon or with Renée, in Paris.

Her daughter Raymonde moved to the Ardèche too – living first in Ruoms but then living in a house on Rue du Temple in Vallon.

A younger relative remembers staying with Raymonde, with her own family, after Raymonde had returned to Vallon. Raymonde was a widow then. She lived alone in a very large house and she locked every internal door at night. In order to get to the kitchen at night from their bedroom, they had to unlock about ten doors!

We can guess Anna was sourcing antiques when she was in France, from both family members and other individuals. An elderly Vallonnaise remembers Anna as 'a very well dressed lady'. She recalls her, on one visit, 'accompanied by Americans who came to buy furniture'. Anna was known locally as 'an antique dealer'.

Several of Anna and her family's Parke-Bernet auction catalogues have survived. Many were two-day events. All the catalogues carry numerous illustrations of the lots being sold and they ranged from forty-five to eighty-five pages. Some are linked to her daughters.

One of Raymonde's auctions was for 'French Provincial Furniture, Ceramics, Including a Group of XVIII Century Meissen Statuettes, Tole & Other Metalwork, Lamps, Clocks, Decorative Objects'. One of Renée's two-day sales was entitled 'French Provincial Furniture and French Garden Furniture and Statuary'. Lots from Avignon, Provence, and Nimes, from Anna's maternal Granier family, were also sold.

Anna's sister Adeline, who had assisted her in Madagascar, possessed many objects brought home from the Island. It might be said Anna awakened a dormant desire for travel in Boulle family members; perhaps it was an existing genetic predisposition that needed to be unlocked. Anna's niece Odette, a daughter of Adeline, nurtured a real admiration for her Aunt Anna.

Anna's travels and endeavours were well-known and souvenir postcards of her in costumes were well thumbed.

Odette sent her daughter on summer language trips to England and Spain. She can see, in retrospect, the spirit of her Great Aunt Anna floating around her bourgeois childhood home.

Anna's wanderlust influence spilled over onto Vallonnaises too. Several left for the United States. The now elderly son of the Vallon mayor, in office in the 1950s, visited America and his father gave him the address of Anna Guérin, in case he had any problems over there.

From 1946 to 1956, Anna took to flying to New York from Paris twice a year, on average. In these years, the Flight Manifest gave her US residence as 957 3rd Avenue, New York. These documents hardly give any information, compared to those of a ship.

I think Anna was travelling for both pleasure and business. I cannot say if she still had her antiques business to oversee but I think that, for as long as she could, she was shipping antiques out to the States – perhaps direct to the Parke-Bernet Auction House in New York.

On 16 April 1961, Anna died at Renée's home in Paris:

> On 16 April, nineteen hundred and sixty-one, twenty three hours forty five minutes, has died, Square Charles Dickens 5, Alix BOULLE Anna, born in Vallon Pont d'Arc (Ardèche) on three February eighteen hundred and seventy eight, without profession, residing in Vallon Pont d'Arc (Ardèche) daughter of Auguste BOULLE and spouse Anna GRANIER, deceased. Divorced first wife of Paul RABANIT, Widow in second marriage to Eugène GUÉRIN. Prepared the eighteen April nineteen hundred and sixty-one, nine hours twenty minutes on the declaration of Aniré BORNENS fifty quarter years old, an employee in Paris, 80 rue de la Pompe, who, made reading and invited to read the act signed with us, Yvonne DELEPINE, official of the town hall of the sixteenth arrondissement of Paris, Officer of the Civil Registry delegated by the mayor.

The cause of her death was cancer; she was 83 years old. The life of a remarkable woman came to an end.

I searched for Anna's cremation or burial, to no avail. Her sister Juliette died at that same address on 26 January 1974. She was obviously on a visit home to the fatherland when she died. She was cremated at the nearby Père-Lachaise Crematorium in Paris on 2 February 1974.

As an American citizen who died abroad, there was documentation for Juliette. Her ashes were interred at Père-Lachaise Cemetery but the law dictated that they 'may be disinterred at any time upon the request of the nearest relative or legal representative of the estate', who was Renée.

Le Père-Lachaise Cemetery told me Juliette's ashes were transported home to Vallon-Pont-d'Arc on 12 April 1977, but there was no record of Anna Alix Boulle in these archives. Likewise, Anna's burial was not to be found in the records in Vallon-Pont-d'Arc Town Hall.

Others searched too, including members of Anna's family, with no success. But the stars were aligning in 2021, the centennial year of the Remembrance Poppy Day. Our French 'team' of three was joined by a fourth. She, a Vallonnaise passionate about local history, had the idea of searching the Protestant archives in Vallon and success was achieved. Anna was buried in the Protestant section of the cemetery in Vallon-Pont-d'Arc on 20 April 1961.

There was no worldwide press release announcing Anna's death. She had been in the shadows for too long. But she has been slowly re-emerging during the past six years. A renaissance is being experienced.

Hopefully, this book will help to shine a brighter light upon Anna's humanitarian achievements and more people will consider her to be the true 'Originator of the Flanders Poppy Day' – as I do.

Epilogue

The World's first National Poppy Day was held in May 1921, in the USA. It was organised by Anna and her charity. America's first veteran-led National Poppy Day was carried out in May 1922, by the Veterans of Foreign Wars of the United States organisation.

November 11, 2021, marked the centennial anniversary of the first National 'Remembrance Day' Poppy Day in Great Britain. It also marked the Centenary of the first National Poppy Days in other Allied nations, such as Australia, Canada, and South Africa. New Zealand's centenary was Anzac Day 2022. In essence, these were Madame Anna Guérin's 'Inter-Allied Poppy Days' … her 'big idea'.

All these countries were First World War Allies, with one common cause, but the degree to which people are wearing poppies today, in remembrance, varies considerably from country to country. The Commonwealth countries have been the most loyal to the Remembrance Poppy.

A proud Canadian lady asked me, in 2015, 'Who put the poppy on your lapel?' I could not answer then but I can today. Now I should like to ask the same question of others. I ask the same question of you. Perhaps you think you know, for sure, or perhaps you know nothing at all but, either way, this book attempts to give you the true answer, as it was known to all those First World War Allied nations in 1921.

What began as possibly a short project, in which I assisted someone with their research but returned to my own, quickly changed to a permanent quest. The more I discovered about Anna Guérin, the more I needed to know. I began as a collator of facts, but I was so captivated by her that I needed to put the record straight. I needed to enlighten as many people as possible about this woman's work.

Madame Guérin was christened 'The Poppy Lady of France' at the American Legion's 1920 convention. For a few years after that, many people of the Allied nations knew exactly who 'The Originator of the National Flanders Fields Poppy Days' was, but she was written out of history. She has been largely unknown within modern generations. It is my quest to prove that it was Anna Alix Boulle, Madame Anna Guérin, who put the poppy on your lapel.

Slowly, Anna Guérin is emerging from the shadows. The centenary year of Remembrance Poppy Day, 2021, saw the light beginning to shine on her again.

France is beginning to discover the remarkable woman who served the country so loyally for many years, during one of its darkest times.

A special homage was given to Anna Guérin on 11 November 2021. The town of Aubigny-sur-Nére, in the Cher department of France, honoured Anna by inaugurating a small renovated square, 'Espace Anna Guérin'. Mayor Laurence Renier led the ceremonies at the War Memorial and the 'Espace'.

Also on 11 November 2021, an exhibition about Anna was held at the Town Hall in Vallon-Pont-d'Arc, in the Ardèche. It was organised by the 'les amis de l'histoire de la région de Vallon' association.

On the morning of 8 March 2022, International Women's Day, a memorial stone was unveiled for Anna at the 'Famille BOULLE-GUIBAL' burial plot, in the Protestant section of the Vallon-Pont-d'Arc cemetery. That afternoon, a plaque was unveiled at the old Boulle home on Rue du Mas des Aires. Mayor Guy Massot led the ceremonies. Family members, townsfolk, and the 'Anciens Combattants of the Ardèche' attended.

To bring the quest up to date, on 18/19 June 2022, an exhibition about Anna was held in Montreuil-sur-Mer, Pas-de-Calais. It was at the invitation of the General Delegation of the Pas-de-Calais Souvenir Français, which wishes to promote Anna Guérin in France. This was the Entente Cordiale weekend which celebrated the restoration of the town's statue of Earl Haig. The ethos of the Souvenir Français is to preserve monuments, graves, and the memory 'of those who have served France well'.

Thanks to the Souvenir Français, there will be a 'Rue Anna Guérin' inaugurated in Annay-sous-Lens, Pas-de Calais, in 1923.

References

Books and Journals

American Legion Weekly, Post-Convention edition of 15 October 1920
American Legion Weekly, edition of 4 February 1921
Bandholtz, Harry Hill, *An Undiplomatic Diary* (Columbia University Press, 1933)
Bowering, C. H., *Service: The Story of the Canadian Legion 1925–1960* (Dominion Command, 1960)
Fairclough, Henry Rushton, *Warming Both Hands: The Autobiography of Henry Rushton Fairclough* (Stanford University Press, 1941)
Harding, Brian, *Keeping Faith: The History of the Royal British Legion* (Pen & Sword, 2001)
Hunt, William Henry, 'African-American Consuls Abroad, 1897–1909', *Foreign Service Journal*, September 2004
Irwin, Julia F., *Making the World Safe: The American Red Cross and a Nation's Humanitarian Awakening* (Oxford University Press, 2013)
Quick March (Official monthly paper of the New Zealand Returned Soldiers' Association)
Scarpaci, Vincenza, *The Journey of the Italians in America* (Pelican, 2008)
Strauss, Gwen, *The Nine: How a Band of Daring Resistance Women Escaped from Nazi Germany* (Manilla Press, 2021)

Websites

https://af-france.fr/en; www.alliancefrancaise.london [Alliance Française]
www.alsace1418.fr [Le Bleuet de France]
www.ancestry.com [Online genealogy research/permissions]
http://archives.ardeche.fr [Ardèche Archives]
http://archives.valdemarne.fr/r/11/pajep [Val de Marne Archives]
www.aucklandlibraries.govt.nz [Auckland Libraries, NZ]
www.awm.gov.au [Australian War Memorial]

www.baltimoresun.com [Baltimore Sun newspaper archives]

www.blackpast.org/african-american-history [William Henry Hunt]

www.britishnewspaperarchive.co.uk [British Library Newspaper Archives]

www.canadiangeographic.ca [Canadian Geographic]

http://cdnc.ucr.edu/cgi-bin/cdnc [California Digital Newspaper Collection]

http://chroniclingamerica.loc.gov [Newspapers – US Library of Congress]

http://collections.mun.ca [Memorial University of Newfoundland Archives]

www.culture.gouv.fr [Ministère de la Culture, France]

http://blogs.denverpost.com/library/category/war [*Denver Post* newspaper]

http://digital.denverlibrary.org [Denver Library, Denver, Colorado]

www.druidhillpark.org [War Mothers convention, Baltimore]

www.elephind.com [Illinois Digital Newspaper Collection]

www.facebook.com/LostButte [Butte, Montana]

https://gallica.bnf.fr [French/French Colony newspapers]

http://gw.geneanet.org [Genealogy Society]

https://history.churchofjesuschrist.org/landing/church-history-library?lang=eng [Latter Day Saints Library, Salt Lake City, Utah]

https://idontblog.ca/forget-me-not-memorial-day-in-newfoundland-labrador

www.ilelongue14-18.eu/?les-captures-en-Alsace-Lorraine [Saint-Rambert-sur-Loire WWI Prisoner of War Camp]

www.legion.ca [Royal Canadian Legion]

www.legion.org [American Legion]

www.lib.umn.edu [University of Minnesota – YMCA Archives]

www.libs.uga.edu/hargrett [Hargrett Library, University of Georgia]

www.loc.gov [U.S. Library of Congress]

www.mairie-vallon.com [Vallon-Pont-d'Arc Town Hall]

https://memoiredhistoires.com/a-propos [Gustave Baussart]

https://mtghawkesbay.wordpress.com [MTG Hawke's Bay Tai Ahuriri Museum, Theatre and Art Gallery, Hawke's Bay, North Island, New Zealand]

http://nebnewspapers.unl.edu [Newspapers – University of Nebraska]

www.nebraskahistory.org/index.shtml [Nebraska State Historical Society]

www.newspapers.com [Online newspaper archive]

https://newspaperarchive.com [Online newspaper archive]

www.nhehs.gdst.net [Notting Hill & Ealing High School]

www.number56.co.uk [Somme historian hosts]

www.onac-vg.fr [Le Bleuet de France]

http://paperspast.natlib.govt.nz [National Library of New Zealand – newspapers]

www.paris.fr [Online services for Paris – Cimetière du Père Lachaise]
https://poppyladymadameguerin.wordpress.com
www.princearthurwaterfront.com [Prince Arthur Hotel, Thunder Bay]
http://releves.free.fr [Ardèche birth/marriage/death register entries]
https://rsa.org.nz [Royal New Zealand Returned and Services Association]
http://rsl.org.au [Returned and Services League of Australia]
https://rwrmuseum.com [Royal Winnipeg Rifles Museum & Archives]
www.service-public.fr [Online public services, France]
www.scrippscollege.edu/denison [Denison Library, Scripps College, Claremont, California – Hartley Burr Alexander papers]
www.shebafilms.com [Thunder Bay Film Production Company]
https://sinclairgenealogy.info [Sir Herbert Brown]
http://tauranga.kete.net.nz [Online newspaper archive]
http://trove.nla.gov.au [National Library of Australia]
www.torontopubliclibrary.ca [*Toronto Star* newspaper archive]
www.tbpl.ca [Thunder Bay Public Library, Ontario, Canada]
www2.ulib.iupui.edu/digitalscholarship [Indiana University – Purdue University]
www.copyright.gov [US Copyright Office]
www.uspto.gov [US Patent and Trademark Office]
http://uwfrenchhouse.org [The French House, Madison, Wisconsin]
www.warmuseum.ca [Canadian War Museum]
www.war-veterans.org/Gold.htm [US Gold Star Mothers]
www.webafriqa.net [General Joseph Simon Galliéni]
www.wdrincorp.com [Ward, Dreshman & Reinhardt, Inc.]
https://en.wikipedia.org

Acknowledgements

American Gold Star Mothers, Inc. (National Archivist)
American Legion National Headquarters
Aubigny-sur-Nère
Auckland Council Library
Australia, National Library of
Australian War Museum
Baltimore Sun Archives
Boirayon, Alain
Boulle/Guibal/Thouard Family
Bouttell, Oliver G.
Brodie Resource Library: Thunder Bay Library, Ontario, Canada
Bruzac, Myriam
Canadian War Museum
Chaloner, Andy and Marilyn
Chante, Andrée
Clark, Emma
Dentice, Jeffrey 'Doc'
Denver Post
Denver Public Library Archives, Denver. Colorado, U.S.A.
Feltin, Carole
Georgia Archives (via L. H. Sizemore; B. E. Walsh; and the late Elinor H. Cook)
Gogos, Frank
Golgath, Marius
Haigh, Ian
Hargrett Library, University of Georgia, USA
History Nebraska (Nebraska State Historical Society), Lincoln, Nebraska, USA
Indiana University – Purdue University, Indianapolis
Irwin, Dr Julia F. (Associate Professor of History, University of South Florida)
Jumas, Sandrine

Klote, James D. (President & CEO, Ward, Dreshman & Reinhardt, Inc.)
LDS Church History Library, Salt Lake City, Utah, USA
MacFarlane, Nancy E. C. (1929–2015)
Mairie de Vallon Pont d'Arc
Mairies de Paris
Malesys, Anthony
Marriott, Gavin
Maurel, Henri
McCully, Terry
Montreuil-sur-Mer
Morris, Wayne
National Library of New Zealand
Notting Hill and Ealing High School Archives
Office Nationale du Bleuet de France
Olszeski, Sandrine
Pere Lachaise Cimetiere de l'Est, Paris, France
Port Arthur News Chronicle, Thunder Bay, Ontario, Canada
Port Arthur Legion Post, Thunder Bay, Ontario, Canada
Portal, Margot
Prince Arthur Waterfront Hotel, Thunder Bay, Ontario, Canada
Ratz, David, CD, PhD, Adjunct, History Department, Lakehead University,
    Thunder Bay, Ontario
Returned Soldiers Association, New Zealand
Returned and Services League of Australia
Rovillain, Pauline
Royal British Legion
Royal Canadian Legion
Royal Winnipeg Museum (Ian Stewart, Curator)
Ryma, Linda
Scott, Jan
Scripps College: Ella Strong Denison Library, Claremont, California, USA
ShebaFilms (Kelly Saxberg and Ron Harpelle)
Simon, Pierre
Sinclair, Peter
Sotheby's, New York
Souvenir Français, General Delegation of the Pas-de-Calais
Stanfield, Chris
Stewart Family
Tauranga City Libraries, New Zealand
Thom Family (Florence, Barry, and Alexandria)

Acknowledgements

Thomson, David and Julie
Thouard, Sylvie
Towler, Anne Campbell
US Copyright Office
US Department of Health & Human Services
US Patent and Trademark Office
Vallon-Pont-d'Arc
Vigoureux, Claude (ONACVG Directeur, Cher département, France)
Vincent, Dorothée
Wisconsin Historical Society
Wisconsin: French House, Madison
YMCA (France; National Secretariat; USA; and World Alliance, Geneva)
Young, George

Index